Jan Morris, *Independent*

'Sattin manages to turn what could be a dull academic treatise into a gripping quest that captures the reader on the first page and does not release him until the final paragraph. We follow him as he bribes his way into moonlit temples in an attempt to surprise women praying to the Pharaonic gods; as he tracks down snake-hunters in their reptilian lairs; even as he travels from the deserts of Luxor as far as the damp streets of Liverpool in search of long-lost manuscripts.

'What ultimately sustains and animates this fascinating and brilliant book is Sattin's boundless love for Egypt and his wonderful ability to convey his enthusiasm for even the most obscure details of the folk religion of Upper Egypt . . . his book is a rarity among modern travel books: a genuine labour of love . . . a marvellous book, and one that any living travel writer would have been proud to write . . . one of the most fascinating and remarkable travel writing debuts to be published for many years' William Dalrymple, *Spectator*

'A compelling portrait of a society which appears to be in the grip of a collective psychosis. This scholarly and well-written book gives a lively and convincing portrait of contemporary Egypt'

Robert Carver, *Times Literary Supplement*

Anthony Sattin is the author of several books of fiction and non-fiction, including *Lifting the Veil: British Society in Egypt 1768-1956* and *Florence Nightingale's Letters from Egypt: A Journey on the Nile 1849-1850*, which he both discovered and edited, and which was recently serialised on BBC Radio 4. He has written for television, radio and for publications around the world, and is a regular contributor to both the travel and the book pages of the *Sunday Times*. He lives in London, and can be contacted via his website, www.sattin.co.uk.

By the same author

An Englishwoman in India:
The Memoirs of Harriet Tytler 1828-1958 (ed.)

Florence Nightingale's Letters from Egypt 1849-1850 (ed.)

Lifting the Veil: British Society in Egypt 1768-1956

Shooting the Breeze

The Pharaoh's Shadow

TRAVELS IN ANCIENT AND MODERN EGYPT

Anthony Sattin

INDIGO

An Indigo paperback

First published in Great Britain by Victor Gollancz in 2000
This paperback edition published in 2001 by Indigo,
an imprint of Orion Books Ltd,
Orion House, 5 Upper St Martin's Lane, London WC2H 9EA

A CIP catalogue record for this book is available from the
British Library.

0 575 402 784

Printed in Great Britain by
The Guernsey Press Co. Ltd, Guernsey, C.I.

For Sylvie, memories of the beautiful place

Contents

Illustrations		xi
Permissions		xiii
Acknowledgements		xvii
1	Chances	1
2	The World and Its End	22
3	Women and the Nile	46
4	The Living and the Dead	76
5	Happy Birthday Abu'l-Hajjaj	99
6	Mr Magic	134
7	The Original Egyptians?	167
8	The Tree at the End of the Book	193
	Glossary	216
	Bibliography	219
	Index	227

Illustrations

(between pages 106 and 107)

The photographs in this book were taken during the 1920s by Winifred Blackman. A few were reproduced in her 1927 book *The Fellahin of Upper Egypt*, but the majority have never before been published. They appear here by kind permission of the School of Archaeology, the University of Liverpool.

1. Winifred Blackman and Hideyb Abdel-Shafy, with whose family she stayed in Fayoum (see chapter 5).
2. Winifred Blackman taking tea with Mansour Bey and Colonel Sherif. Hideyb is standing behind her.
3. Men performing a *zikr* in a crowd at Dimishkin, 1924.
4. The 'servants' of Sheikh Haridi, 'who was originally believed to be a snake'; the Sheikh's tomb is in the background. Some of the servants are his relatives (see chapter 6).
5. A Muslim poet reciting while spinning a disk in the Coptic cemetery at Ezbet al-Muharraq during the Eid al-Ghutas, January 1921.
6. A woman rolling from the stone of Sheikh Habs al-Wehish, Fayoum, December 1925 (see chapter 5).
7. A woman jumping over charms in Winifred Blackman's garden in Fayoum, January 1926.
8. 'On the site of an ancient temple in Middle Egypt is a pool of water ... believed to possess miraculous powers ... [Women] clamber over the stones ... three times, and going more or less in

a circular direction. After this they hope to conceive.' (see chapter 3).

9. A fertility rite involving a flour cake, a candle and a pottery jar, 1925.

10. Women wailing at a graveside, Deir al-Muharraq. Contemporary funeral lamentations have been called 'distillations over time of ancient fragments of Egyptian thought'.

11. People sheltering for *baraka* in the shade of a tree believed to be inhabited by a saint, Fayoum, 1926. Modern Egyptians, like their ancestors, hope to find a shade tree waiting for them in paradise.

12. A youth near Badeh, Fayoum, who Miss Blackman believed showed 'physical features strongly resembling an ancient Egyptian'.

13. The 'servant' of Sheikha Khadra, near Kom Aushim, Fayoum, 1926.

Winifred Blackman's papers are quoted with kind permission of the University of Liverpool and the Umm Seti Manuscript with kind permission of Mrs Jano Fairservis. I am most grateful to the following for permission to quote from copyright works: to Philip R. Amidon, S.J., and Oxford University Press, New York for *Church History* by Tyrannius Rufinus; to Dr Nicolaas Biegman and SDU/Kegan Paul International for *Egypt*; to Warda Bircher and Elias Modern Publishing for *The Date Palm*; to Richard Critchfield and the American University in Cairo Press for *Shahhat, an Egyptian*; to Jonathan Cott and Doubleday, New York for *The Search for Umm Seti*; to Sayed Idries Shah and Octagon Press for *Oriental Magic*; to William J. Murnane and Penguin for *The Penguin Guide to Ancient Egypt*; to Max Rodenbeck and Picador for *Cairo, the City Victorious*; to Routledge & Kegan Paul for Lucie Duff Gordon's *Letters from Egypt*; to Liz Wickett for *For Our Destinies: the Funerary Laments of Upper Egypt*.

It would be difficult to demonstrate that there are still, in these places, survivals from pharaonic Egypt, but it would be dangerous to assume that there aren't any either. The continuity of non-written history exists without interruption, despite the change of masters, the change of religions and even of language.

Jean Capart, preface to Georges Legrain,
Une Famille Copte de Haute Egypte, 1945

About Egypt I shall have a great deal more to relate because of the number of remarkable things which the country contains . . .

Herodotus, *The Histories* 2

Acknowledgements

This story is as old as civilization itself and yet no one in our time has written about it. The question of surviving ancient Egyptian culture touches on Egyptology, anthropology and various other social sciences. I could have written up these encounters from the point of view of either an Egyptologist or an anthropologist (and some members of both disciplines have touched on the subject), but I have training in neither. I am a writer with an interest in travel and history, and have written these encounters as they happened, as a search. I would have liked to have kept myself out of the narrative and for the story to have been driven solely by Egyptians. I had hoped to find an Egyptian who would travel with me, or one who had made this journey through time and space long ago, but in the end that wasn't possible and so it is my curiosity and the Fates themselves that drive the narrative forward. If it feels at times as though the narrative is drifting then I have succeeded in reflecting the way in which my research progressed over the years. There was no direct road to follow, only a start point and a place I wished to reach. As with the best journeys, it was what I found along the way that proved most enlightening.

This book has been longer in the making than most, partly through circumstance and partly through design. Over the years I have been fed, supported and informed by more people than I could list here. I was particularly encouraged by an early conversation with Professor Kent Weeks of the American University in Cairo when he explained that continuity – 'survivals' as he called them – was a subject Egyptologists often talked about but rarely wrote about, because of the difficulties of verifying their claims. 'There are just too many black holes, periods where there are no records. No academic with ambitions is going to put his reputation at risk by trying to accommodate them.'

Two unpublished sources were of great inspiration to me. Professor Elizabeth Slater and Pat Winker of Liverpool University's School of Archaeology, Classics and Oriental Studies kindly allowed me access to the Winifred Blackman archive, while Mrs Jano Fairservis sent me the unpublished Umm Seti manuscript that her late husband, Walter Fairservis, had the foresight to commission. Both sources have been central to developing my thoughts about survivals.

Amongst institutions in the UK, I must thank the staff of the Egypt Exploration Society, the Centre for Near and Middle East Studies at the School of Oriental and African Studies, London, the British Library, the Royal Geographical Society and the London Library. I have a special debt to the Society of Authors who provided me with a grant from the Authors' Foundation which helped stave off debt collectors while I was writing.

Amongst people in the UK, Dr Zaki Bedawi, Peter Clayton, William Dalrymple, Dr Nicholas Gendle, the late Rabbi Hugo Gryn, Derek Hopwood, Director of the Middle East Centre at St Antony's, Oxford, Dr Stephen Quirke, formerly of the British Museum, Professor Jaromir Malek at the Ashmolean, Deborah Manley, Dr Stephane and Monica René, John Ruffle, Keeper of the Oriental Museum, University of Durham, Janet Starkey, also of Durham University, and Liz Wickett all provided help, encouragement or inspiration, and sometimes all three. Mr Peter Willasey of the Harrods Press Office sent me a bottle of Tutankhamun beer which gave me an idea of how the ancients might have spent their evenings. Kate Fenhalls, Zaza and Kadir Guiray, Jane Joseph and Richard and Carol Sattin all provided rooms to work. I also owe many thanks to Mr Wagdi Soliman of Soliman Travel, London, so often the man who got me to Egypt.

In Egypt I have relied on many people. Gamal Abu'l-Hajjaj, Adel Sabet, Colin Clement and Professor Jean-Yves Empereur of the Centre d'Etudes Alexandrines, Lila Abu Lughod, Hassan el-Geretly, Salima Ikram, Michael Jones, Tim Mitchell, Suzy Naga, Youssef Rakha, Dr John Rodenbeck, Muhammad Salem, Dr Boutros Wardieh, Nicholas

ACKNOWLEDGEMENTS

Warner and Professor Kent Weeks all provided great help with my research. Cary Cavness and her staff gave me generous access to the American Research Centre in Egypt (ARCE) Library. Alun Wright did some travelling with me, which was a revelation, and Maria Golia shared her experiences. Siona Jenkins, Karima Khalil, Cydney Roach, Max Rodenbeck, Olivier Sednaoui and David Sims offered generous hospitality and great inspiration whenever I needed it.

Elsewhere in the world, Dr Nicolaas Biegman, whose excellent book on moulids was an inspiration, Professor Valerie J. Hoffman of the University of Illinois, Dr Andreas Reichert at Tübingen University and Dr Jason Thompson of Western Kentucky University all provided help and enthusiasm.

I owe special thanks to Christine Walker and Caroline Gascoigne of the *Sunday Times*, editors who have provided constant support.

This book was shaped at an early stage by the insights of Liz Knights, an inspired editor who died young. I hope that in some way her influence is still evident. Mike Petty took it on and he, Rebecca Porteous and Amira Ghazalla have provided valuable advice and guidance. To them and to my agent Bill Hamilton I am much indebted.

My largest debt is to Sylvie Franquet, who lured me back to the Nile, who opened my eyes and has shown me everything.

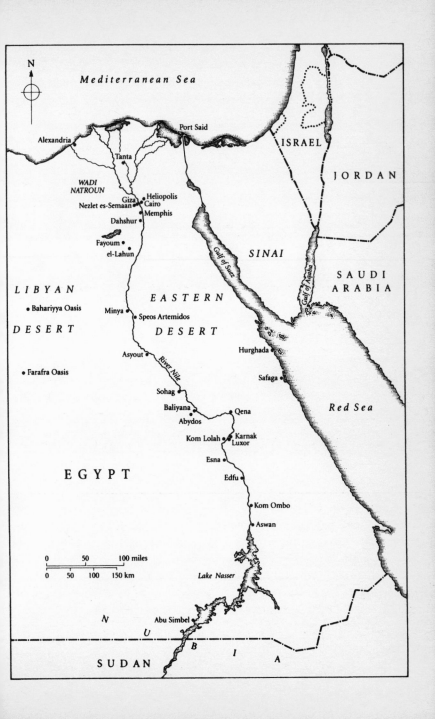

CHAPTER I

Chances

The ultimate meaning to which all stories refer has two faces:
the continuity of life, the inevitability of death.
                    Italo Calvino, *If On A Winter's Night A Traveller*

First, and quite by chance, I met a young guide called Amr, a tall, thin village boy with a beige *galabiyya* and brown knitted cap. Then Amr found me a brown donkey, which he tied up beside his own. We shared black tea and pleasantries in the shade of a date palm and then headed out of the valley into the desert.

The transition from lush garden to arid waste was easy and abrupt. At the edge of the desert the going was still firm, the grey wilderness more rock than sand. The late-morning sun struck like an iron and flattened out the creases from the landscape. The donkeys made a special, plaintive wheeze as if begging to be anywhere but there, but they didn't once turn around, as I did, to gaze wistfully at the Nile valley of Middle Egypt, almost fluorescent green in this light. Its promise of comfort tormented me like the thought of paradise to a troubled soul.

As we got into our stride, Amr brought out a white *kufiyya* and wrapped it round his ears. He shuffled further back on his donkey to let his feet swing loose and when he was sitting comfortably, he began to sing about Antar, one of the great and legendary Arab heroes.

> Then Antar rode across the desert
> And rushed into the fight
> His sword raised above his head . . .

He lifted the meagre bamboo he carried as a crop and sliced through the thick air. Don Quixote could have done no better. The bamboo lisped, imaginary heads rolled and the wheezing donkeys, fearing the worst, picked up their pace, just a little, just for a moment, until the heat melted the edge off their urgency.

We were climbing a gentle incline out of the valley and as we put some distance between ourselves and the fertile land, as we got the overview, it became easy to establish the cardinal points of Egypt. The Nile arrives in Egypt from Sudan in the south and runs more or less due north to its end in the Mediterranean. The sun comes out of the desert in the east and disappears into the desert to the west. Seen like this, the land is in a perfect and harmonious relationship with sunlight and water. Almost wherever you are you can trace the movement of the river and the sun and find that you are at the crossroads of the essentials of life. No wonder ancient Egyptians made gods of these elements and Ra, the sun-god, lorded over all.

The donkeys headed due east, towards a creamy limestone ridge. Even from the river I had been able to make out the line of incisions in the hillside. To the south, signs of a limestone quarry. To the north there were the ancient tombs of Beni Hassan, famous for their terrace with a remarkable view across the valley to the Libyan Desert and for their images of hunting and wrestling, reminders that people who lived long ago enjoyed many of the things we do today.

Amr led us straight ahead and continued to list the virtues of the great Antar. 'He could ride like the wind,' he sang. 'He could fight like the devil. He could love like a prince . . .' The song was incessant and pleading and, as with so many things in Egypt, the longer it continued, the more it began to take on religious significance, a suitable accompaniment for our entry into the hills.

We rode up a ravine and passed the entrances to a string of ancient tombs. Amr slowed and leaned forward on his donkey, as though he was going to get down. This, he explained, was where other foreigners he had taken had wanted to get down. But I was too excited and too happy to stop there and we rode on to the place I had come to see, the temple of Pasht, Speos Artemidos, which Amr, like many Egyptians, called 'the stable of Antar'.

The 'stable' was fronted by a portico of stone pillars, two rows of four. The portico was cut out of the rock, the chamber beyond cut into it, a sudden order and symmetry imposed long ago on the random chaos of nature, its significance lost, its form all that is left to us.

Egyptologists use the name the Greeks gave the place – Speos Artemidos, 'the Grotto of Artemis', the goddess of hunting – but the temple was already old when the Greeks arrived. Their allusion to hunting would have been appropriate because the area was rich in wildlife, and even a hundred and fifty years ago there were still crocodiles to chase this far north. I looked around. The desert is deceptive. At first sight it seems empty, but if you stand still for a few moments, signs of life often begin to emerge, a bird dashing from cover, insects underfoot, small rodents scuffling about. Here, near the grotto dedicated to the Greek goddess of hunting, only flies buzzed around the donkeys.

The little temple was built some three and a half thousand years ago, when wildlife was so abundant and so threatening that it made sense to worship animals as gods. Its foundation details are lost – why it was built here and who commissioned it – but it was dedicated to the ancient lion goddess Pasht. 'Long time ago,' Amr explained as we got closer, 'they found mummified lions and cats buried in deep holes near here.' I was going to ask if people were still finding things, if they were still looking, but he held up a hand to silence me and pointed ahead to some donkeys tied up near the temple.

The donkeys were a disappointment. One of the reasons I had made the journey was that I had been told I would have the place to myself, but here were some tourists, perhaps, or officials from the antiquity service.

Amr thought otherwise. He put a long, slender finger to his lips. 'Wait here. I will go to look.'

Life being strange, indeed, and wonderful, it occurred to me that maybe we had found the hide-out of thieves or hashish smugglers – Ali Baba transported to the banks of the Nile. This I wasn't going to miss. My heels touched the donkey's spare ribs. 'I'm coming with you.'

We left our donkeys tied near the others and walked across the dusty ground as far as the portico, as far as the images of the lion goddess carved on to walls. The temple – think more of a shrine than of the grandeur of Luxor – was gloomy inside after the desert brilliance, but there was no mistaking the two men coming out towards us.

Amr offered greetings. There was a touch of menace about the response. While Amr talked, I looked behind the men and saw a woman in the little chamber. She was dressed in black and merged into the gloom, so it was impossible to see clearly, but she was certainly alone, down on the ground, and she appeared to be rolling across the sand and rock, moving from side to side. I heard her talking, confiding, moaning, softly pleading.

One of the men stood in front of me to block the view.

'Please,' Amr said, turning to me, 'it is not possible for us to stay here right now. We must come back another time.'

My first thought was that this was Amr's elaborate way of getting paid for a second ride and I was going to object, but he took me by the arm and led me out of the portico.

'Why can't we go in?'

'This woman wants to have a baby but she cannot,' he said as plainly as if he had been talking about fixing her washing machine. 'So she has come here for it to be possible.'

'Why here?'

'Because here there is *baraka*, blessing.'

The story, the way Amr explained it as we rode back down into the green valley, was simple. The woman was from a nearby village, had had difficulty in getting pregnant and had visited her sheikh and the doctor. Pills, potions and prayers but still nothing had happened. So now she was placing her faith in the old stones and had come to pray to Pasht to bless her with a child.

'Now she will be OK,' Amr assured me as he used his bamboo to fence with my donkey's tail.

'Why?'

'*Allah karim*. God is generous, ya Antoon,' he replied, using the Coptic version of my name.

'But this is Pasht, the ancient goddess, or Antar, the Arab hero. This isn't Allah.'

'In my country, it is all the same, all Allah.'

'Do many women do this?'

He looked at me in a way he hadn't before, with a touch of suspicion, and then looked ahead. 'Many women? Yes . . . when they need to.'

'And what about men?'

'The men?' He turned away with magnificent disdain as though he could hardly believe I had asked such a dumb question. 'Antar never had trouble with his women.' Then he raised his stick and sliced the thick, hot air in two as though he was bringing the conversation to an end.

We rode on in silence for a few minutes, when Amr again got off his donkey. From one of the openings in the rock he produced a rusty tin of water from which he offered me a drink.

'Thank you,' I declined and, not liking the look of the tin, lied, 'I am not thirsty.'

'You must drink,' he insisted. 'This water is from the Nile. They take it from the centre, where the river is fast, so there is no problem. And you know what we say here in my country? That if you drink the water of the Nile then you will always return.'

He offered the tin again, having so loaded the gesture with significance that to refuse would have been to admit that I never wanted to return to the Nile. The water was surprisingly cool and, not so surprising, tasted of mud and rust. I must have looked uneasy when I handed back the tin because Amr slapped me on the back and congratulated me.

'And when you come back, you remember you friend Amr who's showed you all these places.'

By the time I reached Cairo I had less generous thoughts as the first symptoms of amoebic dysentery appeared.

I met Amr in May 1987. Late the following year, passing through Cairo, another chance meeting led to my falling in love, after which only the most pressing of reasons – a book about to be published and my first novel needing to be prepared for the printer – dragged me back to London. The subject and object of my passion was a Belgian girl, an Arabist who had been living in Cairo for some five years. As she wasn't about to leave, I had no choice but to get back there myself. By the beginning of 1989, we were living together on the top floor of a riverside apartment on an island in the Nile. This was a smart part of Cairo. But as well as looking down on the gardens of embassies and a magnificent palm tree on which birds fed during the day and round which fruit bats swung each night, we looked across the river to the rundown port district of Bulaq, and beyond it to downtown minarets and towers. With such a view, the city seemed open to us. Some days we would pinpoint a landmark we could see from our terrace and then head off for it on foot, not knowing what we would find on the way. It was with this spirit of curiosity and easy encounter that I answered the phone one morning. I didn't recognize the man's voice, so asked to whom he wanted to speak.

'To anyone,' he replied. 'To you.'

I resisted the urge to hang up and asked how he had got my number.

'I dialled at random. I often do this. Thanks be to God, today I find a *khawaga*, a foreigner. I need to speak to someone. My name is Khalid.'

Khalid had recently finished his medical studies. It had been hard. His father had died when Khalid was two years old and he had lived then, as now, with his mother in Sayyida Zaynab, one of Cairo's poorer neighbourhoods, named after the saint believed to be buried there.

'Money isn't everything. I worked hard and when it was time for the examinations it was me, Khalid, who did well . . . better than others with money and good clothes. I passed with some of the highest grades of the year.'

He paused, perhaps to allow me time to congratulate him.

'Then what happened?'

His voice lost its opening confidence, became hard, brittle, building towards a crescendo. 'You want to know something? There is a sickness destroying my country. I studied seven years, I got top marks, but I got no job. Good jobs go to people with connections not top marks. This is what I wanted to say and it is good to say it to someone like you. There is no hope.'

Khalid invited me to his house, 'To visit, and because,' he explained, 'I am a professor at making tea.' When we met some days later at Midan Tahrir, Cairo's chaotic central square, it was clear from his expression that I wasn't quite what he had expected from his *khawaga*. Too young, perhaps, or hair too long. I was also surprised: he looked more like a failed prize fighter than a doctor. He had a thick-set face and a thicker, high-calorie body, his fitted shirt gaped at the buttons and his tight, white trousers pulled at the seams. He was tall, taller than his friend, a sharp and lively electronics engineer called Hamdi.

While Khalid was timid at first, Hamdi was only too happy to talk. He explained that this night was the climax of a *moulid*, a festival to celebrate the birth of the Sayyida Zaynab. 'These are days when we remember our saints and pray for their blessings. We also take the opportunity to get together and enjoy ourselves, like you do at the birthday of the Prophet Eissa (Jesus).' Khalid glowered at him as he talked, and he walked off ahead when his friend asked me about Michael Jackson.

It was more like carnival than Christmas. Closer to Sayyida Zaynab's mosque, the lights became brighter and the sound of car horns was buried beneath Koran recitals blaring from speakers mounted above shop fronts and over mosques. The million-strong crowd was diverse, a few wealthy Cairenes taking a stroll, farmers on a rare outing to the capital settled in groups along the streets, young men looking for a laugh running circles round clean, well-dressed families who held each other's hands like paper cut-outs. Old sheikhs with long robes, high turbans and an almost tangible air of dignity processed towards the mosque while their followers crowded behind them. Khalid became increasingly tense as he and Hamdi led me through the crowd of celebrants.

On the pavements, on plastic mats, women squatted over primus stoves to prepare food and simmer tea, while cross-legged men smoked from tin-can waterpipes. Along the main streets, *mawalidiya* – the traders, holy men and beggars who make a living out of these occasions – were offering sweets, boiled beans, cakes, blessings, circumcisions and mystic moments complete with incense, while bringing down free and profuse praise on the spirit of the saint.

Sayyida Zaynab was born in Medina in 628, the granddaughter of the Prophet Muhammad through his daughter Fatima. In 679, she received such a warm welcome when she arrived in Cairo that she decided to stay. She died there the following year, at fifty-two years old, and, in the centuries after her death, she became the city's second most popular saint, after her brother, the martyr Husayn.

Sayyida Zaynab's mosque and tomb, the focus of the crowd's attention, appeared ahead of us decorated like a sideshow in an amusement park. The high stone walls were beaded with white lights, the curvaceous outline of the tomb hung with strings of red, green and yellow bulbs. A single neon-lit word – Allah – appeared above the wall. If this was religion, it was easy to see why it was so popular.

As the crowd moved towards the mosque, Khalid stood in front of me, pushing people away. Each time I slowed to look at men at prayer, at women and children, at dancing and laughter, he seemed embarrassed and said, 'Come. *Come*. It is not safe,' as though something

7

terrible was about to happen. But his words were wasted and so were his efforts. When the crowd moved towards the mosque they took us with them, Khalid mouthing words at me and abandoning himself to the force of people as though it was the will of God.

At the steps to the mosque, the pushing became frantic, a matter of hands and knees as well as elbows and shoulders, as people struggled to get close to the silver fence surrounding the holy woman's tomb. We were almost among them, near enough to cast a wish or two, but Khalid managed to drag us into the stream of people leaving the mosque and the crowd led us away.

The side streets and narrowing alleys were quieter, though not quiet. Around one corner a family held up discs of bread and small pyramids of salt and spice in invitation. Around another, from a makeshift platform brilliant with the neighbourhood's power, a man was chanting a single word: Al*lah*, Al*lah*, Al*lah*, his voice rippling through the fetid air. As though in answer, the PA system whined with feedback.

The street was blocked by men of all ages swinging from side to side in time with the chanting. When the chants came faster, the men joined in the chorus, believing the words would bring them closer to God.

'These men . . .' Khalid said, as though he had been hoping to get to bed early. 'They will go on all night.'

We entered a building behind the stage. The power had been diverted to the platform outside and we walked up the two flights of concrete stairs to Khalid's home in darkness.

In a small, candlelit sitting room – velour sofas and chairs around a low table, everything covered with dust – four men were talking in hushed tones, inaudible over the street noise. Their faces looked sinister in the candlelight.

Khalid introduced me.

'From London,' they repeated, without the enthusiasm I had met elsewhere in Egypt. Several packets of cigarettes were pointed towards me, then the men continued their whispering.

Khalid went into the next room and I heard women's voices. He returned carrying a tray of black tea. 'It is an honour to have you in my house. I am very happy.'

He was even happier when the electricity came back on. On the whitewashed wall there was a glittering inscription from the Koran, mounted in a golden plastic frame, and a faded black and white photograph of a man who might have been Khalid's late father. In the light I also noticed Khalid's nervous tics, his twitching eyebrow, one slow-blinking eye and the constant jigging of his right leg, like a sprinter loosening up before a race.

The other men left, furtively, and when they had gone, Khalid closed the door and the window. 'Too much noise,' he said of the chanting, although I would have preferred the street to confinement in the room.

I had expected Khalid to continue with our phone conversation, with another rant about corruption and the unfairness of life for people without contacts. Instead he asked what I thought of his country.

I gave the standard answer. 'I think it is beautiful.' I also used the Arabic word *helwa*, sweet.

He smiled, as if flattered, and in his fluid English began a speech about Islam and the Koran. The revolutionary turned to religion. 'Islam has given me back my life. Now . . . once again . . . thanks to God . . . I have something I can believe in.'

Hamdi said nothing.

'We must live by the laws of the Prophet – peace be upon him. We have done wrong and look what has happened to us. Our country is in trouble and our leaders are bad. I tell you, if we follow the Koran, Egypt will be strong again, God willing.'

'Are you suggesting a fundamentalist state?' I asked naively – this was before the current violence had started. Before Khalid could answer, Hamdi butted in. 'If . . . if . . . if . . . Look around you, ya Khalid. It's not just *khawagas* who ignore the teachings of our Prophet.' He waved his hands around, to indicate the scene outside the window.

Khalid raised his right hand to silence him and kept it raised for several minutes, his eyes closed, right leg jigging.

I was beginning to worry about him, when he turned to me. 'You know the Koran . . . the word of God given to the Prophet?' He paused, perhaps thinking he had been presumptuous, and took a step back in his reasoning. 'You know our Prophet? Muhammad, may God bless him and grant him salvation?'

I assured him I had even read some of the Koran. He was encouraged. 'How can people not believe it? I don't understand. How can they not see the truth and obey? Why will they not follow the *Sharia*, the True Way? What they are doing outside, here, tonight . . . this is not Islam. This is not what Allah has told us to do, so why are they doing it? Why are they allowed to do it? They must be stopped. And if the government won't take action then the government must be stopped. I tell you, my country is finished unless we start to obey our Prophet.'

That was what he had invited me to hear – that and to give me tea – and now that he had done so, he had nothing else to say. A little later, he led me back through the celebrations, just as wild, though the crowd was a bit thinner, and left me near Tahrir Square.

It took me several years to see the link between a woman rolling on the ground among the ruins of an ancient shrine and a young man in one of the densest parts of Cairo insisting that Egyptians must be true to the Koran. The link became clear to me one day in the spring of 1997 when I was visiting the ruins of the ancient workers' village of Deir al-Medina in Luxor.

The fresh early light had been pure and dazzling, touched with some of the brilliance of creation. It had made everything look young, had brought out the best in dusty trees, run-down buildings, and gave a sheen to the rusting tubs floating on the Nile. And it had stirred up all sorts of thoughts in my head.

In the tomb of an ancient sculptor named Iphy, I was joined by a group of Italian tourists. Their young Egyptian guide had a booming voice and in the confined space of the tomb, slightly cooler than the furnace building up outside, I had no choice but to follow his lead.

'Iphy was a sculptor from the time of Ramses the Second. Ramses, as we know, was a pharaoh from the New Kingdom, from the Nineteenth Dynasty, and he reigned from 1279 until 1212 BC. Which means that this tomb could be as much as three thousand, two hundred and sixty-six years old.'

The group, who had been woken at 5 a.m. and had already visited half a dozen tombs and a temple, were slow to react.

'That's very old, no?' the guide prodded. A few people responded with a nod.

'If you look over here you will see what makes this tomb different from the royal ones we visited earlier in the Valley of the Kings. Here we have Iphy going about the business of an Egyptian village. Here you can see that he is ploughing, here he is cutting his food, leading his animals, picking his grapes . . .'

'How can this be so old?' one man interrupted. 'This man with his plough – he looks like the farmer we saw as we came up here this morning.' They had seen people who tucked up their white robes when they were working. They had seen them hitting their animals to make them pull wooden ploughs. They had seen the women walking behind.

'Very good,' said the guide, eager to capitalize on the moment. 'And you are right: in Egypt, in different ways, and for all people, many things have not changed since the time of the Pharaohs.'

'In different ways, and for all people . . .' I thought about that challenging statement as I climbed the slope above the ancient village, past a late Ptolemaic temple, to a huge pit which I assumed had been dug in antiquity. The path wound down from the rim of the pit, but then suddenly dropped off, which was enough of a discouragement. I remembered a story I had been told – a true one? a scene from a film? – about a woman who fell down a pit in this area and couldn't get out. She was found eventually, weeks or months later, and with her the piece of paper on which she had recorded her last thoughts. She knew she was going to die, that the odds were heavily against anyone passing that way and looking down into the pit – I couldn't even see over the edge – and for as long as she survived down there she lived with a vision of the heaven she had had in her life and the hell she was facing.

I skirted round the edge of the pit, my eyes on the ground, taking an inventory of what passed beneath my feet: fragments of pottery that could have been made last year or five thousand years ago, chunks of limestone from the cliff face above me, Cleopatra cigarette packets, fossilized clams, other shells and a few strange, soft lumps. I stooped to pick one up. It was warm from the sun. With its bobbles and nodules, it looked like a piece of a planet visited by Antoine de Saint-Exupéry's Little Prince. When I tapped it, the lump cracked open and, as often happens in Egypt, the truth turned out to be more fantastic than I had imagined. It was hematite, a soft rock with a strong streak of ferrous oxide, the colour of dried blood. I crushed a small piece between my fingers and it easily broke down into fine powder. Higher up I found a piece of limonite, another ferrous oxide which broke down into yellow pigment. From these pigments, the workers of Deir al-Medina created the colours they used to decorate the tombs of their kings. I had just walked across an ancient paint box.

Closer to the cliff wall, the slope became steeper. Stones, sand and dust were loose underfoot and I slid back every few steps. When I reached the cliff, the rock rose hundreds of feet above me towards the withering midday sun. Dripping sweat, I climbed into an alcove in the rock. As my eyes adjusted to the gloom, I saw I was standing in the mouth of a cave. I went in only as far as the last of the dazzling light could reach, nervous about what might be lying in the inner darkness, about not seeing a pit below me or having a rockslide close off the mouth while I was in there. No one knew where I was. No one would know to come looking for me. I wasn't ready to move to the Place of Truth.

When I saw more clearly I realized I was surrounded by human remains, bits of bone. What had I stumbled on? The remains of a murder? How long did it take in that desiccating air for a body to be reduced to its final elements, to dust and bone? The wild dogs and jackals that hung around there – you don't usually see them, but you hear them at night – might have helped the process. Then I spotted shreds of brown fabric on the ground. I took a piece back towards the light. It was a loosely woven linen, the sort of cloth used for mummy wrappings, though it could just as well have been from clothing or packaging. There was no way I could tell the age of the human remains just by looking at them, but I suspected that the linen was from long ago; only crepe bandages use the same weave these days.

Outside, by the mouth of the cave, there was a tomb, and further along the ridge more mummy pits, more scraps and bones. The mountainside was riddled with pits and caves, the last resting places of the anonymous, of people for whom posterity was never guaranteed, who had no funerary temples built in their honour, no pyramids raised over their remains. The winding sheet and a common grave were their fate, as they are for many Egyptians today.

I worked my way along the ridge, back past the temple, until I was up above the ruined, ancient village. I settled in the shadow of an overhanging rock and turned the piece of linen over in my hands. Little flecks crumbled to dust and I put a hand down to collect them as they fell, just as I tried to collect my wild thoughts and observations. I was searching for a way to order them. The past seemed to live on here in so many different ways. The woman at Speos Artemidos was doing what women had been doing there for thousands of years, begging God, the gods, whoever, to make her fertile. Down in Iphy's tomb, the Italian tourists had made the connection between the picture of a man who died three thousand years ago and farmers they had just seen in the Egyptian countryside. So why, seeing that I had stumbled upon this without really looking, and given that there had been more written about Egypt than almost any other place in the world, had I neither read nor heard more than a few words about Egypt's surviving ancient culture? And why did I feel that I was being drawn into it? Why me? Why now?

I come from a family of migrants. My mother is an American and my father's family came from Poland and Russia. My father's father lived to be seventy-seven, yet in all the years he spent in London he never learned to read or write English. I was brought up in a stationary environment – we moved house only four times in the years I lived with my parents – and apart from the annual drive down to the Mediterranean, we stayed put. Yet my roots are shallow and travelling is part of my life. I find nothing strange in the fact that I move all over the world, that my brother lives in New York, my sister-in-law in Hong Kong, that my brother-in-law is married to a South African. Holding that scrap of linen in my hand, feeling it, turning it, seeing it begin to crumble, it made perfect sense that I should be fascinated by a people whose 'strength', in the words of the prophet Isaiah, 'is to sit still'. In the shadows cast by the pharaohs and their subjects, in the habits and customs, the beliefs and superstitions that had survived, in the continuity in the lives of Egyptians I met, I recognized something that was missing from mine. A glimpse of the eternal.

Sitting up there on the mountain, I decided on the quest that later became an obsession. I wanted to know what sort of manners and customs had survived from ancient Egypt and, if at all possible, to find out how they had survived. Also, and by no means less important, I wanted to know how Egyptians felt about these survivals, how Muslims and Christians responded when they looked in the mirror of time and recognized some of their own lives in the world of the pagans.

I also wanted to identify the powerful forces ranged against these old traditions; particularly the growing pace of western influence. In the 1960s many villages along the Nile had no electricity, but after President Sadat's modernization programme, the entire Nile valley and delta had been plugged into television, into free US soap operas. The rate of change had accelerated in the past few years. In the aftermath of the Gulf War and the freeing of controls over the movement of money into and out of the country, Egypt – at least in its cities – had experienced a social revolution, a revolution that was implicitly opposed to the old traditions.

Khalid had been embarrassed by the carnival atmosphere at the moulid of Sayyida Zaynab because he thought it had little to do with Muslim celebrations. Soon after the moulid, after Khalid had pleaded his case for a return to fundamentalism, Islamist leaders called for an end to what they considered un-Islamic practices. Among these were the sort of customs that Amr, my guide at Speos Artemidos, regarded as entirely natural, the sort of customs in which I was interested. The Islamists insisted that it was time for Egyptians to abandon these outdated traditions. A couple of years after I met Khalid, in the wake of the Gulf War, Islamists began a campaign of violence which they hoped would bring fundamentalist Islam to the country and bring an end to many of the survivals I was looking for.

The prospect of the sort of changes these influences might bring gave an urgency to my search, for it was possible that customs and beliefs that had survived millennia were going to disappear within a generation. This generation.

During the past few years I had understood the inevitability of things passing. I had fallen so deeply in love that I knew for sure one lifetime wasn't going to be enough. That feeling of the preciousness of time was heightened when a friend of mine was killed in a plane crash. What were the odds of that happening? So small that they weren't worth reckoning. I hadn't reckoned on them and yet it had happened. I already knew about transience, but with love and death in my life I wanted to believe that some sort of continuity, some sort of eternity was possible.

Up on the mountain above the burial ground of the pharaohs, I turned all this over in my head as I turned the piece of linen over between my fingers. Only a few threads were left, like the few clues I had about life in ancient Egypt.

'Eh, mister.'

I looked up into the blaze of light and colour of the valley.

'Mister.'

Below me, among the browns and beiges dancing in the thermals on the hill slope, the guardian of the nearby temple was waving. '*Mamnouh!*'

'*Mamnouh?*'

'*Mamnouh!* It is forbidden. You must come down.'

So I did.

At the end of that winter I was back in England, sitting on a train in the brown countryside, nothing else moving beneath a terrible, pressing sky. It wasn't raining, but the clouds were so low that the country was wet. In Liverpool, I walked past the gloomy Adelphi Hotel, beneath the concrete folly of the cathedral, to the university, on my way to see the papers of a woman who had died in 1950.

Winifred Blackman was an archetypal blue-stocking. The daughter of a Welsh clergyman and sister of Aylward Blackman, later Professor of Egyptology at Liverpool University, she studied anthropology at Oxford University and first travelled to Egypt attached to the Percy Sladen archaeological mission. She arrived in Egypt in 1920, two years before Howard Carter discovered Tutankhamun's tomb and made the Valley of the Kings in Luxor and the study of Egyptology a headline-grabber around the world.

The next ten years were spent collecting information about local beliefs and customs and making analogies with ancient Egypt. She stands out from most foreigners in Egypt at that time for her ability to speak Arabic, for her understanding of both modern and ancient Egypt, and her interest in the *fellahin* and willingness to live in their villages; for several years she rented a room in a house in Fayoum.

Blackman spent the winters in Egypt, but each summer she returned to England to work on her notes, do background research and write her articles about customs, superstitions, magic and saints, which she published in anthropology publications such as *MAN*, *Discovery* and *Folklore*, and in the journal of the Egypt Exploration Society. Presumably she also did some networking to ensure that grants were forthcoming for the following year. All this was a prelude to *The Fellahin of Upper Egypt*, her study of 'their religious, social and industrial life today with special references to survivals from ancient times'. Published in 1927, it was a ground-breaking study, the first from a trained anthropologist, and still one of the best.

'These customs and beliefs are of great importance and interest in themselves,' she wrote, 'but the fact that most of them are very ancient makes it still more urgent that they should be adequately studied and recorded.' Yet *Fellahin* contained only one chapter devoted to analogies between past and present, and it began with an emphatic statement: 'I wish to make it quite clear that in this chapter I am by no means supplying a full list of the ancient analogies with which I am acquainted . . . In my strictly scientific account of the *fellahin* (to appear later) the question of survivals will be dealt with very fully. (As I am shortly publishing a book which deals exclusively with Coptic saints and Muslim sheikhs, to be followed later by a book on modern Egyptian medicine-men and their remedies, I am here omitting all references to the numerous and important survivals connected with the cults of the saints and sheikhs, and I am only just touching on the resemblances of the modern to the ancient magico-medical prescriptions.)' All this sounded fine, but *The Fellahin of Upper Egypt* was the only book Winifred Blackman published. I was travelling to Liverpool in the hope of finding out what had happened to the rest of her material.

Aylward M. Blackman was Professor of Egyptology at the University of Liverpool from 1934 to 1948, and as part of the legacy of his tenure, the department had received Winifred Blackman's archive. It filled a bank of filing cabinets, which sat in the middle of a large room where the School of Archaeology, Classics and Oriental Studies displayed some of its antiquities, the ancient resting on the more modern. An information sheet listed the contents of the archive, the notebooks, manuscripts, price lists, ringbinders, letters, thousands of photographs and negatives, many strange objects; the woman's life-work numbered, labelled and locked away. When the cabinets were unlocked, I found coins and buttons, animal dung, skin and hair, written charms, medicines and potions, published books, old journals, letters in Arabic, old wires and pieces of metal whose uses can now only be guessed at. But there was no further manuscript, no book on Muslim sheikhs and

Coptic saints, no book on analogies with ancient Egypt. Her research notes were there, all neatly written out in longhand, but if she had worked them up into books, then they were either elsewhere or destroyed. Instead, I started going through the notebooks, spending as many hours in the room as I was allowed, reading fast, making my own notes on anything that looked like it might be of interest.

On my second morning, I found a file of Aylward's papers where, along with some choice press cuttings from the 1930s – 'Professor A. M. Blackman declared, "Times without number in Egypt I have slept with mummies all round me – even under the bed – yet I've never had any ill luck"' – I read Winifred's obituaries. On 16 December 1950, the *Abergele Visitor* (incorporating the *Colwyn Bay Gazette*) reported that her death 'took place in hospital last Tuesday'. *The Times*, two days earlier, had given her a small paragraph and referred to her first-hand study of the *fellahin* and to her book, 'a remarkable work in that it was at once of use to the scholar and of interest to the general reader'.

What happened to Winifred Blackman between 1927, when she published her first book, and her death in 1950? What caused her silence after 1927? What happened to the books she had announced in *The Fellahin*, her 'strictly scientific account of the *fellahin*', the other 'book which deals exclusively with Coptic saints and Muslim sheikhs' and the later volume 'on modern Egyptian medicine-men and their remedies'? Did all those years living and working alone get to her? Did something happen to her in Egypt? There were rumours that she had had an affair with one of the villagers who had been helping her, so a broken heart, perhaps?

Just before I left, I found a slip of paper with four lines written in Arabic and English. It might have been a translation of something she had heard. It might have been her own composition. 'Hell is hot,' it read. 'Hell is cold. Hell is thirsty. Hell is hungry.'

Back in Cairo, digging through the libraries of the German Archaeological Institute, the Netherlands Institute and the American Research Center, I came across the name of another Englishwoman, a near-contemporary of Winifred Blackman, Dorothy Eady.

Dorothy Eady's story has been well told in a biography, *The Search for Umm Seti*, by Jonathan Cott. In 1907, when she was three, she fell down the stairs of her family home in Blackheath, south London. When the doctor arrived, the girl was pronounced dead from 'a brain concussion in an accidental fall'. An hour later, however, she was up and running. Happiness and joy! But there was a problem. Soon afterwards her dreams began to be crowded with images of a massive, colonnaded building surrounded by gardens of flowers and fruit trees. By day she would cry and tell her parents that she wanted to go home. But you are home, they pointed out. No, she insisted, to my real home. And where was that? She didn't know.

The following year, on a trip to the British Museum, she ran to kiss the feet of Egyptian statues and announced that these were her people. A few months later, when her father brought home an issue of *The Children's Encyclopaedia*, part of which was devoted to ancient Egypt, Dorothy announced that she used to be able to read hieroglyphs, but had forgotten how to do so. When she was seven, she saw a photograph of the temple of Seti I at Abydos in Middle Egypt. 'That is my home,' she announced to her incredulous and increasingly concerned parents. 'That is where I used to live.'

By the age of ten, she was skiving off school to hang around the British Museum, where she was spotted by Sir E. A. Wallis Budge, the Keeper of Egyptian Antiquities. Budge, an eccentric character, had asked why the little girl wasn't at school and been told that she wanted to learn how to read hieroglyphs. He offered to teach her.

At the age of fourteen, she was woken one night by a man leaning over her with his hands on the neck of her nightgown. She told a friend many years later that she had mixed reactions to this arrival. She was scared for obvious reasons, but she was also happy, because she knew who the man was. He was the pharaoh Seti I.

From this point on there is a sense of inevitability about Dorothy Eady's life. At the age of twenty-seven she met an Egyptian who was studying in London. He proposed to her, and two years later she was on her way to Cairo to be married. A year after that she gave birth to a son, whom she called Seti, and from then on she was known, according to Egyptian custom, as Umm Seti, mother of Seti.

She also began to enjoy regular nocturnal 'visitations' from the pharaoh Seti. Others saw him as well, including her mother, who then insisted that 'Egypt is not a safe place to be in.' Umm Seti thought, on the contrary, that Egypt was a wonderful place to be because of him.

From the pharaoh she learned that she had lived another life more than 3000 years ago. In that earlier life, she had been brought up in a temple. Her ancient *alter ego* had been called Bentreshyt. When she was twelve, the priests gave her the choice of leaving the temple and finding a husband or remaining in the temple and dedicating her life to Isis. Bentreshyt chose the latter and took a vow of chastity, but hadn't counted on having a pharaoh fall for her. Some years later she became pregnant by Seti and, rather than expose the king to scandal, she chose to commit suicide. Now that he had rediscovered her, the pharaoh appeared regularly in night-time visions, explained what had happened in her previous life and promised not to leave her this time.

While Umm Seti was happy, this was too much for her husband, and he left her. Some years later he won custody of their son.

In 1952, the year in which Egypt's monarchy was overthrown, Umm Seti finally made it to Abydos. But it wasn't until 1956, the year of the nationalization of the Suez Canal Company and the failed Anglo-Israeli invasion to 'liberate' it, that she was transferred there by the Egyptian Antiquities Organization. She was fifty-two years old and until her death in 1981, at the age of seventy-seven, she remained in Abydos and maintained the ancient religious rites in Seti's temple.

When I first read about Umm Seti I was sceptical, to say the least, about her claims that she had lived in ancient Egypt and that she went astral travelling with Seti I. But the more I read, the less incredible her story sounded. I mentioned her to Egyptologists, people who were by training if not by nature cautious, conservative and tight-lipped. The ones who had known her all responded the same way: they smiled a broad, unambiguously joyful smile. 'Oh, Umm Seti . . .' said Professor Kent Weeks when I visited him in his computer-packed office on the American University campus in downtown Cairo, 'she was a wonderful, wonderful person.' Weeks worked with her back in the 1960s when he was new to Egyptological field research. He was interested in ancient medical practices and discovered that she had a wealth of specific information. What's more, she had tried many of the ancient remedies herself. 'It was easy to be cynical about Umm Seti, until you saw her. I'd heard all sorts of fantastic stories about her and frankly I didn't believe them. But then again, you couldn't ignore her either because her inside information, as you could call it, led to some important discoveries being made at Abydos.'

One of the most important of the discoveries Kent Weeks mentioned concerned the gardens where Bentreshyt remembered playing and where she first met Seti I. In 1956, when Umm Seti took up her post in Abydos, the temple was being restored. 'I had kept on and on about that garden until I came here,' Jonathan Cott recorded Umm Seti as having said, 'and then the foreman found it exactly where I said it was – to the southwest of the temple – tree roots, vine roots, little channels for watering . . . even the well; and the well *still* had water in it.'

'In the end,' Kent Weeks concluded cautiously, not wishing to commit himself, 'you have to make of her what you will, but you can't write off her knowledge of ancient Egypt.'

In a back issue of the American Research Center in Egypt's newsletter, dated winter 1981/2, I came across Umm Seti's obituary, written by Dr Labib Habachi, an eminent Egyptologist. Habachi acknowledged that Umm Seti was already well known for her book *Abydos, Holy City of Ancient Egypt*, which had appeared that year. But she would, he was sure, be even better known in the near future. 'Her other book, *Survivals from Ancient Egypt*, encouraged and sponsored by ARCE, will appear soon.'

Apparently not so soon. There was no listing of Umm Seti's manuscript in the Center's library catalogue and the librarian knew nothing of it. As a long shot, I wrote a letter to the director of ARCE in New York who replied to suggest that I contact Jano Fairservis, widow of Professor Walter Fairservis Jr, an Egyptologist who had done much fieldwork in Egypt and who had known Umm Seti.

Jano Fairservis was quick to reply. Yes, she did have what she called 'the Omm Sety [*sic*] Manuscript'. She also offered an explanation of how she came by it. 'My husband commissioned the articles from Omm Sety and sent the money for them. He recognized her unique position and her story-telling ability – and she was struggling to support herself. The American Research Center in Egypt handled the money and she sent the manuscripts there – where they sat. We expected ARCE to publish them, but they did not.'

Jano Fairservis agreed to put a copy of the manuscript in the post. When it arrived, I felt like celebrating. Winifred Blackman had provided many clues and pointers and textual markers for me to follow, and now Umm Seti's writing had appeared as some sort of animating spirit. Had she been alive, I would have swum the Nile to get to her door. Instead, here was her manuscript, an expression of her views and experiences of many aspects of survivals. Through her writing, she had another – a third? – life.

I put her ream of loose pages on top of the books and magazines, photocopies and foolscap sheets I had collected during my research. Beside them were the spiral-bound reporter's pads and small black notebooks I had filled with my own thoughts, experiences and observations, and some blank ones for the record of my encounters. I was as ready as I would ever be to peer into the shadows of Egypt's living past. To celebrate, I went to a party.

CHAPTER 2

The World and Its End

Those who worship Serapis are Christians.

Emperor Hadrian

Professor As-Said Abdel-Aziz Salem was sitting behind a large desk in
his office on the first floor of Alexandria University's concrete arts
building, a sofa and two armchairs in front of him, a student standing
beside them. He gestured for me to sit, to wait, as I had sat and waited
in similarly furnished offices of officials from the departments of
Antiquities, Information and State Security. Professor Salem's office
differed from those in one notable way: the accumulations of paper and
impressive mountains of books had taken many years to form.
Whether Professor Salem intended it or not, they gave the impression
that he had completed a great deal of work during his tenure at the
university and that he intended to complete a great deal more. He
wasn't about to move.

When the student left us alone, Professor Salem came and sat on the
sofa opposite me. His was an unusual mixture of elegance and
academic shabbiness and he exuded a sense of well-being; the metal
rim of his glasses sparkled. 'I was born in Alexandria, but I completed
my Ph.D. in Paris. You know the Sorbonne?' He was an expert on
Islamic Spain, had been director of the Islamic Institute in Madrid and
Cultural Attaché at the Egyptian Embassy there. He had excavated at
Medina Azhara in Cordoba. He was a member of the Spanish Royal
Academy of Arts and had been teaching at the university in Alexandria
for decades.

Professor Salem had studied enough of the rise and fall of cultures to
believe that history repeats itself; oblivion was hard to conceive of, a

denial of his subject, in contradiction of the facts as he understood them; eternity was everything. Not a stable, static affair as we are tempted to think the ancient Egyptians conceived it, but a great and glorious, desperate and terrible, never-ending story.

I asked my questions. How best to understand Alexandria's survival from antiquity, how best to see it? And then I sat back in the enormous armchair, so low that I could barely see the surface of his desk, the mandatory black sweet tea in front of me, and waited for his safe vision of history to envelop me.

'Have you seen my book on Alex? No?' He was genuinely surprised, as though I was the only person in the world who hadn't. He started excavating around the base of a pile behind his desk, on the bookshelves, the window ledge, in the hope of finding a copy. '*Dos minutos*.' He phoned the university press.

While Professor Salem was running through the extensive list of his other published work, we were joined by a couple of young lecturers, to whom I repeated my question. 'Has anything survived from ancient Alexandria?' I mentioned the Arab general Amr's report of marble palaces, baths and theatres, 1200 greengrocers and 40,000 Jews. Add in Greeks, Egyptians and Levantines, traders and scholars from elsewhere, and you have a big, cosmopolitan city. When E. M. Forster lived here earlier this century, the city was just as mixed, with Greeks and Italians, eastern Europeans, Britons – 400,000 people lived in Alex then. And now there are how many – four million? Five million? Probably more. But since the 1960s, most of them have been Egyptian.

'Completely Egyptian,' one of the lecturers corrected, 'and many more than five millions.'

In which case, what could possibly be left of Alexandria's cosmopolitan spirit? Professor Salem was stirred by this. 'Alexandria is not how it used to be. Before, it was the best town in the Mediterranean. Now it is dirty and the houses – everything – left to fall down.'

I suspected that Professor Salem had not understood my question, but before I could correct him, the thinner of the two lecturers said, 'The problem is one of economics—'

'Ah! The economic factor!' the professor mocked.

'—because the government handed over to the private sector who are motivated by profit.'

At this Professor Salem started shouting. 'Forget about profit. What of our traditions? What has happened to the old style of building? I myself live in a villa – my bedroom is twice the size of this room . . . We Alexandrians need space. We are not born for this. Our ceilings must be high or the air won't circulate. But these new buildings.' He shook his head. 'Boxes . . . just boxes. Alexandria has lost her face and you tell me there has been profit. Allah!'

The mention of God put a seal on the conversation and no one dared to disagree. A gloom settled on the academics. A runner from the University Press fought through it to deliver the book.

'But . . .' Professor Salem added, handing me the volume as though it was a lifesaver, 'she has not lost her memory.'

Just as I opened the book, two more professors arrived. They had heard that a special meeting was in progress and didn't want to miss out. One of them, a tall, tanned man with wiry grey hair and a perfectly round and smiling face, introduced himself as Dr Lutfallah. While Professor Salem continued his dispute, Dr Lutfallah asked, 'Are you by any chance a historian?'

'No,' I replied, 'a writer. I just came to ask where or how or if I can see what is left of the ancient city.'

Dr Lutfallah, Professor of Graeco-Roman History, moved closer. 'That depends what you mean by ancient. Alexandria is a classical city, and although you can find traces of the old pharaonic heritage here, there aren't many of them now.'

'So, classical then,' I agreed.

In a voice that was quiet enough to be conspiratorial, as though he was broaching a subject he dared not speak out loud, Dr Lutfallah began to explain how sites and their functions had lived on in Alexandria. 'Don't be fooled by the apparent lack of monuments and material remains in the city. Because the city has always been inhabited, people have used old stones for new buildings. But there is another and perhaps more important way in which things have survived. In Alexandria we have a tradition of urbanism, of living in this space. It might sound obvious, but I'm not sure that it is. Certainly very few people have written about it.'

'Can you give me an example?'

'Well, take this building. The university has been built where the Mouseion, home of the great Alexandrian library, stood, in the grounds of the royal palace. The market is where the market always was. The main streets, the two that cut the city in half, still follow the line of streets laid out by Alexander. It's the same with Alexander's tomb. The site around the Mosque of Nebi Danial, where some people believe Alexander's tomb will be found, has always been a royal burial ground. That's where many of the royal family were buried before the 1952 revolution. And why is this? Because we like a continuity in these things. Beneath the mosque there is a medieval church and beneath the church . . . who knows? Maybe there is a tomb, a temple. It makes sense that Alexander and the Ptolemies are buried there. No? If not there then where? No, I really think they are there.'

Strabo, the Greek geographer who saw Alexandria around the time of Jesus, described the city as having two particularly impressive streets, 'of greater breadth than the rest, being upwards of a plethron [100 feet] wide, and these intersect each other at right angles.' A crossroads in the centre of the city, in other words. Although Alexandria is recorded as having been designed by the architect Dimocrates and laid out in the presence of Alexander the Great himself, its basic plan looks surprisingly similar to the Egyptian ideal of a city. The ancient hieroglyph for 'city' was an oval or a circle cut through by a cross, two lines dividing it into four quarters, just like Alexandria.

Alexander the Great was buried, according to several visitors who saw his tomb, at that central crossroads, in a building called the Soma. The original tomb structure was most probably a pyramid, with a temple complex around it. Wanting to test Dr Lutfallah's claim to continuity – knowing that it was one of several theories – I walked along the seafront, beyond the huge site where the new, high-tech Alexandria Library was under construction, past crumbling early twentieth-century buildings and under the palms outside the Cecil Hotel. In the 1960s, the writer Jan Morris found an echo of the city's more recent past there in the shape of an old colonial couple, 'relics of the summery thirties', the wife blind and bedridden, her husband 'still sometimes to be encountered descending the dark staircase with a careful soldierly tread'. Now the stairs were busy with European businessmen and a few tourists, and colonial memories no longer shone as brilliantly as the wood and brass on the hotel's ornate lift cage.

From the corniche I turned into a busy shopping street that was unusually long and straight. It fitted, as Dr Lutfallah had suggested it would, the description of the ancient street of the Soma, which ran from the eastern harbour towards the lake at the back of the city. Like the street of the Soma, it was named after a burial site, in this case that of the Nebi or prophet Danial. And like Alexander, who was buried near the crossroads of the ancient city, the prophet Danial was at rest at one of the principal crossroads of the modern city.

For more than a hundred years, archaeologists and tourists have attempted to fix the location of Alexander's tomb. There were, in fact, two tombs of Alexander in the city, the one in which he was buried by Ptolemy I in 320 BC, and another, a sort of Ptolemaic family grave, built a hundred years later by Ptolemy IV. In the first century AD, the Emperor Augustus paid his respects to his hero – and is memorably quoted as having told attendants who offered to show him the remains of Alexander's successors: 'I wished to see a king. I did not wish to see corpses.' The Emperor Caracalla followed suit in 215. After that, there are no records. So what happened? Perhaps, as has often been suggested, his tomb was destroyed in one of the many riots which upset the city's balance in the third and fourth centuries. Or perhaps the pagan priests moved his remains to a safer place when they could no longer guarantee his safety at the shrine. The priests of Thebes had done the same thing to the mummies of the pharaohs, abandoning their grand tombs in favour of an anonymous but safe pit, so why not to Alexander? But the thought that he might still be buried beneath the city's crossroads was a seductive one and it worked on me as I went around the city until, in the end, I felt the need at least to see the disputed site.

Visitors to the ancient city were struck by the breadth and elegance of its main streets. Achilles Tatius, a fifth-century bishop, wrote: 'A range of columns went from one end of it to the other. Advancing down them, I came in time to the place that bears the name of Alexander, and there I could see the other half of the town, which was equally beautiful. For just as the colonnades stretched ahead of me, so did other colonnades now appear at right angles to them.' Earlier this century, E. M. Forster still considered it an elegant part of town. But the money has moved out to suburbs, many of the more fashionable shops have gone with them and now there is something forlorn about the street that led to the mosque and tomb of the Nebi Danial, its shops filled with shoes, clothes and cheap toys.

Along the street outside the mosque, there was a flea market of sorts, with secondhand books, clothes, videos and stationery laid out on sheets of cardboard. Across from the mosque, the entrance to the French Cultural Centre was flanked by pillars that originally supported a Ptolemaic building. Curious about the tombs of Egypt's more recent royalty, which Dr Lutfallah had mentioned were nearby, I asked a man selling old books on the pavement outside the Cultural Centre if he knew where they were.

'No royal tombs here,' he said with certainty. But I wasn't to be so easily deflected. 'Well how about Said Pasha?' I asked, mentioning Egypt's nineteenth-century ruler who had given his approval for the Suez Canal and his name to the canal's Mediterranean port. 'Do you know where he is buried?'

'Said who? Never heard of him.'

By this time several people had stopped to listen. 'Surely somebody here must have heard about the royal tombs, just over this wall here? Someone must have heard of Said Pasha?'

Nothing. Then a wizened old man came and took my arm. 'Lookee lookee,' he said in English and led me across the road to a small gap between two buildings where, under some rubbish and discarded building materials, I could make out some old pillars. 'Romani,' he offered by way of explanation, then he shook my hand and disappeared.

I abandoned my search for the tombs, crossed the road and walked up a concrete path behind a sweet shop to the unremarkable, whitewashed mosque of Nebi Danial. Inside, half a dozen men were prostrated in an attitude of sleep rather than prayer. I made the mistake of assuming that, because no one had paid me any attention, I hadn't been noticed. I sat down against an empty pillar and closed my eyes. When I opened them a couple of minutes later, a small man in a white *galabiyya* was standing over me, wiping his short, damp hair with a handkerchief.

'Yes?' he asked in English and then proceeded to answer his own question. 'You want to see the Prophet Danial's tomb.' He produced an outsize key and unlocked the door to the mosque's side hall. The hall had an opening in the middle of its floor, surrounded by a green railing. He walked over to the railing and looked down on to a tomb wrapped in a blue cloth, embroidered with an Arabic inscription. 'The Prophet

Danial,' the guardian assured me and then pointed to the neighbouring tomb: 'Lukman, the Wise.'

He talked for a few minutes about some of the people who had been to visit, including television crews from England who, he complained, never paid enough for his services. Having broached the subject of reward, he then suggested that I climb down the ladder for a closer inspection. I didn't take much persuasion, though once I was bouncing and swinging on the ladder I wished I had asked whether it was safe.

I jumped the last of the ten feet down into the tomb. The opening was large enough and the day bright enough for the crypt to be fully lit. The guardian had assumed that I wanted to see the Prophet Danial's tomb, but I already knew that it wasn't the lion-tamer who was buried here, but a fourteenth-century Shafei sheikh who happened to enjoy the same name. Nor was Lukman the Wise the subject of my attention. This according to many was where Alexander lay buried. In the 1880s the great antiquity detective Heinrich Schliemann, flushed with success and international acclaim following his discovery of the treasures of Troy, arrived in Alexandria to find the hero's tomb. Schliemann considered the lie of the land, the ancient texts and the results of digs elsewhere, and announced that Alexander was buried beneath the Nebi Danial mosque. That was as far as he got, for he was refused permission to excavate the holy site for fear of offending Muslims.

There was no proof that anyone had seen the tomb since the second century, unless we believe the 'gossipy story' of a dragoman from the Russian consulate, recorded by E. M. Forster, who reported having found 'a human body in a sort of glass cage with a diadem on its head and half bowed in a sort of elevation or throne'. That was in 1850, but neither he nor anyone else found the place again.

The crypt in which Danial and Lukman were buried looked like a cruciform chapel. The ceiling was vaulted, and the venerable sheikh's tomb sat in the middle of the cross while Lukman occupied one of the transepts. Then I noticed that behind me, at the end of what seemed to be the nave, there were some steps. The guardian, who had been watching from above, lost sight of me as I walked over to them. I could hear him shuffling around the rail trying to get a better view.

The steps led up to what looked like the beginning of a passage, blocked off by tightly fitted rocks. I got up close to the rocks and peered through a crack, hoping that I too would see the great Macedonian hero seated on his gold throne, but it was dark and I was unable to see anything at all.

So what were these steps? If this was originally a chapel, why was there a flight of steps into the nave? Perhaps instead I was standing in one of the ancient cisterns or underground chambers with which Alexandria is said to be riddled and into which a young woman disappeared some twenty years ago, having fallen down a hole in the road. Perhaps if I pulled aside the stones blocking the way I would find not Alexander's tomb but more passages, more turns, more beginnings.

In the end only one thing was certain: the same force that had stopped every Alexander-hunter from James Bruce and Heinrich Schliemann to Michael Palin and Michael Wood also stopped me. The guardian, perhaps knowing what I was up to, called out, 'O friend, where are you? You must to come where I can see you.'

'I was just looking to see what else is down there,' I explained as I climbed back up the ladder.

'There is nothing,' he said, and repeated more firmly, 'Nothing.'

Three o'clock on that breezy, brilliant Alexandria afternoon, the traffic was playing its traditional melody, drivers honked each time they saw another car and the old tram thundered along its worn tracks. I was walking through the stalls of a textile and home-goods market, set up across the tree-lined street from the gates of a cemetery. Beyond the cemetery, Pompey's Pillar, one of Alexandria's main sights, stood on a rise said to be the site of the original fishing settlement of Rhakotis. If that is true – and few things in this city of legend are ever strictly, historically accurate – then this smashed-up, broken-down quarter I was walking through, this discarded kernel, was the oldest inhabited part of the city.

The pillar had become the centrepiece of an archaeological park, an area of unexpected order in a chaotic city. The flowering bushes were watered daily, the trees clipped, paths swept, a neat yet unassuming site, and a strangely inappropriate one, considering that this was where ancient Egypt finally ended.

Guards chatted at the entrance and the woman at the ticket office barely raised her head from her magazine nor her hand from a bag of beans as she served me. I was alone inside the enclosure and took my time to look at neatly laid architectural fragments and broken statues along the path, the single, surviving column always in the background, its height exaggerated from my position at the bottom of its hill. The brilliant sun gave it a sheen, a touch of glamour.

The Arabs called it *Amoud as-Sawari*, the Pillar of the Horseman, the name it still carries in the city. The horseman is a reference to a porphyry statue of the third-century Roman Emperor Diocletian which stood on the pillar as late as the eighteenth century. To foreigners this column remains Pompey's Pillar, the name given by Crusaders who believed, wrongly, that it held the ashes of Julius Caesar's rival, Pompey, who was murdered in Egypt in 48 BC. According to the fifteenth-century Arab historian al-Maqrizi, the pillar originally stood in a portico surrounded by some four hundred columns. In more recent times it was considered one of the city's most satisfying antiquities, its celebrity confirmed in the 1840s by the complaint of the British Egyptologist Sir John Gardner Wilkinson at the number of people whose names were carved or written in boot-black on its base. Wilkinson, in his *Modern Egypt and Thebes*, the first comprehensive guidebook to Egypt, implied that it was he who solved the mystery of the pillar's origins, as 'Mr Salt [the British consul] and I were enabled, with the assistance of a ladder, and by chalking out the letters, to make a complete copy.' 'To the most just Emperor,' Wilkinson read, 'the tutelary God of Alexandria, Diocletian the invincible: Postumus, prefect of Egypt.' The pillar was raised in AD298. The memory would have been a bitter one for Alexandrians, for that was the year in which Diocletian punished them for their disloyalty by laying siege to the city for eight months. When his legions finally got inside, helped by an opportunistic Alexandrian, there was a massacre. Being Egypt, there is a contrary and equally plausible story in which the statue was raised by Alexandrians to thank the emperor for having responded to news of a famine in the city by allowing them to hold back some of the corn usually sent to Rome in tribute.

Whatever the truth, I knew that the pillar was, in the words of E. M. Forster, 'a subordinate monument'. The more significant ruins lay around the base of the pillar and the incident that interested me occurred almost a hundred years after Diocletian's legions smashed through the city gates.

I had just started walking up the looping path towards the pillar when a man hurried past me and said, as he went, 'Closed now.'

'But you don't close till 4 p.m. and it has just passed lunchtime.'

'Not today. Today we close early. Holiday. So you come back another day. Closed.'

Academics and Egyptologists dispute the date of the end of ancient Egypt as they dispute almost everything about the past, with the passion of ambition. Some claim the end came in 667 BC when the Assyrians invaded Egypt and left the capital of Thebes burning. Others point to 525 BC as the date when the lights went out on the culture of the pharaohs, when the Persian King Cambyses not only invaded, but incorporated Egypt into his empire. Graeco-Roman scholars often argue for 332 BC, when Macedonian Alexander invaded and put Hellenism into the mix, while others insist that Cleopatra was the last of the pharaohs. So, was ancient Egypt brought to an end when those asps fulfilled the queen's 'immortal longings', as William Shakespeare would have us believe? Many would say not, for although Egypt was absorbed into the Roman Empire after Cleopatra's death, and Augustus added Pharaoh to his long list of titles, Egypt's religion and culture survived Roman rule and even outlived Roman power in the Mediterranean. I preferred to set the date for the end of ancient Egyptian culture as some time during the rule of Christians in Egypt, between the conversion of the Byzantine Emperor Constantine (AD 323–37) and the arrival of the great Arab general Amr Ibn al-As in AD 641.

When the Byzantine garrison surrendered the city to the invading Arabs, Amr, an imaginative and educated man, was clearly impressed by what he found. Streets paved with marble, shaded by colonnades, a city, he wrote to his master the Caliph Omar in Arabia, 'of 4,000 palaces, 4,000 baths, 400 theatres'. We can read some of the awe of the desert-dweller for the city into those words. We can make allowances for poetic licence and trim the figures down a little. But we are still left with a city of world importance. So what happened to it?

Neglect and natural disasters brought down most of ancient Alexandria. The Pharos, the great lighthouse, one of the seven wonders of the ancient world, slowly crumbled around a people who had neither the means nor the ability to repair it. Eventually, it was levelled by a series of earthquakes and fell into the Mediterranean, its base remodelled into a chocolate-box fortress in the fifteenth century as part of Sultan Qayt Bey's coastal defences. The royal quarter with its palaces, temples and Mouseion (museum), the epicentre of Alexandria's intellectual establishment, was in part destroyed by fire and fighting; the remainder was also tipped into the sea by an earthquake. Elsewhere in the city, the story was much the same. But that isn't to say that nothing remains. Because Alexandria has been continuously occupied, always with an eye to the future, very little has been excavated. When you walk the streets the past is literally under your feet; when you lie in bed, your head rests on history.

The lack of visible monuments has had the unexpected effect of adding to Alexandria's mystique. The name is still evocative. It imposes on some people and inspires others to live up to it. Alexandria still prides itself on its intellectual achievements, even though most of them are millennia old, still thinks of itself as a cosmopolis, even though most foreigners were chased out in the 1950s and 1960s, still wants to be a trading centre, though the port lost much of its international trade to the Suez Canal. There are traces of the dash of Ptolemaic times to be found in the way the girls of Alexandria walk with a swing, the way the old men in berets or black sunglasses pass with a swagger. And even taxis are a more colourful orange and black than the black and white of Cairo.

What I saw when I arrived at the Eastern Harbour was not the royal palace, not Cleopatra's playground or deathbed, but a line of late nineteenth- or early twentieth-century buildings. Even in these it was impossible to miss the hallmark of Alexandria, an unashamed, cosmopolitan eclecticism that felt entirely at ease mixing elements from Renaissance Italy with Louis XVI's France, Henry Tudor's England with Alexander's Macedonia and Ramses's Thebes. Along with many of the city's more interesting buildings, they belonged to the nineteenth-century revival, one of Alexandria's great periods of prosperity and one that it had waited all the long years of the Arab and Ottoman occupation to see. When it came – starting with the pro-European policies of Muhammad Ali in the early 1800s and flourishing in the 1860s thanks to a worldwide cotton shortage which Egypt was able to fill – the boom transformed the city. Some efforts were taken to protect and excavate promising sites as Alexandria was transformed from a neglected Levantine town to a major international port. But in the scramble to develop, most of the city's antiquities were merely built over.

Yet Alexandria's was a grand myth, one which the city's newly rich elite wished to know about, and there were several talented writers on hand to tell it, from the Alexandrian-born poet Constantin Cavafy, to E. M. Forster, Lawrence Durrell and Naguib Mahfouz. In their accounts the myth was embroidered to such epic proportions that they colour the way we look at the city today. So much so that even though I had done my research, even though I knew better than to bring hopes and expectations, I was disappointed as I stood at the harbour and watched a fishing boat coming in from the Mediterranean, a paper kite hovering above Qayt Bey's fort, fishermen on the concrete breakwaters dreaming of catching something worth eating for dinner. I had hoped for something substantial and conclusive, something that might throw light on to my search for survivals, but all I found were dreams and longings and strange irrevocable decisions.

Walking away from the waterfront, I came across several caged vans and a heavy presence of armed police. A demonstration perhaps? Had there been an accident? Was the governor out visiting someone? I crossed the road and found that they were guarding the synagogue, a grand neo-classical building with a massive portico, set back from the street behind a high wrought-iron gate. It was an unlikely home for an unexpected survival.

The soldiers at the gate were wearing steel helmets, though even the troops at the Iraqi Embassy wore only berets. They were aggressive when I asked what was happening. 'Are you Jew?' one of them asked. 'Of course,' I replied flippantly and smiled. He took me at my word. 'Jews this side.' He pointed to the next turning down the street, then turned his back on me.

At the side gate a short man in a green sweater, a walkie-talkie in hand, asked the same question. 'Are you really a Jew? From where?' He asked for my passport, perhaps in the hope that it would state my religion, then called the watchman. A tall, thin man in a white *galabiyya* and knitted cap appeared and beckoned for me to follow.

Like the Serapeum in the Christian era, the large and well laid out

Great Synagogue belonged to another time, when Jews made up one of the most active and wealthiest of Alexandria's many minority groups. The doorman was loath for me to see it. 'Come,' he barked and led me to a side building, the administrative offices or, as the inscription announced, the 'Grand Rabbinat Communauté Israelite'. I stopped to read the dedication in the entrance hall, the record of sponsors whose generosity had paid for the construction of the building in the 1890s, their names carved on white marble tablets that were so clean they looked as though they had just been hung. Again the doorman wanted me to hurry, not to look or touch. He knocked on a closed door and led me in.

There were three people in the room, an elderly lady, a grey-haired man with glasses and an older man, in his eighties at least, who could only move by shuffling his feet. The old man was slowly making his way to the chair behind his desk, from where he would head the meeting.

When the old man was seated, the lady turned to me. I asked if there was someone who could tell me about the Jewish community and its histories.

'What does he want?' the old man asked the lady.

'He wants to speak to Balasseano,' she replied loudly, leaning close to him.

'Ha,' said the other man, 'Balasseano and his stories.'

'That's who you want,' the lady said. 'Balasseano. He is famous for his stories. But he's not here now. And he won't be for at least an hour, an hour and a half . . .'

In case I had any ideas about hanging around until he did show up, she added, 'And this is not a waiting room.'

I sat in a nearby café and when I went back to the Rabbinate, Balasseano had arrived.

Victor Balasseano was forty-six years old, a native Alexandrian of Italian descent, greying, softening, and with a limp that made him reliant on his stick. We started speaking in English, but after a few minutes he slipped into French. 'It is the language we prefer to speak here. Even the Hebrew School is conducted in French.'

'The Hebrew School?' I knew there had been several highly regarded Jewish schools in Alexandria earlier this century, from the four-storey community school, which prepared students for the Arabic baccalaureate, to the private, French-speaking École Fondation de Mensce. But I had assumed that these institutions had closed down during the Arab–Israeli wars, that they had ceased to exist along with Alexandria's Jewish community.

'Oh yes. In the 1940s we had 1500 students.'

'And now?'

'Now?' I had surprised him by being so literal. 'We have given it— no! We have loaned it to Egyptians. What are we to do with a school? We have no children.'

When I asked about the history of Alexandria's Jews, Balasseano let out a long breath. 'There have been Jews here since – since the beginning.'

It wasn't an exaggeration. Soon after Alexander the Great laid out the city, Jews from elsewhere in the Empire, particularly from Jerusalem, were relocated to Alexandria and allowed to settle along the ancient Canopic Way, just around the corner from where Balasseano and I were sitting. According to legend, those first Jews arriving in Alexandria became so Hellenized that the third-century BC Egyptian ruler Ptolemy Philadelphus ordered the Pentateuch, the five books of Moses and the first five of the Bible, to be translated into Greek so that younger Jews who no longer spoke Hebrew could still practise their religion. To ensure the accuracy of the translation, seventy huts were built on the island of Pharos and seventy scholarly rabbis locked up in them to translate the ancient scriptures. When they emerged, they had finished seventy identical translations, now known as the Septuagint. That, at least, is the legend, though E. M. Forster added a more realistic note by pointing out that the Septuagint was made 'over many years, and not completed till BC 130'.

Even the synagogue had a history. The present building was finished in 1856, thanks to the permission of the Egyptian ruler Muhammad Ali and the money of Jewish philanthropist Sir Moses Montefiore. It replaced a building that was destroyed in 1798 when Napoleon Bonaparte's army occupied Alexandria. The philosopher Moses Maimonaides mentioned visiting the earlier building, the Eliahou Hanabi, in 1165, while an ancient Jewish writer, presumably referring to another building, noted that 'the person who has not seen the synagogue of Alexandria and the enfilade of its double colonnades hasn't seen the glory of the children of Israel.'

A couple of years earlier I had met an Alexandrian exile on an Italian island. His parents were Italian Jews living in Alexandria and in 1948, when Israel declared statehood and was attacked by its Arab neighbours, he had chosen to fight with the Israelis. His family subsequently had their property taken from them by the government and he hadn't been back to the city since, but he still spoke of it with unbearable longing. Balasseano knew him. 'Tilche? Of course I remember him. He was on the committee in . . . when was it? . . . 1946.'

While we were talking, a young Egyptian wearing a beige shirt and grey trousers appeared. 'Put your notebook away,' Balasseano said. I closed my bag just as the man came over. He asked who I was and spent a while flicking through my passport, though it wasn't obvious that he could read English. The man worked for the Interior Ministry, and Balasseano took the opportunity to ask about opening the synagogue on extra days. My friend was suddenly nervous. I noticed that he had started talking faster, told too many jokes and awarded the man too many honorifics. '*Ya bey, ya habibi, ya pasha.*' When they had agreed on the amount of time the Jews could spend in their synagogue, the agent said to me, 'And you are leaving. Now.'

I knew from listening to Balasseano's conversation with the Interior Ministry agent that a service was to be held the following evening, the start of a Jewish holiday. Balasseano had admitted that they rarely had the ten men required to hold a service on the sabbath; I was curious to see how large a community would turn out on a holiday.

Security outside the synagogue had been extended to include an antiquated fire truck that couldn't have put out a fire in a burning bush. Inside the compound I was questioned by several plain-clothed agents, who referred to me as the British Jew. One of them noted down the details of my passport before waving me in.

The interior of the synagogue was as grand as the outside. The walls were oak-panelled and the upper galleries supported by marble pillars. But there was something abandoned about the place. The air was thick with the must of age, and the upper galleries and most of the pews on the ground floor were empty. The focus of the room, as in all synagogues, was a cupboard, the Ark, where the scrolls of the Torah, the Jewish holy text, were kept. The room was so large, the congregation so small, that the distance between the people in the synagogue and the Ark seemed impossible to cover.

A couple of women sat to the left of the central aisle, two men to the right. The women were talking in the strange babel of tongues that had characterized the Levant in the early nineteen twenties. *'Izzayyik, cherie,'* said one to the other, *'bonne fête* and may you have many more years.' 'Did you take the Royal Jelly?' 'Did you see what she was wearing last week?'

As the service wasn't going to start on time, I walked along the rows to read the brass name-plates on the seats, a roll call of the Jewish community, from Chedid to Mizrahi. A few more people arrived, the men walked up the aisle to the front while the women hung back. As I waited, I became increasingly concerned about my safety. Why the need for the fire truck and soldiers on duty outside? Was it likely that an Islamist group would attack a synagogue in Egypt? Why was it that the only representative from the Israeli Embassy was a security man, a young *sabra*? The women appeared to have no such concerns, or if they did they hid them well beneath their chatter about vitamins and clothes.

I went to greet the men at the front, including the shuffling old man and the grey-haired one I had seen in the office, who seemed to be conducting the evening and acting as cantor.

'Did Balasseano talk to you?' he asked with hostility.

'He had some good stories to tell.'

'Stories are all he has . . .'

At the appointed hour they were still several men short, so the Israeli agent took out his mobile phone and started dialling.

I hadn't planned on attending the service, believing that I would be intruding, but as I made up one of the necessary ten, I felt obliged to stay. The grey-haired cantor still wasn't going to welcome me, and made a few comments about the fact that I wasn't wearing a tie and hadn't brought my own headgear. 'This is a synagogue, you know.' But the others greeted me and shook my hand.

Balasseano was the last to arrive. With him was his wife and their two children, the only young people in the synagogue. As soon as they were in their places, the cantor began to sing his way through the service, Balasseano started on one of his stories and the women resumed their trade of gossip, advice and opinion.

The cantor sang in Hebrew, his voice rising and falling within a tight range. There was little variation. I knew nothing about the possible heritage of this sort of singing, but when, at a prescribed point in the service, everyone stood up and two men walked forward to open the Ark, it occurred to me that there must be parallels between this Ark and the shrines of pagan gods in ancient Egypt; the ancient Egyptian belief that their gods actually inhabited the shrines was echoed in Exodus when the Lord instructed Moses to get his people to build an ark 'that I may dwell among them'. I closed my eyes and listened to the cantor and the sudden silence that accompanied the two men as they approached the Ark. This sequence of sounds – the low incantations followed by the sound of people walking silently through a crowd – had been heard in Alexandria since its foundation more than 2300 years earlier, since before the end of ancient Egypt. The sound of worship in this place was a survival of sorts, although it wasn't one I had expected to find. It also wasn't one that I expected to last. Given the age of the community and that Balasseano's was the only young family, it would have taken more than an optimist to believe that these sounds would still be heard there in ten years' time.

The service lasted an hour, and when it was over, most of the group, the twenty-five or thirty surviving Jews of Alexandria, the elderly, the ancient and the few young ones, went to eat together. Balasseano limped over and invited me to join them. But although my fears for my own security had passed, I found the whole scene depressing. I had heard enough stories for one day, enough memories, enough comments on the past, enough hints at the lack of a future. The lights were already being turned off and the grand building was in darkness. I wished Balasseano happy holiday, left him on the steps under the neo-classical facade and walked across the dim compound to the gate.

Alexander the Great had intended his new city to be a meeting place, a melting pot. In antiquity, nothing showed off the extent to which it succeeded better than the cult of Serapis, a composite god with an Egyptian theology and a benign, bearded Greek face. Concocted during the reign of the first Ptolemy, Alexander's successor in Egypt, it was hoped Serapis would unite the colonizing Greeks and native Egyptians. He was a god for his time, and his cult was immediately popular. Royal patronage must have helped then as it does now; inscriptions, written like the famous Rosetta Stone in hieroglyphs and Greek, record that Ptolemy III Euergetes (246–222 BC) dedicated a temple and its sacred enclosure to Serapis at Rhakotis. Another temple to Serapis, on the peninsula of Canopus several miles east of the city, was also dedicated by the king. In the end, the cult had such universal appeal that shrines and temples to Serapis were built across the known world, from Athens and the Greek holy isle of Delos to India.

Ptolemy III carried the name of 'the Well-doer'. He was, in E. M. Forster's words, 'a sensible and successful soldier, with a taste for science' and he married his cousin Berenice, 'the most highly praised of all the Ptolemaic Queens'. 'In their reign,' Forster concludes, 'the power of Egypt and the splendour of Alexandria come to their height.' The cult and temples of Serapis were part of that flowering.

The original Serapis temple on Rhakotis hill was built along classical Greek lines, more Parthenon than Karnak. As a series of secondary buildings was added over the centuries, the appearance changed, became less strictly ordered. In among the later buildings there was a generously endowed library which became the world's largest depository for ancient texts – some three or four hundred thousand of them – after the famous 'Mother Library' in the palace enclosure burned down. At its height in the early centuries BC, the Serapeum, as the temple was known, and its companion out at Canopus, were among the most sacred places in the Mediterranean. The seeds of their destruction were sown several hundred years later by the arrival from nearby Palestine of a man called Mark.

No sooner off the boat than Mark began his mission by converting a Jewish cobbler by the name of Annianus to a new cult called Christianity. With such an auspicious start, according to Coptic legend, Christianity found its first home in Egypt in AD 45. Seventeen years later – again according to legend – Mark was executed for speaking out against the worship of Serapis, another name to be added to the growing list of early Christian martyr–saints and proof, if proof were needed, that the pagans still had the upper hand and that Serapis was a god to be reckoned with.

For the next three hundred years, Christians, Jews, pagans, neo-platonists and the adherents of a host of other sects, cults and creeds jostled on the marble pavements of cosmopolitan Alexandria. With so many different beliefs rubbing against each other there was bound to be a transferance of ideas as well as differences of opinion. The differences were clear to the people concerned and they often went further than a mere exchange of words. To many outsiders, however, the fighting was incomprehensible, as a letter ascribed to Trajan's successor, the Emperor Hadrian, written in Alexandria in AD 134, makes clear: 'Those who worship Serapis are Christians,' he declared, 'and those who call themselves bishops of Christ are devoted to Serapis.' Clearly in the emperor's eyes they amounted to the same thing. But there were differences, and not just of doctrine. For one thing, Christians were good at organizing themselves. More significant, the cult of Serapis had royal backing, while Christians were touched by the stigma of their founder's execution by the Romans for being a troublemaker. All that changed at the end of the third century.

Constantine had served as an officer in the army Diocletian sent against Alexandria. By 306 he was joint ruler of the Roman empire, and six years later he met his rival in battle outside Rome. On his way to the fight, Constantine saw a flaming cross in the sky on which were written the words *In this conquer*. He did, and after he had dealt with his rival and become lord of the known world, Constantine converted to Christianity. The following year he issued an edict which gave tolerance to Christians, and in 324 he used his power to make Christianity the imperial religion.

Constantine still held back from persecuting pagans and it was not until the end of the fourth century that the Emperor Theodosius the Great issued a series of increasingly restrictive edicts against pagans. Even then he stopped short of ordering the old temples destroyed. By that time, however, a man by the name of Theophilus had become Patriarch in Alexandria. It was for Theophilus and the destruction he wrought that I went back to Pompey's Pillar.

I was up early and ate breakfast looking out across the busy palm-lined square to the Eastern Harbour. I had wanted to be back at the Pillar when its shadow was still long, but the city conspired against me and the sun was high above Rhakotis hill, the gatekeeper already retreated into the shade by the time I walked the tended path and up the ramp to the base of Pompey's Pillar. The pillar was built on a small rock outcrop, and from the vantage point near the base of the pillar I could make out the rough extent of the temple of Serapis, one of the most famous and spectacular temples of the classical world. Or rather I could make out the totality of its destruction.

Below the column, a sign indicated where archaeologists had uncovered the foundation deposits and therefore the outline of the original temple building. All over the site there were holes and shafts, the edge of limestone blocks sticking out of the mound, the remains of crumbling brick walls from the Roman period. The limestone on which the pillar rested had become riddled and taken on the cellular appearance of honeycomb. Around the back of the site, over towards the Muslim cemetery, a smaller column had been reconstructed. Beside it, steps led down to a dressed-stone court. At the bottom, a sign: 'Leading to Galleries for Religious Ceremonies'. The doors were locked but through the mesh I could see down a long subterranean corridor where niches had been cut into the rock, to hold figures of the gods. It was here that the life-size basalt statue of a bull, sacred to Serapis and carved in the second century AD, waited out the long dark centuries, right foot forward, ears flapping, solar disc on its head, before it was discovered and moved to the Alexandrian Museum. Elsewhere, more holes, more shafts, the odd water channel. What went on here? For clues I had to turn to the church historians.

By the time of Theophilus the Patriarch, the hub of the city had shifted away from the Serapeum, eastwards towards the newer Roman suburbs. Temple life throughout the country had also declined, partly because state and religion had been separated and temples were now cut off from the central administration. But the world-famous Serapeum was too important to be eclipsed. Rufinus of Aquileia gave a convincing and, for a Christian, strangely flattering description of it in his *Church History* of 402. 'The site was elevated, not naturally but artificially, to a height of a hundred or more steps, its enormous rectangular premises extending in every direction. All the rooms up to the floor on top were vaulted, and being furnished with ceiling lights and concealed inner chambers separate from one another, were used for various services and secret functions. On the upper level, furthermore, the outermost structures in the whole circumference provided space for halls and shrines and for lofty apartments which normally housed either the temple staff or those . . . who kept themselves pure. Behind these in turn were porticoes arranged in rectangles which ran around the whole circumference on the inside. In the middle of the entire area rose the sanctuary with priceless columns, the exterior fashioned of marble, spacious and magnificent to behold . . . The interior walls of the shrine were believed to have been covered with plates of gold overlaid with silver and then bronze.' The eighteenth century English historian, Edward Gibbon thought it 'rivalled the pride and magnificence of the Capitol' in Rome.

The real treasure of the temple was the great image of Serapis, said to have been fashioned in precious metals by the Greek master-sculptor Bryaxis and so large, according to Rufinus, that 'its right hand touched one wall and its left the other'. It was the stuff of many legends, of which the most popular was that it had been brought to Alexandria after the god had indicated, in a dream to King Ptolemy I, that its statue could be found in a place called Sinope. The statue was also an object of veneration and fear, and the focus of Christian loathing. In AD 391, in the wake of Emperor Theodosius's edicts against pagans, things came to a head.

Rufinus makes no comment about the character of Theophilus, but Theodoret, Bishop of Cyrrus, a small Syrian city, and author of another, not necessarily unbiased church history, described Theophilus as 'a man both of excellent wisdom, and also imbued with a great courage, by whose diligence the City of Alexandria was delivered from the worshipping of idols'. That was in the mid-fifth century, some fifty years after the event. Edward Gibbon had other thoughts. He described Theophilus as 'the perpetual enemy of peace and virtue; a bald, bad man, whose hands were alternately polluted with gold and with blood'. Both were devout Christians and no doubt applauded the closing of the pagan temple. What turned Gibbon against Theophilus – apart from the qualities he mentions – was the knowledge that he did more than just bring an end to service in the house of Serapis. He effectively destroyed the god. And once the great Serapis had been shown to be weak, the entire Egyptian pantheon began to slip off its pedestal.

As is often the case with momentous events, it happened more by chance than design. Against a background of temple closures around the Mediterranean, workmen building a new Christian church elsewhere in Alexandria discovered an old pagan sanctuary. It was too good an opportunity for Theophilus to pass by and he had the cult objects paraded round town. Predictably this outraged the pagans and the ensuing street fights ended with pagans taking Christian hostages and locking themselves in the Serapeum.

Realizing that their days were numbered, and encouraged by a pagan philosopher by the name of Olympius, the devotees of Serapis vowed to defend their temple at all costs. 'These Pagan fanatics,' as Gibbon described them, 'fortified themselves in the temple, or rather fortress, of Serapis, repelled the besiegers by daring sallies and a resolute defence.' He also mentions inhuman cruelties wrought on Christian prisoners. Rufinus was more specific: they were 'forced to offer sacrifice on the altars where fire was kindled; those who refused they put to death with new and refined tortures, fastening some to gibbets and breaking the legs of others and pitching them into the caverns . . . built to receive the blood of sacrifices'.

Finally on to the field of battle rode the city's magistrate, or perhaps his messenger. A ceasefire was brokered while the Emperor Theodosius himself was petitioned. Christians and pagans crowded unarmed into the city's main square to hear the imperial verdict. The emperor had drafted what he must have thought a perfect diplomatic resolution: the dead Christians were to be made martyrs, the pagans were offered amnesty and the cult of Serapis was to be suppressed.

There are no eyewitness accounts of the suppression, which is not entirely surprising given the upheavals that followed. But Theodoret, who was born around the time of the temple's destruction, described events this way. First there were the lesser shrines, as there are side chapels and lesser altars in many Christian churches today, where the images of the gods issued orders and prophecies by means of a priest, hidden in a secret passage behind the idols. 'These, the most wise bishop overthrew, and disclosed the cunning of the priests to the people.'

Beyond the outer halls, the patriarch Theophilus approached the sanctuary of the god Serapis. The god had been abandoned by his followers, who knew the fight was lost, but he was still wrapped round with an aura of mighty and mysterious power. Theodoret mentions 'a false report, that if any man should come near unto it, an earthquake would suddenly arise, and destroy the people', an echo of the ancient belief that world order was only maintained by the will of the gods and by the upkeep of their cults.

While the Christian crowd behind him held back, terrified by the possible consequences of their actions, one of Theophilus's men raised his axe against the statue. The crowd drew its breath, and no doubt uttered a few hasty prayers to Serapis and the rest of the pagan pantheon – just in case they turned out to be more powerful than the patriarch had claimed. The statue, Theodoret reported, felt no pain and uttered no cry 'for it had no life'. In an age when gods were believed to inhabit their statues, when statues were effectively incarnations of the gods, this must have been deeply unsettling news. Worse was to come. Some reports mention that the statue itself was rotten and that when its head was lopped off, a horde of mice came scurrying out. The body of the statue then had more indignities heaped upon it. Theodoret wrote that it was 'drawn about the City, so as they who had before adored the Image, did now behold, and laugh at the feebleness of their God'. Parts of the god were burned in various quarters of the city. The final insult came when Theophilus built churches over the temple sanctuary which later were said to house the relics of St John the Baptist and the Prophet Elijah.

Soon after the death of Serapis, Emperor Theodosius issued another edict that 'no person shall be granted the right to perform sacrifices; no person shall go around the temples; no person shall revere the shrines'. With the Serapeum converted to Christianity it was only a matter of time before the remaining cult centres were closed. As Rufinus put it, 'After the death of Serapis, who had never been alive, what temples of any other demon could remain standing?'

Burning statues was one thing, but as I soon discovered, changing minds wasn't so easy. On my way down from the pillar, I noticed that a set of steps led below the platform and through a small arch to where a Nilometer had stood, a measure by which the benevolence of Serapis – the annual rising of the Nile – was gauged and the prospects for prosperity assessed. As part of the destruction of the temple and a sign of his risen power, Bishop Theophilus moved the Nilometer to one of his new churches.

Ancient Egyptians believed that the Nile rose according to the will of the gods. At first Osiris and later Serapis were thought to exert the greatest influence over the life-giving inundation. When the rites were stopped at the Serapeum, there was a fear that Alexandrians would be punished with a low Nile and subsequent famine for their part in this blasphemy. But the following year the Nile rose so high that Alexandrians started to worry about flooding. Rufinus said it had happened 'so that God could show that it was he who ordered the waters of the river to rise in season, and not Serapis . . .' The way Rufinus saw it, the old order was dead. He was wrong.

After the Nilometer was moved from the Serapeum to a church, and after the Nile continued to rise, Rufinus wrote that there began a practice 'of bringing that very measuring rod [the Nilometer] . . . to the Lord of waters in the church'. The old belief about the gods deciding whether or not the Nile would rise had not gone up in smoke with Serapis. Instead, this and other attributes of the old god had been grafted on to the new religion, perhaps as a way of making it more acceptable to the conservative Egyptians. Whether this was the case or not, the belief that the Christian, and later Muslim, God could control the river's flood survived into the twentieth century. In the 1930s, Egyptologist Margaret Murray reported that the 'people pray as of old to the Ruler of the river, no longer Osiris, but Christ; and as of old they pray for a blessing upon their children, and their homes.' I took this as encouragement to look for survivals in the relationship between Egyptians and their river.

CHAPTER 3

Women and the Nile

'The peasants appear to believe that ancient things are specially
endowed with *barakeh*, and that on that account they may be
efficacious in curing childless women of their barrenness.'

Winifred Blackman, *The Fellahin of Upper Egypt*

Early in the morning, fishermen were out with their patched-up
rowing boats, their crude dugouts, their dangerous slips of flotsam,
balancing on the edge of rotten boards that passed for prows to throw a
net or beating the surface of the Nile, as paintings show their
ancestors doing thousands of years ago. Mid-morning, when I went to
the river to release a mouse which had been feasting in our kitchen,
the bank was busy with rats picking over the remains of the city's
breakfast. Later, passenger boats passed on their way to the barrage, so
crowded that there was barely room to dance, so noisy with their
drums and rattles and singers that they could wake me from the
deepest dream-filled slumber. River buses hurried towards Old Cairo,
barges shunted gravel, wood and occasionally food up and down the
river and river police scuttled close to the banks in their inflatables.
The occasional waterskier took a turn round the island. Egyptian
sailors were forced to swim upstream as part of some frightening
initiation test. And when the river was flat, the Zamalek rowing club's
eight shot past my window in their sleek boat, their eight oars leaving
circles on the surface like needle marks from stitches around an old
surgical wound.

At night the river came into its own, its surface reflecting the city's
lights, little pleasure boats making a tour of the banks. I sat on our
terrace overlooking the water, listened to the sounds from a nightclub
come wafting across the river's mercurial top and considered, as

ancient Egyptians had done close by, long before, that I was at the epicentre of the world.

The Nile is longer than any other river on earth and it also functions in a unique way. In summer, when other rivers are falling, the Nile begins to rise and continues to do so throughout the period of heat. The ancient New Year started at the time when the river began to rise. The Nile dictated the three seasons and with them the pattern of life in the country. And because Egyptians relied entirely for their well-being on the Nile flood, many ceremonies and festivals were held to mark the rise and fall of the water and many more superstitions were attached to the various levels the river reached. The river may have lost some of its significance in recent years, but it was still the thread that held its parts together and I was confident of finding survivals connected with it.

It is not known whether ancient Egyptians ever found the source of the river. There is no tangible evidence, no inscriptions high upstream, no references in Egyptian texts to suggest that they knew, nor that they had heard from people of the south about the rainfall in Ethiopia, Kenya and Uganda. But whether they had unlocked the secret of the river or not, as I had seen in Alexandria, ancient Egyptians believed the Nile rose – or didn't – at the will or whim of the gods. The Nile itself was venerated in several ways, often as a fat-bellied, saggy-bosomed deity called Hapi. You can get a sense of the extent to which the river was revered from *A Hymn to the Nile*, a New Kingdom text:

Hail to thee, O Nile, that risest from the earth, out of mysterious darkness to the light of the day where men hymn thy coming: who waterest the fields, whom Ra has created to feed all the cattle, who waterest even the desert, which is far from the water, for it is thy dew that falls from heaven. If the Nile is sluggish, men's noses are stopped up, all men are wretched, the sacrifices vanish, millions die. If it riseth, the earth rejoiceth, every back laugheth, every mouth is glad, every tooth is to be seen.

Osiris, one of the most popular and long-lasting of the ancient gods, was killed when his brother Seth threw him into the Nile, locked inside a wooden casket. Osiris's faithful wife Isis recovered his body, but Seth again found it and this time went as far as to cut it into thirteen pieces, which he threw back into the Nile. Again Isis went searching for him. Ten . . . eleven . . . twelve pieces were recovered, but the thirteenth, his penis, was never found. According to one version of the legend, it was eaten by fish.

As the cult grew in popularity, Osiris became known as Lord of the River and was associated with the natural cycle, with renewal and regeneration. But it was a woman, Isis, his wife, who was credited with making the Nile begin to rise. Legends stated that it was her tears, shed in sadness at Osiris's death, which made the difference. The Copts have kept an echo of this tradition alive by calling the eleventh day of their month of Bauna (mid June) *lailet an-nuqta*, the night of the drop, that drop being a tear.

Lailet an-nuqta used to be a night of great celebration, when many people sailed boats on the river. The ancient chronicler Heliodorus described it as one of the country's main festivals. The fourth-century historian Libianus went further and noted that people believed that if the rites were not performed in the proper way then the river simply would not rise. In villages throughout the country there was song and dance, and statues of the river god Hapi were paraded around the houses to celebrate the blessing.

Being superstitious by nature, Egyptians did more than just make offerings to the river gods. They also attempted to divine how high the river would flood. One way of doing this was to leave unleavened dough overnight on the flat roofs of their houses. If the dough had risen by the morning, the year would be a good one. The state had more scientific ways of gauging the rise in the water level.

Along the river between Aswan and Cairo there was a series of Nilometers. As at the Serapeum, these were columns against which the levels of the rising water level could be gauged. Beside the columns stood the records of previous years. The historian Strabo, a contemporary of Julius Caesar, wrote that there was 'nothing in Egypt so useful as these Nilometers'. One of the *savants* who accompanied Napoleon Bonaparte on his 1798 expedition went as far as to call them 'holy relics'. Thanks to these gauges we know the detailed history of the river's rise to the seventh century AD, while less complete records date far back into the pharaonic period. They tell a tale of feast and famine.

The ancients prayed for the river to rise to sixteen ells. The Roman writer Pliny spelled out the significance of the number. Considering the notches along the side of a Nilometer, he wrote that '12 ells mean hunger, 13 sufficiency, 15 security, 16 abundance.'

To encourage the abundant sixteen, Egyptians prayed to their gods. Amr Ibn al-As, the great Arab general, discovered after the conquest of Egypt that they went further. Amr was told that each year, when the river began to rise, Egyptians made an offering to the Nile god by drowning a young virgin. Amr found this practice barbaric and ordered that it be stopped and so it was, but not without dramatic consequences: three months after its traditional flood season, the river hadn't risen. For once the all-conquering general was uncertain what to do. He wrote to his master, the Caliph Omar in Medina, and received a suitably regal reply. Omar praised Amr for stopping the human sacrifice and enclosed a letter which he ordered be thrown into the river in the place of the young girl. The letter read thus: 'From Abd-Allah Omar, Prince of the Faithful, to the Nile of Egypt. If thou flow of thine own accord, flow not; but if it be God, the One, the Mighty, who causeth thee to flow, we implore God, the One, the Mighty, to make thee flow.' And, praise be to God, the Nile responded by rising to the blessed sixteen of abundance.

Although the caliph had stopped the sacrifice, what his letter had shown was that he too believed, as the ancients had done, that the river was controlled by a deity who – like the pagan gods – could be petitioned to intervene and make the river rise for the benefit of the country. And although, as a result of Amr's decree, young virgins could walk the summer streets of Cairo without fear of being trussed up and drowned to please the river god, the tradition of sacrifice survived, as Edward Lane discovered in 1834, some twelve hundred years after Amr's decree.

Lane noticed that while the Nile was still low, an earth dam was built across the mouth of the canal that linked the river to the city of Cairo, which then sat back on the valley. The dam stood about seven metres above the river's low-water mark. In front of the dam, Cairenes built 'a round pillar of earth, diminishing towards the top, in the form of a truncated cone, and not quite so high as the dam. This is called the "arooseh" (or bride). Corn or millet was then planted on the bride's flat head, to confirm her fertility.

The *arusa* was a sacrifice to the river, a substitute for the virgin of old, and when the river rose it consumed her. But even this substitute had ancient leanings: in pharaonic Egypt dolls were also thrown into the Nile, in the words of Egyptologist Guillemette Andreu, to arouse the Nile god's 'desire to swell up and inundate the land'.

One night at a party I gave a serious reply to the question of what I was doing. I was talking to a tall, dark Roman by the name of Marina, who had been living in Egypt for many years.

'I've got a story for you,' she said in reply, 'about when I first arrived, when I was with Alex.' She lit a cigarette. 'This being Egypt and Egyptians being the way they are, people wanted to know why we had no children. At that time I knew some people out by the pyramids and one day, when I was visiting them, the woman asked if we had a problem – you know – with getting pregnant.'

Marina said she was so out of her head at the time that there were, no doubt, many problems, but she didn't think conception was one of them. Still, she was curious to know where all this was going to lead and intimated that well, yes, maybe something was wrong, but – hey! – what could she do?

'The woman, whose name was Karima, knew someone there in the village who could help with these things. Maybe she could also help me. She said she would arrange for me to visit her.'

And then?

That's as far as she got when we were interrupted. Maybe we needed to fill our glasses or someone else came to talk to us, but either way the conversation drifted elsewhere.

Marina didn't forget, however, and when we parted she said, 'Come and talk to me if you want to know more about it. Some time this week.'

Most Egyptians I had contact with in Cairo were young and male, and the astronomical cost of providing a suitable home for a wife in an increasingly dense city had prevented many of them from marrying as young as they would have liked. Most men I met outside the city were married by the time they were twenty-five. 'And children?' I'd ask. 'Ye-es,' came the country reply, 'four.' Or sometimes five or more. 'And you?' they'd then ask.

When this first happened I said I had no children. 'God willing, one day . . . ,' was the generous answer, but I noticed that a certain distance was kept between those who had and those who didn't. Later I was able to say that I had two children. 'Boys?' the men asked hopefully. 'Yes, both boys.' 'Thank God,' was the reply, and, 'The Prophet is with you.' I put this down to chauvinism. Daughters were going to be trouble to look after and keep pure, and they cost money when it came time to marry. What's more, with a daughter the family name ended. Sons were a whole different proposition. Yet there was something worse than daughters. To have no children at all – as I had admitted – was a calamity beyond endurance. No one to carry the name or continue the blood, no one to look after you in old age (if they couldn't afford a place of their own, a newly wed girl tended to move to her mother-in-law's home), no one to remember you in that uniquely filial way when you died.

'We all want to believe that there is a power out there, or up there, who can help us out of those difficult moments,' Marina said, 'especially if we think we have some hotline to them. Egyptians are just like everyone else in this respect. The difference is that they have been doing it the same way for so goddam long.'

Marina lived on the top floor of a nineteenth-century Italianate building in the centre of Cairo, an ultimate urban experience. To get to the antiquated wood-cage lift, which might, if it was working and if no one had left the door open at one of the six floors, carry me to the top, I passed a secondhand-book dealer, his stock laid out on the pavement, a cart selling some sort of instant carbohydrate burst and, up the steep flight of stairs, a couple enjoying a stolen moment of courtship. I had come to hear the rest of Marina's story.

'So I was telling you about this woman, this sheikha I met,' she said as though she had broken off only a couple of minutes ago. 'She lived near the Pyramids and it was agreed that I should go and see her. This was a long time ago, you know, when I was still new to the city – and my memory is not what it used to be, so you must be patient.'

I was beginning to wonder whether she had had second thoughts about telling me. 'Anything you can remember will be interesting.'

She went to the kitchen, stirred something in a jug and came back at speed, her voluminous *galabiyya* billowing behind her. She had poured tequila cocktails. 'This should help the memory.

51

'I can't tell you what happened with the sheikha without telling you about Alex. The two might be unconnected in every other way, but in my memories of what happened they are inseparable.

'I had what you could call a turbulent relationship with Alex. He could be a dangerous man to be around. Some people said he was the sort who would die young, and that's what happened. Although I was with him, he wanted me to give more of myself. He wanted me to have a child and I suppose I wanted to have one to please him. The child was to be the irrevocable bond between us.'

Marina went to get a packet of cigarettes and then crouched back down on the floor cushion. There was something absent about her, as though she had been released from the room, as though she wasn't talking to me, just talking and I happened to be there.

'Alex was leaving for India to perform what we might call an illicit commercial transaction and I was to wait for him in Cairo. The anxiety of separation was alleviated for both of us by the knowledge that early each day I was going to make my way to the Pyramids to visit the sheikha, a couple of kilometres away from Karima's village. It pleased me to think that while Alex took his chances, I took mine in the name of a child, a proof of love.'

The sheikha turned out to be an enormous woman who smelled of spices, an albina with the face of a frog. She received Marina in the courtyard of her concrete home, full of children, mostly girls, and women going about their work, shouting and scolding, all health and fertility. Karima pleaded Marina's case and the sheikha agreed to treat her.

'We went to a bedroom and sat on the floor. A small girl came and climbed on the bed to close the shutters as the visit of a white woman had drawn a bit of a crowd outside. The girl left and came back with a tin covered with great clam shells, a bowl and a bar of red soap. The sheikha motioned for me to lie down. Karima told me not to be afraid. The sheikha started mumbling the obligatory *be izn illah*s, then uncovered my stomach and washed it heartily with red suds, taking handfuls of flesh and kneading my belly. My womb, she said, was *mish mafrusha*, unfurnished. Stranger things were to follow.'

Right on cue the phone rang and Marina hurried to answer it – again the sail-like billowing of her *galabiyya*. When she came back, she continued without a pause.

'The sheikha made me sit up and bend over my outstretched legs seven times while she chanted and pushed me in my back. Now she addressed herself to the contents of the tin – some beads and shells and a cloth package from which she extracted a tiny sachet of herbs, tied with a thread. She motioned with her finger for me to come closer. I did. She motioned again, curling her index finger inwards. I kept on going and was practically on top of her when Karima explained that I was supposed to put the sachet inside me. So I stood there and did it.'

The sheikha's girl was called, the tin of charms taken away. Marina was told not to ride horses, to remove the sachet the following morning at Karima's house before going to visit the skeikha, and to dispose of it as she passed the pyramids. 'No drink,' the sheikha said, waving her glass, 'and no breakfast.'

'I had no word from Alex. I returned three days running, leaving downtown still sleeping, taking a cab to the end of the city, stomach empty, proud of myself for doing this. It was a long walk from Karima's to the sheikha's house, but I enjoyed it and Karima encouraged me with stories of her own experiences with the sheikha. "Look at my son Eid," she would say proudly, as though he was living testimony to the sheikha's powers.

'On the third and last day, the sheikha handed me a sachet as usual, but this time she told me to keep it until my husband returned. She made a point about that. After we had made love, she told me, I had to insert it and this time I must leave it there all night long. Two days afterwards I should come back to the sheikha and then . . . what a magnificent son I would surely present to my husband, *inshaallah*. First, I needed my husband back.

'Several days later the doorbell rang. Alex in a suit, sweating after the six flights. I burst into tears. "But wait," says he. "*C'est pas fini.*" His luggage, the merchandise, the whole point of the trip, had been lost and he had to return to the airport. He wouldn't let me come and I was sure I'd never see him again. I went repeatedly to my room to handle the sachet, crying, until he came back with the bag.'

She paused to light up, perhaps because she sensed she was becoming maudlin, or because she was uneasy about sharing her confidences. I kept silent. When she continued, she was more matter-of-fact.

'After Alex returned, I went back to see the sheikha. This time, she took a little fetish doll from the bottom of her tin, took me into the courtyard, placed the doll on the ground and told me to jump over it seven times.'

'Do you know why seven?'

'Days of the week? Magic number?'

'Deadly sins?' I suggested. 'Circles of hell?'

'Anyway,' said Marina, returning to her story, 'after I'd jumped the seventh time, she called for a pitcher of water, dipped the doll into it and told me to drink seven times. The rest of the water went into a jar which she said I had to wash with at sundown – and until then I wasn't to talk to a man.'

'I went home in silence and washed with the water . . .'

'And?'

'And what?'

'Did it work? Did you get pregnant?'

'Of course. I had triplets. What do you think? Of course it didn't work. And several months later later Alex died here in Cairo. I had no child. End of story.'

Only it wasn't over because later, after we had eaten pasta and drunk whatever was left in the cupboard, I asked if she thought the fertility ritual she had performed had anything to do with ancient Egypt.

'I don't know,' she said easily, 'but why don't we go and ask the sheikha? I haven't been there for, oh, at least ten years, but I have a box of old papers here somewhere and I'm sure I'll find her address.'

She didn't. Instead, she found a photograph of Karima's husband, Samy, as a young man. How, I wondered, were we going to track him down from an out-of-date photograph? I mentioned my concern.

'Have faith,' Marina told me.

Edward Lane referred to what he called a 'very singular and disgusting practice' regarding infertility in *The Manners and Customs of the Modern Egyptians*. In the nineteenth century, criminals sentenced to death in Cairo were beheaded at the foot of the citadel. Their corpses were then taken across the square to a nearby stone table where they were washed and prepared for burial. The water drained into a trough. 'Some women,' Lane added, 'step over the body of a decapitated man seven times, without speaking, to become pregnant. And some, with the same desire, dip in the blood a piece of cotton wool, of which they

54

afterwards make use in a manner I must decline mentioning.' Was the ritual Marina had performed, I wondered, in some way an echo of this?

In Cairo in the 1890s there appeared a treatise called *Tibb ar-Rukka*, the Medicine of Old Women – old wives' tales. The work, published in Arabic in two volumes, was written by an Egyptian doctor by the name of Abd ar-Rahman Efendi Ismail. Efendi Ismail had been trained in western medicine and appears to have looked on folk medicine with the eye of a sceptic. Entry XIX is entitled '*Ukm*, barrenness'. 'One of the best "remedies" for barrenness is to walk over a person who has been killed. This is a famous old "remedy", even with inhabitants of large towns. It is long since we used to see, when our professors were lecturing on Anatomy in the Kasr al-Aini College [Cairo], many ladies coming to the dissecting room in order that they might pass over the dead, with this object in view.'

Marina was sitting with Alan, a solid, dark-haired Scot with an explosive manner, who had lived in Cairo for more than ten years. Alan, who had friends near the Pyramids, stared at the old photograph of Samy and shared Marina's view that we had a good chance of finding him.

We took a taxi to the village, which had become a large town, grown fat on its proximity to the Sphinx and the auditorium for the nightly Sound and Light Show. The main street and some side streets were lined with papyrus factories, carpet bazaars, souvenir emporia and stables.

As soon as we arrived at the stables in front of the Pyramids, Alan was spotted by one of his friends. We received the usual hospitality – much shaking of hands, an insistence that we sit down, cold drinks opened and bottles passed round. After the formalities, Alan brought out the photograph of long-ago Samy. His friend looked at it, squinted, blinked, squinted again. Others came and soon there were ten of us huddled round the old photo and, yes, they thought they did know him. Twenty minutes later, Samy was there.

He had aged badly since the photograph had been taken, had lost some teeth, some hair, his shape, his looks, but there was no mistaking him. He recognized Marina immediately.

Again there was the insistence of hospitality and we all climbed into his friend's car to go to his house, where there was more embracing with his wife Karima. On the mat in their small room, more drinks were offered while Marina swapped memories and news. Then she mentioned the sheikha.

'She is no longer with us,' Karima replied, 'God have mercy upon her. She died some years ago.'

Marina reminded her of the ritual they had gone through although there was clearly no need; Karima remembered it all as a bright time in her life.

'Does someone else perform that sort of thing now?' Marina asked.

Karima looked puzzled, as though she was wondering why Marina would want to go through all that again.

When Marina explained why we had come and what I was trying to do, that I thought there might be a link between the sheikha's 'cure' and ancient Egyptian rituals, there was a mood change.

Samy stopped smiling for the first time. 'No one does that sort of thing any more.'

Later he explained that there was another sheikha, but that he was loath to approach her. 'She will want money,' he explained, 'a lot of money, a hundred dollars or more, and for what? What is there in all that?'

Karima said nothing.

'*Maalesh*,' Marina told them, 'never mind.'

I wasn't surprised by Samy's reluctance to help. I didn't know whether his response was because he was loath to discuss personal matters in front of a stranger, or another instance of the shift in public perception. Did Samy think there was something wrong, something unIslamic in these rituals?

I didn't want to let it drop. In London, some years earlier, Dr Zaki Bedawi, a Muslim scholar, had told me that, with ancient cultures, customs related to the essential mysteries of life, to fertility and death, were the last to change or be abandoned. I held on to that hope and called Mona, one of the people I had met on my first trip to Egypt in 1987. Mona seemed about as far removed from ancient cults as it was possible for a person to be. She belonged to modern, cosmopolitan, forward-looking, mobile-toting Egypt.

Born into a wealthy and well-known Muslim family, educated at the

American University in Cairo, well groomed and well travelled, Mona worked in public relations, a job to which she was perfectly suited. It was some time since I had seen her, but on the phone she was as welcoming as ever. She suggested we meet on a Nile-side terrace.

The café–restaurant was spread out over terraces up the river bank. I chose a table near the waterline and watched small pleasure boats filled beyond safety with loud young Cairenes pass close to the bank. A felucca glided upriver towards the jetty over by the Meridien hotel. A man and his child paddled a small rowing boat to within a few feet of me, then pulled in the fishing net they had just dragged across the river, to no avail. Behind me, waiters carried trays burdened with late lunches, early dinners, copious snacks, huge ice-cream sundaes, pots of tea, cold hibiscus drinks. Beyond them, I spotted Mona.

She was a confident thirty-something woman, her large brown eyes highlighted with kohl, as ancient Egyptian women used to do. She was dressed to the nines in a tight-fitting blouse, long, figure-hugging skirt and she turned heads as she walked. She was also both married and without a child, but I had no idea how I would ever get the subject around to fertility rites.

When we had ordered, and exchanged news, Mona asked what I was working on and I explained about my search for this living past. I mentioned some of the connections I had made.

'But Anthony,' she laughed, 'how is it that you know about these things when most of us who live in Cairo never even get to hear about them?'

'Put it down to the advantage of the outsider. I know more about what goes on here than I do about my own country.'

When she heard about the woman at Speos Artemidos, where Amr and I had arrived by donkey, Mona was pensive for a moment, as if she wasn't sure that she had understood me.

'It's very interesting that you ask me about this, Anthony. Two or three years ago I would not have known what you were talking about. In fact I would have said that you have made it all up. The past is past. After all, I was brought up here in Cairo and we didn't know about these things. But recently friends of mine have started talking about them too. They are worried that they don't yet have children and they want them very much. What can they do? They go to see the doctors and they go to pray in the mosque – maybe somewhere special like at

Husayn or Sayyida Zaynab. But if this doesn't work? Well, then they go out into the countryside, to an old temple or perhaps to a tomb, and they will pray there for a child. This really happens,' she added in case I didn't believe her.

Mona was clearly uneasy about the conversation, but she was also a little elated. Each time a waiter came to pour more tea or empty the ashtray, she stopped talking. As she was known and liked at this café, she stopped often.

'Who do they pray to?'

'To Allah,' she said. 'To God.'

'Not the old gods?' I asked, although I knew I was pushing too hard.

'Old gods, new gods,' she shrugged and repeated the formula, 'there is no God but God. Just different names, no?'

In her intonation, there was an appeal for understanding. I began to wonder whether while telling me about her friends she wasn't also describing her own experience. I took it as a cue.

'Have you been with them? To these places?'

She laughed at me for even suggesting such a thing. 'Anthony. Of course not,' and then a little less easily added, 'but I think I would. If it came to it. Yes, I think I would.'

The desire to procreate has particularly sharp teeth in Egypt because under Islamic law a man may divorce his wife for many reasons and one of them could be her inability to bear children. This is a many-sided calamity for a woman. She will lose her husband – often her financial support, she will have no children and she will carry the stigma of having been divorced for being infertile, making it difficult to remarry. Under such pressure, it was understandable that a woman might put her trust in things blessed with age, that had been tried and tested, that had the patina of use, especially if they touched on religion.

Winifred Blackman described several rites she had witnessed or heard about. During her first visit, in 1920, she was working on an archaeological dig at Meir, near Asyut, when several women came to the camp to ask for ancient bones; they believed that if they stepped over them they would become pregnant. Later in the season, she announced that she had some charms which had proved helpful with conception. Women began arriving in groups, as many as ten at a time, all wanting to try them out.

The charms were inch-high, blue-glazed figures of the goddess Isis, a mummified but unidentified god, a scarab and a cat. 'The ritual,' Blackman recorded in her notebook, 'was as follows. The women first repaired to one of the ancient decorated tomb-chapels. On entering, each stepped seven times backwards and forwards over what she supposed to be the mouth of the shaft admitting to the subterranean burial chamber. When this performance was over she returned to the undecorated tomb-chapel in which I lived. Here I produced the charms, two of which were placed on the ground at a time. Then each woman solemnly stepped over them backwards and forwards seven times. Four charms in all were used . . . When this was accomplished the lower jaw-bone of an ancient Egyptian skull was placed on the ground. The same ceremony was yet again performed, being repeated with two complete ancient Egyptian heads, one a well-preserved mummified head, the other a skull. A glass of water was then brought, into which the blue glazed charms were dropped. Each woman drank some of the water, and then picked out the charms and sucked them. Some rubbed their bodies with these magical objects, and also applied the water to their persons.'

When she returned to Egypt after a summer spent in England, Blackman heard that some of these women had become pregnant.

Oxford-based Professor J. Gwyn Griffiths described a similar ritual in this letter to the anthropological journal *MAN*: 'On 23 February, 1937, during a visit to the temple of Deir al-Bahari, on the western bank of the Nile, opposite Thebes in Middle Egypt, I witnessed an interesting fertility rite.

'I was looking at a mummy which lay on the floor in the temple, when I noticed that three young native women, who appeared to be near me, were taking a special interest in that object. One of them, who was dressed, like her friends, in the European manner, took her stand near the mummy and, raising her dress a little, she stepped over it, backwards and forwards some three or four times, saying the while, *En sha'la Rabbina yiddi ni' wahid walud* (May the Lord give me a little boy).' Griffiths then went on to note that this rite was found throughout Egypt, but had not been recorded elsewhere.

Umm Seti recorded several fertility rites in her manuscript, although it seems that in neither her present nor her past life did she have need of them herself. She made no comment about ancient Egyptian fertility rites, although as she claimed to have been reincarnated she was presumably in a position to know. But she did notice that in our time Egyptian women believed certain monuments could make them fertile.

The pyramids of Giza attracted their share of supplicants, some of whom slid down the surviving limestone casing blocks on the Third Pyramid. Others slept in the entrance to the Second Pyramid. One of these was a woman whom Umm Seti knew well, who had been married for four years but was still childless. We are left to imagine the trials and tribulations the woman must have gone through, the monthly disappointments, the self-doubt, before she walked up that slope – she and her husband – past the Sphinx, on to the ridge, all Cairo at her back, the pyramids in front and beyond them the desert.

The guards challenged them, then recognized them as neighbours and knew why they had come. The man helped his wife scramble over the tall blocks of the Pyramid, up the man-high courses to the opening, settled her there and then climbed down. Strangely, Umm Seti makes no mention of the woman's fear of the great monument, of the *djinn* and *afarit* who were said to treat it as home, the unknown powers it was believed to contain and which one might glimpse if one stayed there alone. Paul Brunton, who spent a night inside the Great Pyramid in the 1930s, described 'spectral figures', 'grey, gliding, vaporous forms', 'malevolent ghostly invaders' creeping around him in the darkness. But the woman Umm Seti knew 'slept soundly all night in the upper entrance, while her husband and one of the guards sat outside, smoking and drinking tea until the dawn came.' Nine months later, the woman gave birth to a daughter.

In the Egyptian Museum in Cairo, there is a green schist statuette of the goddess Ta-urt, represented as a pregnant hippopotamus standing on her hind legs. In ancient Egypt she was the goddess of pregnancy and childbirth and was worshipped across the country and down through the centuries. Umm Seti noticed that the statue had an uncharacteristic polish to it, a sheen created in recent times by women rubbing their hands over the goddess's belly and then over their own.

At Dendera, in a small temple beside the main one, where the sons of the main gods of the place were worshipped, there were two basalt statues of the god Ihy, portrayed as a naked boy. 'In order to obtain a child,' Umm Seti wrote, 'the would-be mother must walk clockwise seven times around each statue in turn. After that she must step seven times over each figure, taking care to pass directly over the phallus.'

In 1978, another Egyptian fertility rite – one with no apparent connection to Osiris – became celebrated around the world when American anthropologist Richard Critchfield published his study of a *fellah* called Shahhat, a villager from the west bank near Luxor.

Shahhat's beginning had a sensational angle to it. His mother, Umm Muhammad, had already given birth to four sons, so fertility didn't appear to be a problem for her, but all of them had died during infancy or childhood. Umm Muhammad was worried that her husband would divorce her if she didn't produce a male heir. 'She was frantic,' Critchfield wrote. 'She sacrificed sheep at the holiest of shrines. She bought amulets and magic written charms, that, burned in a pot of incense, were said to make a wish reality. She consulted sorcerers and *sufis* and the most revered old sheikhs. She prayed incessantly to Allah. She even sought the help of Christian Coptic priests, for her whole position as a woman, wife, and mother was at stake. At last, when all else failed, she crept late one night into the walled grounds of the great stone mortuary temple of Ramses III to appeal to the ancient god.'

Critchfield described how the woman slunk through the darkness to the temple's sacred lake, circled round it seven times, 'now begging Allah to forgive her, now fervently calling upon Ammon-Ra, the Unknown, to help her conceive a son.' Eventually, after collapsing in a panting, trembling heap, she drank some of the water. A year later her son was born. Critchfield reports that she told no one what she had done. She named her son Muhammad, but to protect him from the Evil Eye she called him by another name: Shahhat, the beggar.

Critchfield's study of Shahhat's life was a great success and soon became a standard text for anthropology undergraduates studying Third World development. But not all the attention it received was favourable. Timothy Mitchell, a British academic, accused Critchfield of believing tall stories at best and at worst of making up part of his book. Mitchell was well placed to make the accusations because he too had lived in Shahhat's village, had met Umm Muhammad and knew the circumstances of the *fellahin*. He had also spoken to many of the people Critchfield had written about. They had told him they had made up stories because they thought that was what Critchfield had wanted to hear.

Sitting in the apartment in Cairo, watching the first of the fruit bats swinging round the dates on the palm tree below the window, it occurred to me that whatever else Mitchell and the villagers had said none of them had doubted the idea that women went to the pharaonic temple to pray for fertility. I decided to go and ask people in Shahhat's village. There was still time to catch the night train to Luxor. I called a friend who lived near Shahhat's village, to warn him I was coming, packed a bag and hurried downstairs.

Ibrahim, our local taxi driver, was passing a cloth over the immaculate bonnet of his old Peugeot. There was something strange, awkward about his movements, as though he was afraid that by applying too much pressure he would wear away the metal or rub off the paint. Without appearing to look up, he knew I was there. 'Aywa missiou,' he bellowed across the road at me, as if I would have dared go with anyone else while he was standing there. 'Off again? Where to this time?'

I told him about my book. 'In Luxor, women go to the pharaonic temples because they cannot become pregnant.'

'Why do they do that?'

'They believe that pharaonic things have some sort of power. What do you think?'

If Ibrahim had been a singer, his voice would have been described as *basso profundo*, although it had acquired its profundity through neither talent nor training, but by smoking with dedication from an early age. His laugh was similarly low-hung and he replied with ridicule. 'I've heard of that sort of thing, but I don't believe it.' Then he went religious on me. 'Why go to the old temples when there is a mosque. There is no God but God—'

I finished the sentence for him, '—and Muhammad is his messenger.'

'But for Saiidis,' he added, bringing out the old prejudice of northerners for people of Upper Egypt, 'nothing is too stupid.' All the way along Fouad Street he told me stories that were either completely untrue or seriously distorted, and ended by cracking a few Saiidi jokes, similar in nature to those told about Poles, Irish and Belgians elsewhere in the world. 'It's not too late to change your mind,' he said, as I got out at Cairo Central Station. 'I can drive you home again.'

I paid less than he wanted but more than he deserved, said goodbye and made it on to the night train to Luxor with a couple of minutes to spare.

Zeitoun's house was on the west bank of the Nile at Luxor. A large mudbrick villa fronted by palm trees, it was built in Egyptian style, by which I mean like a fortress, with few openings on the ground floor. But while other houses in the hamlet had flat roofs laid over palm-trunk beams, Zeitoun's house was covered by large domes, which made it look like something out of an Orientalist's dream. The fact that it stood between the desert and fields, beneath the holy Theban mountains, beside the great temple of Medinet Habu, added to the fantasy.

Dogs barked to announce my arrival and Zeitoun appeared in jeans and pyjama top, his face, hair and clothes covered in mud. 'Just in time. We are doing some building.'

'You haven't finished the house?'

'A house like this is never finished. It is always growing, growing.'

Zeitoun was a product of the Levant. His family were famous traders before and after World War II, at the time of the last king, Farouk. In the aftermath of the revolution, which saw Farouk sail out of Alexandria in a treasure-laden ship, Zeitoun's family fled to Lebanon and France, 'Which explains how I was educated in Beirut, have a French passport but am Egyptian.'

He was the first of his family to return to Egypt. While studying architecture in London, Zeitoun was influenced by the Egyptian architect Hassan Fathy. Fathy had led a revival in mudbrick architecture. Zeitoun and David, an American friend who had studied with him in Beirut and was at that time working in Egypt, decided to build themselves a house. It was to be a showpiece, an experiment to see how far they could push Fathy's principles of mudbrick architecture. The answer, they discovered, was very far indeed.

Zeitoun, David and several villagers worked until midday, by which time they had raised the wall they were building by several feet. After that they rested and after the rest Zeitoun walked me round the house.

'As you are looking for . . . what do you call those things?'

'Survivals.'

'*Survivances*. Well, you've come to the right place. The whole house is a survival, one way or another. Did you see how we were working, the way the bricks were made and left in the sun to bake? The way we stuck them together with more mud? Just like the olden days. And here's something else you must put down in your notebook: many people have written that the ancient Egyptians had no arches, that all their roofs were flat. For temples that was true because they were building with stone. But it was not so for domestic architecture. In houses they definitely used vaults like the ones we have here' – he pointed to massive vaults covering the entrance to the house. 'And if you go to the Ramesseum you will see that near the temple there are storerooms which had mudbrick vaults and parts of them are still standing after how many thousand years? It's fantastic, no?'

On the upper terrace, we stretched out on *mastabas*, brick benches on which ancient Egyptians also liked to sit after work. The sun was low but it was still warm. People from the village were in the fields, cutting fodder which they bundled up and took home to feed their animals, as the ancients had done in this place. Some girls were laughing by a waterpump across the field. Zeitoun, who had a reputation for chasing girls, smiled when he heard them. 'Listen to that!' he said, trying to feign disapproval.

Most obvious of all, from where we were sitting, was the mortuary temple of Ramses III, one of many built by pharaohs in front of the tomb-laden hills. It was there, according to Critchfield, that Shahhat's mother prayed to the ancient god Amun-Ra. I was itching to see inside it.

'There's no hurry,' Zeitoun assured me. 'In fact I think we should wait till tonight.'

'But then it will be closed.'

'That's no problem. The guards all know Zeitoun. So relax, have a beer, and I'll tell you about Shahhat.'

Zeitoun met Shahhat when he first arrived in the village back in the 1970s. 'Shahhat and me, we were bad young men. Oh, the nights we spent together . . .'

He reminisced for a while and then, before he disappeared into the past all together, I brought him back and reminded him that I was interested in the circumstances of Shahhat's conception. 'Sure,' he said, 'why not? Just look at the architecture. Look at the relationship between the temple and the village, the one so big, so old, so beautiful in its decoration, while the houses – *paf!* – you make them out of mud in a couple of days and if you don't keep them up, or if the rains are bad, then they fall down.

'No,' he corrected himself, 'not fall down. They get worn down by the wind, the rain, the sun. Compared to their houses, the temple is everything that God stands for – solid and eternal. So why not go there to ask for help when you need it? It's no more bizarre' he said, pointing to the coming night, 'than wishing on a star.'

We lay back on the *mastabas*, sipping beers, watching the light fade. After Cairo, the place was intoxicatingly calm and I caught the slightest sounds – children crying in a house a long way off, a dog barking on the hill, the neighbours bringing their animals in for the night and getting their food ready. As night fell a thick silence wrapped itself around the house, and then other sounds came with the darkness. A breeze rustled palms on the edge of the field and the eucalyptus which had grown out of the courtyard and now towered over the house. Muhammad, one of the neighbours, was sitting out talking softly to one of his brothers. An animal screeched up in the hills and I sat up to look. The great limestone crags were glowing in the night as if the pharaohs and queens buried in their hillside tombs still had the power to command life and light. The glow was reflected moonlight. When Zeitoun saw it, he decided it was time to visit the temple. First he went looking for his stick, 'In case we meet a snake or something.'

Black dogs outside the neighbours' houses showed their teeth and snarled. I shushed them; Zeitoun waved his stick. We cut across the fields, along the ridge of an irrigation channel, and climbed over the mound of earth that had covered the temple's ancient outer wall. From the top I could see the whole complex, the fortress-like main temple, its walls slanting inwards as they rose to exaggerate the sense of their mass and solidity. To the right, the slender trunk of a single palm supported an extravagance of fronds. All around lay the architectural salvage of ages past: stone lintels and basins, pools and well heads. And around the perimeter wall for much of its course there were still remains of the medina, the town, of Djeme which the Copts built over Ramses's sacred compound after the old rites had been abandoned.

Zeitoun pointed out the lie of the land with his stick, how the fields behind us were slightly sunken, the remaining trace of a huge artificial lake connected by a canal to the Nile, along which the pharaoh sailed to his temple in the wet season. As in Ramses III's day, there were guards at the entrance to the temple. Zeitoun didn't wait for them to find us or to be roused by the wild dogs which we were sure were prowling nearby. Instead he went into their hut.

After the handshakes, the slapping of backs, we had tea and a smoke, and then Zeitoun announced that we were going to have a quick look at the temple.

'But *mudir*, boss,' said one of the guards who didn't share a history with him, 'the temple is closed. It's forbidden.'

'Never mind,' Zeitoun replied, 'the professor and I will not disturb anyone,' and he handed out another round of cigarettes to smooth further objections.

Medinet Habu was built as a power base during Ramses III's lifetime, and as the centre of his cult, where prayers to his memory were to be said, after his death. Like his predecessors, Ramses III didn't want to be buried near his temple. The place was too obvious. And like his people, he believed that his corpse and his many funerary objects had to be kept intact to ensure a happy afterlife. So, more than 1500 years after the height of the pyramid age, Ramses had himself buried in secrecy alongside the other dead pharaohs in the Valley of the Kings. The temple, therefore, stood in for the grave as the place where Ramses, now deified, could be worshipped.

All this cost money, of course, and as his predecessors had done, Ramses III made the necessary donations to support the temple complex. He also kept careful records of his gifts, so that he could refer to them when he came face to face with the god Osiris on judgement day. At the time of his death, the papyrus recording all the donations he had made to temples throughout the country was 133 feet long. The details are staggering, as is the idea of the bureaucracy needed to keep such a record. Ramses gave some 169 towns, 113,433 slaves, almost half a million head of cattle, a million plots of land, more than 19 million bouquets of flowers, 2756 images of gods. There were thousands of kilograms of gold and silver, hundreds of thousands of animals and millions of jars of wine, honey, oil and incense. One half of the total revenues of Egypt and its colonies, which at the time included a large swathe of the Middle East, went to build, maintain and ensure the future of temples such as Medinet Habu.

Nothing I have seen in the world compares to Medinet Habu by moonlight for pure wonder and spookiness. Beneath the bright sky, the temple looked squat, as permanent as anything made by man can be, its limestone walls washed with silver. We walked away from the gatehouse, a two-storey Syrian-inspired structure, which Ramses commissioned to commemorate a Middle East victory that must have been fictitious, for by the time of his reign, Syria was no longer worth fighting. Across the outer courtyard we passed between two smaller chapels and approached the main building. The massive gate was shut, so we walked around the outside, clockwise, coming first to the remains of the palace. The sand and scrub were littered with stone fragments. Like desert and delta, and pharaoh and *fellah*, destruction and survival go hand in hand.

We walked over the destroyed palace area. The basic floorplan of the rooms had been recreated, and Zeitoun tried to give me an idea of what the place might have looked like. It seemed small to me. We peered into the inner temple through the window of royal audience, where Ramses stood if he was watching a ceremony rather than taking part. Then we studied the inscriptions and images that cover the outer walls, the calendar of sacrifices that were to be made here in the period after the anniversary of the pharaoh's accession, the exaggerated accounts of Ramses's military achievements (suggestions of a Syrian campaign might have been misleading, but Ramses III did win considerable victories against the Libyans and 'Sea Peoples'), great images of the pharaoh hunting wild goats, asses and bulls. Zeitoun had seen it all many times before, but he was an architect and he was still impressed. 'Look at the way they cut this stone.' He ran a hand over the join between two of the great blocks. 'How did they know to cut their blocks so accurately? Look how they fit together. And see how the moonlight comes from the side and brings the pictures to life.'

We moved away towards the south-east corner of the compound. The main temple had reflected enough moonlight off its creamy walls to light up the ground around it, but the moon had sunk, and in the far corner it was dark. Zeitoun began to brandish his stick and I trod carefully, imagining snakes and scorpions and some of the beasts which terrorized the nights of the ancients.

'The sacred lake is somewhere near here,' he warned, 'so be careful. You don't want to fall in.'

As my eyes adjusted, I saw several things rising out of the black ground, one of which looked like the entrance to an air-raid shelter. Zeitoun thought it was the Nilometer. Inside, a flight of steps led down to water. The air was dank. I threw in a stone to see how deep it was and heard something – some things – scuttling around. 'Just some snakes,' Zeitoun said offhandedly, 'or maybe scorpions, or bats, or . . .' In the half-light I saw his broad smile.

The sacred lake stood near the stone wall which separated the temple compound from the village of Kom Lolah where Shahhat and his mother lived. We stood and listened to the sounds of life, of someone praying, a rustling nearby (someone moving away from us?), a man calling out (one of the guards accosting someone?) A few feet below us, the black fetid water of the sacred lake bubbled like soup. My thoughts fractured and divided, went back thousands of years to midnight rituals performed for the gods, back a few decades to Shahhat's mother petitioning the gods here, in this place, to give her a healthy son and then back to Zeitoun and me standing at the water's edge.

I was beyond pretending: I was scared. 'I think,' I whispered into the darkness towards Zeitoun, 'that we should get out of here.'

I waited another moment.

'Zeitoun,' I whispered more loudly, 'let's go.'

There was no reply. He had already gone.

Boutros, the local doctor, came for dinner at the house the following evening. He was a complex, cultured man who spoke good English and French, could hold his own in a conversation about the latest films or exhibitions in London or New York, although he clearly hadn't seen them, and who held strong opinions about everything from the price and quality of the local Stella beer to American cultural imperialism. It occurred to me that the local doctor would know better than anyone else what went on in the village.

After dinner, I asked him about Shahhat's mother and whether he knew women who had performed fertility rites at the temple.

'It's not interesting,' he replied, offhand almost to the point of being rude. 'Whether they do or don't is of no interest.'

'Maybe to you it isn't, because you live here . . .'

He was clearly annoyed. 'Why does everyone who comes here want to push this point about "the footsteps of the pharaohs"?'

I had already sorted out my theory on that. 'I am interested because I have a sense of having lost touch with my history. Because in Egypt, I see people who can draw a line straight back to pre-history. And – most important – who still have documentary evidence to support it. Don't you think that's exciting?'

'All I see is what happens when these things people in the village do, fail. They come to me for help. "Please doctor, give me some of your medicine." It's all nonsense.'

Critchfield described Kom Lolah as a traditional Egyptian village, a place where there had been little change over the centuries but which was about to be transformed by electricity and the Aswan dam. Transformed it was, but by a different force: tourism. One day in the café I found a Dutch girl lying on her back on a wooden bench with one of the villagers on top of her. On another day, outside the same café, a middle-aged American woman laughed while a young man from the village massaged her breasts.

Kom Lolah's location near the ancient burial ground of pharaohs and nobles made it far from typical. For years, travellers had been going there in search of enlightenment or wealth, and now for sex. It was too famous, too well known to be typical. Villagers had become used to contact with foreigners. And since Critchfield's book was published in 1978 and became a standard anthropology text, Shahhat and the other characters in the book had enjoyed some sort of celebrity; they were no longer surprised by people asking for them by name.

I was thinking of going to talk to Shahhat about fertility rites, but then I remembered what he had told Timothy Mitchell, that he had said whatever he said to Critchfield because he thought that was what Critchfield wanted to hear. So how could I know whether what he would tell me was the truth? I decided to ask elsewhere in the village.

Hamida watched my face with her hazel-brown eyes. 'I hear you went to the temple the other night.'

I wasn't surprised she knew; word travelled fast in such a small community. 'I've heard that women go to the sacred lake to help them get pregnant. Do you know about this?'

She knew, that much was obvious, but it was mid-morning and she had things to do in the house. 'Come back another day,' she suggested.

'Tomorrow? I could bring Zeitoun.'

She hadn't seen him for a long time. 'Come for lunch,' she said.

I objected, knowing she could ill afford the extra food. Critchfield reckoned that Upper Egyptian families spent twice as much each month as villagers in the delta, the extra expense being the cigarettes, meat, tea and sugar offered to friends and neighbours. Hamida was no exception to this tradition of hospitality and she insisted to the point where I would have insulted her had I refused.

Hamida was as strong-willed and hard-working as other women in the village, but she was unusual in that her husband was absent; I didn't know if he had left her, died or gone elsewhere to work. She would never have invited us had her husband been at home – he would have done the inviting – and she risked gossip by having two men in her house. Perhaps that was why she chose a time when the children would also be there.

The design of the village buildings had changed so little over the centuries that it was hard to tell whether the row of two-storey mudbrick buildings facing the entrance to the temple were ten, a hundred or a thousand years old. A clue was provided by a photograph taken by British photographer Francis Frith on 18 March 1862, which showed the temple's 'castle gate' and a large swathe of ploughed land where the houses now stood; so perhaps even the oldest was no more than a hundred and thirty years old. Not that this proved people weren't living there. At that time villagers still lived inside the temple, moving out later in the century when the Egyptologists moved in.

Hamida's house had three rooms and a large yard on the ground floor, and two bedrooms upstairs. The largest room was the one we stepped into from the street, which had *mastabas* along two walls. The family's animals passed this way when they were brought in at night. Zeitoun looked the place over with his architect's eye, saw where she had covered the mudbrick plaster with concrete, where she had added burned-brick walls to the upper floor. 'After the bad rains,' she explained defensively, 'we had to do something to stop the house falling down.' Zeitoun said he doubted whether laying concrete over mud was the answer. 'She'll be doing it again before long,' he said quietly to me and then offered to work on the house for her. Hamida seemed flattered rather than offended by his comments, because she considered Zeitoun a foreigner – he wasn't pure Egyptian – and because it was rare for someone of his standing to show this sort of interest.

She was an attractive woman. What you could see of her skin was the colour of milk chocolate, but most of her was hidden beneath several layers of clothing, the outer one being black. Many women in the village in their thirties, with several children, looked worn down, but Hamida still had a bounce in her step, a sense of determination about her. She sat on the bench across the room, a block of sunlight separating us, the door open so that anyone passing would see how innocent was the meeting, and started to talk about the temple.

'When a woman wants to have a baby but has a problem, she goes with someone, a friend, another woman, and they go in through the main gate and walk around to see all of the temple.

'This must be on the last day of her period and she must not have washed herself or have been with her husband. After they have looked around, they go straight to the lake, where the woman who has come to help must throw a stone into the water. The woman who wants the baby then has to wash herself in the lake, both her face and her body.'

I remembered the sound of bubbles rising through the lake's fetid water. 'You mean, she has to get into the lake?'

Hamida laughed at the idea. 'No, no. She takes some water and smears it over herself. Then she has to take a bottle of water home with her, which she heats up and uses to wash herself.'

'And all this happens at night?'

'Only during the day,' she replied, contrary to Critchfield's description of Shahhat's mother's visit.

'And does it work?'

'Oh yes, definitely.'

'Did you try it?'

She pointed to her children. 'Thank God I didn't need to. But recently there was a woman who came all the way from Sohag with her husband. They knew about it because they have a friend in the village. She had been trying to have a child for years and had been to see several doctors, but nothing seemed to work. Then she came to the temple and did as I told you and you know what? She had a baby.'

'Is Habu the only temple where this sort of thing is possible?'

'No, there are others, but this is the best.' She smiled with proprietorial pride. 'Some time ago some officials tried to forbid it, but then someone quite high up in the antiquity service came with his wife. She couldn't have children, so she went to the lake and soon after became pregnant. And she is the one who has made sure that women can still go to the temple.'

One of Hamida's daughters appeared from the kitchen. 'I have something I want to show you,' Hamida said. 'Later, down by the temple. But first you must eat.'

Lunch was served on a *tabliah*, a low table; Zeitoun and I sat on a mat around it. At other country meals, the hosts had always left me to eat or had stayed only to serve me, but Hamida hitched up her black dress and sat down with us. The food was good and there was plenty of it – fried beef, vegetables in a tomato sauce, coarse Egyptian rice, white beans and flat bread. Hamida piled our plates with vegetables and then sifted through the meat with her fingers to find us the largest chunks.

'Look at this,' Zeitoun said in English so Hamida wouldn't understand, 'this is their food for the next days. They want us to eat it all and yet at the same time they will be happy if we don't.' When Hamida wasn't looking, we slipped some meat back into the bowl.

There was no ceremony over the meal and little conversation. When we finished we merely gave the traditional *alhamdulillah* – thanks be to God – stood up and went to wash our hands.

Hamida's younger son brought tea and we moved to a windowless room, cooler than the others, where the children were watching a black-and-white musical on the television. The film, from the 1960s, was set in Alexandria. I wondered what Hamida, living in her mudbrick house, farming her land where the soil is part Nile silt, part human remains, above all living in the shadow of the pharaoh's temple, made of the film. For her, the Egypt of the movie was another country where women wore short skirts and tight blouses. She assumed Zeitoun and I belonged to that other world and, pointing to the female star, she asked if I knew her.

We dozed through the heat of the afternoon and then Hamida took us out to show us something we had missed. We walked past the temple's main gate, past the guards, the armed police, a driver asleep in his car, a couple of tourists drinking tea at the café, the empty terrace of the Habu Hotel and the houses where people were beginning to stir.

I asked Hamida why villagers still went to the ancient temple. 'You are Muslims, yet you go to the pharaonic temple. Why?'

'Why not?' she replied with the same lack of interest that Dr Boutros had expressed. 'We have always done these things. Since the time of the pharaohs. And there is and has always been only one God.'

At the side of the temple compound, the high stone outer wall disappeared beneath an unexcavated mound. On top of this mound a new mudbrick wall, little more than a metre high, had been freshly whitewashed. Hamida pointed to a small break in the wall, something which Zeitoun had never noticed before, though he had often passed that way.

We climbed the bank and found ourselves in an open-roofed shrine, eight or ten feet square. An elderly lady was sitting in one corner.

'This,' Hamida explained, 'is the place of Sheikh Alaa ad-Din.'

Zeitoun, who had lived on the other side of the temple for more than twenty years and had never heard mention of the sheikh, was speechless, for once. He rubbed his jaw, shook his head, shrugged his shoulders and held out his hands, palms up.

We sat barefoot on the rough coir mat.

'Tell me, ya Hamida,' Zeitoun begged with a look of childish wonder, 'who is your Sheikh Aladin?'

Hamida began to relate a story *min zamaan*, from long ago, about the child Alaa ad-Din, who came here, as she put it, 'like a bird who makes his nest'. He stayed for a while and then passed on. Since then the place had been sacred to him. 'At one point,' Hamida continued, pointing to some wooden planks stacked to one side, 'there was a roof over this place, but it fell down. And this woman,' she said, touching the sleeve of the elderly woman, 'comes every Monday and Thursday from the village at the crossroads down there and looks after him,' by which she meant the shrine. 'She brings water and lights candles.'

At this cue, the other woman, whose skin had sun-dried to parchment, handed me a candle. There were niches in the middle of each of the four walls and I chose one in which to make the offering, the women keeping silent as I honoured the sheikh.

When I crouched back down on the mat, she offered me water. 'Sheikh Alaa ad-Din makes miracles,' she assured me. 'When we are in trouble and we ask the sheikh what to do then he helps us and solves our problems.'

Alhamdulillah, we all murmured.

'Sheikh Alaa ad-Din comes like a phantom in the night. Sometimes some of us see him and then we know that he has the *baraka* for us.'

Hamida and the old woman continued to extol the many virtues of the sheikh who came there long ago as a boy and went no one knew where. When due tribute had been paid, we stood up. Before leaving, I walked to the north side of the shrine to look over at the temple. It was late afternoon and the sun, low over the ridge of the Theban hills, cast a honeyed, orange light. Majestic palms, standing alone at intervals in the temple forecourt, had fronds the colour of emeralds. The sky was a deep blue. Like the moonlight, the slanting sun raised the reliefs on the temple and once again the old gods seemed to rise out of the walls. It was only then that I noticed the sacred lake, immediately below me. It seemed more than coincidence that the shrine had been built above the lake, more than coincidence that the child-sheikh had chosen this place, out of more than a kilometre of perimeter wall, to kneel and pray.

I looked down at the lake. 'Hamida, where does the water in the sacred lake come from? There isn't regular rain here to fill it. Does someone,' and I nodded towards the elderly woman, 'come and fill it up?'

'No, no. It comes from the Nile. From the Nile, as before.'

A few metres from the lake stood the ancient Nilometer that Zeitoun and I had seen on our moonlit walk.

I thought of the stories of festivals celebrating the rise of the Nile, the sacrifice of the virgin and the planting of grain on the *arusa*, the bride of the river, to rouse the river to the magic number 16, the 16 cubits of water which promised an abundant harvest. I thought of Marina drinking seven times from the sheikha's water, of the women anointing themselves with water in Winifred Blackman's camp, of something else Umm Seti had written about women going to the Osirion, the supposed tomb of Osiris at Abydos temple and washing themselves with the clear water. I thought too of Theophilus, the Alexandrian patriarch who had destroyed the temple of pagan Serapis, but had moved its Nilometer into his church. As in antiquity, the same powers which helped the Nile make the land fertile were called upon to help women in need.

Beyond the low wall of the sheikh's shrine, the sun dipped behind the hills. Zeitoun put a hand on my shoulder. 'I think these ladies want to go home now.'

CHAPTER 4

The Living and the Dead

The house of death is for life.
Hardjedef, Old Kingdom sage

During the '*Eid* to celebrate the end of the fasting month of Ramadan in 1834, Edward Lane passed through Báb an-Nasr, Cairo's great Gate of Victory, and out into the cemetery. That night the British Arabist and Cairo resident made the following entry in his diary: 'This day I accompanied my neighbour 'Osmán to visit the tomb of the sheikh Ibrahim, in the cemetery of Báb en-Nasr, on the north of the city, to see that the monument was in good repair, and to pay to the memory of the lamented traveller that tribute of respect which is customary on the 'Eed.'

This 'lamented traveller' Sheikh Ibrahim whom Lane had gone to honour was known in Europe as Jean Louis Burckhardt. Twenty-five years earlier, the young, intelligent Swiss man had set out on one of the world's great adventures. He had been commissioned by the London-based African Association to find the source of the river Niger and the fabled town of Timbuktu. At the time, neither the course of the river nor the whereabouts of the town could be located on any known map. But that year of 1809, James G. Jackson, an English trader in Morocco, had published a fantastic description of the place whose ruler possessed 'an immense quantity of gold'.

The plan was for Burckhardt to travel to Cairo and join one of the annual caravans of pilgrims returning from Mecca to west Africa and, it was hoped, to the Niger. As a plan it was both vague and dangerous, an indication of the Association's desperation to succeed, for they had already sent several expeditions to Africa and almost all had ended badly. The last and most famous, launched in 1805, teamed the explorer Mungo Park with forty-four British redcoats. Park had already managed to reach the Niger on an earlier expedition in 1795, so he was not unaware of the risks, yet thirty-nine of his soldiers died before even getting to the river and Park himself was killed with the rest of his party soon after.

In spite of the risks Burckhardt was convinced he could complete the quest. He was described as a strong and solid man, so the natural dangers – the inhospitable landscape, the crossing of the Sahara and the many deadly diseases of the Niger – did not daunt him. But the people of the countries he wanted to pass through did and he decided that the only way to ensure his safety was to pose as a Muslim. In England he began to study Arabic and when he reached Syria, he adopted the dress of a pious Levantine and the name of Sheikh Ibrahim Ibn Abdallah.

On his way from Syria to Egypt, Burckhardt struck lucky and became the first European for at least five hundred years to see the ancient Nabatean capital of Petra, the 'rose-red city half as old as time'. When he reached Cairo in 1812, his disguise was so convincing that even the British agent failed to recognize him as a European. It was there that he faced what he anticipated would be his biggest problem: finding a caravan that would take him across the desert.

As there was no immediate prospect of a caravan, Burckhardt went south along the Nile into Nubia. The British MP Thomas Legh, who met him en route, described him as having 'all the exterior of a common Arab . . . He told us he had been living for many days with the sheiks of the villages.' Burckhardt continued into Nubia, where he was the first westerner since the Graeco-Roman era to record seeing the great work of Pharaoh Ramses III, the temple of Abu Simbel. He went even further south, as far as Shendi in Sudan, in the company of Arab slavers. Still no news of westbound caravans, so from Shendi he headed across the Red Sea and made the pilgrimage to Mecca. In Mecca he hoped to find people travelling to the Niger river. He was also adding credibility to his disguise by becoming a *hajj*, a pilgrim.

In Arabia things started to go wrong. He was received by Muhammad Ali, the ruler of Egypt who was then in Taif, and helped his legend by impressing the learned imams with his knowledge of the Koran, but he also contracted dysentery. A second bout was so serious that he confessed himself 'now unable to rise from my carpet . . . I had by this time lost all hope of returning to Egypt, and had prepared myself for dying here.' He did recover, however, and re-entered Cairo in June 1815, two and a half years after his departure and a few days after Napoleon had been defeated at Waterloo. For the next two years, Burckhardt planned his Niger journey (ignorant that the British Navy had initiated another attempt, via the Congo River in 1816) and worked on his journals, which were later published. In 1817, while the maverick Egyptologist Giovanni Belzoni was capitalizing on Burckhardt's discovery in Nubia by forcing his way into the main temple at Abu Simbel, Burckhardt had a relapse of dysentery and died.

Foreigners who died in Egypt were usually buried in the cemeteries allocated to their religious denominations. But as Burckhardt lay dying in his house in the old city, he told Henry Salt, the British agent, 'The Turks will take my body – I know it – perhaps you had better let them.' So the man whom Salt called 'the perfect Arab' was buried under his assumed name just outside the city's great gates, in the northern cemetery.

Out of respect for Burckhardt's memory, on the first *Eid* I spent in Cairo I went to visit his tomb with Sylvie, the girl who had lured me to the city in the first place.

The guidebook I had at that time, a previous edition of the *Blue Guide*, stated that 'the exact site of his [Burckhardt's] tomb is unknown.'

'But this is Cairo, a city of marvels and wonders,' Sylvie said by way of encouragement as we walked through the city gate into the cemetery, 'and I've found stranger things here than a lost tomb.'

The cemetery was busy, the main track into it reduced to slush. We slipped between a couple of tomb houses and in among the graves, where it was calm and quieter. In several tombs families were talking, food was being prepared, prayers chanted.

We asked some old men standing by one of the cemetery's bigger tombs if they had heard of Burckhardt, on the assumption that they might know more than the young ones. It was a good guess. The men introduced us to the guardian of the large tomb. He couldn't help, but he did point out another tomb where we should ask. We were passed from person to person, tomb to tomb – 'Ask Hassan.' 'Go to my neighbour.' '*Maalesh*, never mind, I don't know.' – until we came to the broad reception hall of another large mausoleum, where three men were drinking tea and watching a television propped up on a grave. Through the doors on the far side of the room we could see other marble tombs. A man in a dark grey *galabiyya* and knitted white cap introduced himself as the guardian and invited us to join him on the wooden benches. *Etfaddal. Shukran. Afwan.* (Please join us. Thank you. You are welcome.)

The guardian laughed when he heard why we had come. He didn't see many foreigners round there, and he found it awkward talking to a tall blonde like Sylvie so he addressed himself to me. 'There are no written records. If you want to know who has been buried in this section of the cemetery in the last ten years then I can tell you, for I have it in my head. If you want to know the people from the last eighty years, then this too I can tell you, for my grandfather told it to my father and my father told me. I have it all here.' He tapped his temple.

'The tomb we are looking for belongs to a man who came from Switzerland. But he died here long before your grandfather. One hundred and eighty years ago to be precise.'

Sylvie thought it would be wise to embellish the story a little. 'This man,' she said, pointing at me, 'is from his family and wishes to visit the tomb for the *Eid*.'

'*Ya salaam.* That is a long time ago,' said the guardian. He wasn't sure he could help. 'But I have heard of a *khawaga* buried somewhere on the edge of the cemetery whose grave is kept up by a foreign government – the British, I think.'

He called a boy over and told him to make enquiries for us. Half an hour later the boy returned with a couple of men. One of them, who carried two bundles of keys tied to a string round his neck, thought he knew what we were looking for. We followed him through a maze of small mausoleums and simple graves into a place we would never have found – or found our way out of – on our own. We passed a series of wooden shacks, like garden sheds, their doors open, families sitting on mats inside, the men smoking waterpipes made from old jars and hollowed bamboo stalks, women preparing tea or food on primus stoves. It was impossible to tell just by looking whether these people were newly arrived refugees, had come for the holiday weekend or lived there all year round.

The cemetery looked like a rambling and disorganized place, but it did have divisions, demarcations and boundaries, mostly invisible to the eye but seared into the memories of the guardians. The man with the keys took us to Area 30, on the edge of the great cemetery, and called for the guardian.

We asked if he knew of a foreign sheikh buried here.

The guardian, an elderly, toothless, friendly man by the name of Gomaa, Friday, reacted as though it was the most normal request in the world and led us to a tomb built against the cemetery's back wall. 'That's him,' he said, 'but he's locked. Wait here a little and I'll go get the key.'

If we had come across this tomb by chance we might have suspected it was Burckhardt's for it was as different in style from the other buildings as a church is from a mosque. It was a small, square construction, sun-faded yellow on the outside, with plain mouldings around two covered windows and big cracks in an old wooden door. In a cemetery full of domes, it was the only tomb with a pointed, European-style roof. By the time Gomaa returned with the key, we had been joined by three children, curious to watch the foreigners.

Gomaa swung the door open, wiped his hands on his blue *galabiyya*, smiled wide enough to show his toothless gums and shook my hand again. '*Ahlan wa sahlan*. You are most welcome.'

The tomb was in a good state, but the roof had lost its tiles and strips of sunlight fell through the wooden slats. The white marble grave was raised several feet off the ground, with vertical blocks at the head and feet. The block at the head was capped in the Turkish style with a marble turban. The inscription around the side of the grave, carved in elaborate characters, confirmed that this was the grave of 'Al-sheikh al-hajj; Ibrahim al-Mahdi Ibn Abdallah Burckhardt al-Luzani'.

'*Ya salaam*,' I said, happy to have found this greatest of all Middle East travellers.

'There is no God but God,' Gomaa replied, and while we sent one of the children to buy flowers, he brushed the dust off the marble.

This wasn't the tomb Lane saw in 1834. In the 1850s the British explorer Richard Burton wrote in his journal, 'Some years ago, the sum of £20 (I am informed) was collected, in order to raise a fitting monument over the discoverer of Petra's humble grave. Some objection, however, was started, because Moslems are supposed to claim Burckhardt as one of their own saints.' Perhaps as a result of the squabbling, the new tomb, the one we were visiting, was not finished until 1871.

When the grave had been cleaned, while we waited for the dust to settle and the flowers to arrive, we sat against the wall and I asked Gomaa what he knew about this sheikh from Lausanne.

'The sheikh was a very good man. Another guardian, who lived long ago, was sleeping in the tomb one day when he dreamed of white light and holy apparitions.' He studied my face to see if this was the right course to be taking. 'He was afraid of this – who of us is not disturbed by thoughts of *afarit* and *djinn*? – but then four men in white clothes appeared before him and assured him there was no need to be afraid. Indeed, they said that it was a blessing to see the white light.' By implication, therefore, Burckhardt himself was blessed on account of the white light having appeared in his tomb. 'They called him *al-muslimayn*, the two Muslims, because he was so devout.'

We arranged palm leaves and the orange flowers of Cairo's brief spring on the cold marble and when everything was done, we stood in silence, thinking about the great man until Gomaa began coughing and hawking extravagantly and we knew it was time to leave.

If you were a wealthy or powerful ancient Egyptian then you built a tomb to house your body and placed in it the many objects and symbolic helpers you hoped you would have need for in the next life as well as an earthy priest to say prayers and make offerings to the dead. The Old Kingdom sage Hardjedef, whose fame lived on long after his tomb had been desecrated, advised his son to 'beautify your house in the necropolis and make excellent your place in the West. Accept [this maxim], for death is bitter for us. Accept [this maxim], for life is exalted for us. The house of death is for life.' What he was telling his son was that if he didn't manage to preserve his mummy in its tomb then he would not be able to enjoy a happy afterlife.

The appointment of a ka-servant, as the priest was known, was also a way of ensuring that tombs were maintained and protected from tomb robbers, but this sort of service didn't come cheap. The ka-servant would be supported by income from an endowment of land. 'Choose for him a plot amongst your fields, well-watered every year,' Hardjedef wrote. 'He profits you more than your own son. Prefer him even to your heir.'

There were no guarantees, of course, and even the best-laid plans sometimes went wrong. Families intervened or the endowments made for the ka-servant were embezzled or failed to generate enough income to maintain the tomb. What is certain is that, by the New Kingdom, Hardjedef's advice was looking naive to say the least. It is referred to in a text called 'Harpists' Songs': 'Those who built tombs, their places are gone. See, what has been made of them? I have heard the words of Imhotep and Hardjedef, whose sayings men recite so much. What are their places (now)? Their walls are crumbled, their places are gone, as though they had never been.'

But in spite of the difficulties, the cult of the dead thrived throughout ancient Egypt and by the time of the advent of Christianity it was central to everyday life: in Alexandria, Alexander the Great and the Ptolemaic kings who succeeded him reinforced the cult when they were buried in a central position – the main crossroads – of the living city. Coptic Christians defiled the old tombs yet they maintained the cult and many monastic churches still contain the remains of fourth-century Coptic saints whose bodies, it is claimed, have not in any way decomposed.

When the Arabs took control, it would have been safe to assume that all this would come to an end. Yet it didn't.

The Koran is quite specific in its instructions for burial. The corpse should be wrapped in a winding sheet and buried that same day before the sun sets. Although the burial may be marked by a stone, the way the Prophet saw it 'the best grave is one you can rub away with your hand'. The implication was that as a Muslim you shouldn't bother about the physical remains after a death. And with good reason, because graves tended to become the focus of veneration, which often led to idolatry. But this injunction flew in the face of the longer-held Egyptian view that if physical remains were not properly looked after, then future happiness in the afterlife might be in jeopardy.

When Amr Ibn al-As, general of the Arab army that conquered Egypt in 641, described the place he had taken for his master in Arabia, he made one serious omission. There was no mention of the remarkable funerary monuments which towered over the living throughout the country, from the Pyramids at Giza, the most recognizable monuments in the world, to tombs cut into the limestone cliffs of the Nile, from the pits for mummified bulls near Cairo to the Valley of the Kings and the funerary temples in Luxor. Perhaps they didn't strike him as significant.

Early Muslim burials were straightforward affairs. Gone were the life-long preparations, the elaborate processions, the complicated rites and rituals of the pagan world. When Sidi Oqbah, a companion of the Prophet, died in Cairo in the seventh century, he was wrapped in a shroud and buried quickly in the desert south of the new city. In contrast to the pharaonic tradition, his grave was dug on the east bank and he was laid on his side facing Mecca, pointing away from the western gate of the ancient underworld.

But there was another tradition for Islamic burials and it was one which could be traced back to Muhammad himself: the Prophet was buried beneath the floor of his wife's house. Amr's son Abdallah, who ruled Egypt for a year after his father's death, followed Muhammad's example and was similarly buried in his own house, beside Amr's mosque. When the mosque was enlarged, the tomb was incorporated into it, the mosque becoming effectively a funerary monument.

A series of magnificent tombs was built for the Fatimid sultans and princes who arrived from Tunisia in 969 with the bones of their ancestors. But these were eclipsed by the grandeur of the tombs built after the creation of the *waqf*, a system of religious endowment that was exempt from taxes and government meddling (in Cairo there is, now, a Ministry of Waqfs which administers the religious endowments). The *waqf* system provided the pious with a model for charitable activities and the unscrupulous with another set of laws to exploit. It also led to a boom in the building of magnificent tombs.

During the thirteenth and fourteenth centuries, after the Fatimids and their successors the Ayyubids (Saladin and his descendants) had lost power, Egypt was under the control of Mamelukes. Mamelukes were slaves bought in the markets of Central Asia and the Caucasus, who were then trained by the emirs of Cairo in the art of warfare and the principles of Islam and drafted into what became a formidable army. The emirs believed that as Mamelukes had no blood ties or family obligations, they would be loyal to their masters, and on this principle many of them were freed. Under the Mameluke system, there was no automatic hereditary succession and, theoretically at least, the sultan was chosen by his peers, although in fact he was often chosen by power brokers. It was possible, therefore, for a slave in some Central Asian market to be shipped as part of a consignment headed for Cairo and brought up by an emir, then to be freed and to rise through the ranks to become an emir himself and maybe even sultan of Egypt. Rather than foster security, it became an invitation for the ambitious to master the art of poison, to learn how to brandish knives in the dark. During a one-hundred-and-fifty-year period of Mameluke rule, no less than thirty different sultans rose to the throne. Thirteen were executed or assassinated, ten were deposed, three abdicated and only four of them enjoyed a natural death while still in power.

Mameluke rule had serious consequences for the City of the Dead. Although there were, as always, exceptions, Mamelukes were forbidden from bequeathing their wealth to their children. In consequence, many of them tried to dispose of their wealth before death. One of the most popular ways of doing this was to build a tomb with a mosque, a *madrassa* (Koran school) or hospital attached and endow it with a *waqf* to ensure its upkeep. That way the name of the Mameluke was preserved as long as the building survived and there was the bonus that however mean and bloody a man had been in life, he might still be remembered as a generous benefactor.

Mamelukes gave Cairo some of its finest buildings and most generous *waqfs*. Historian Max Rodenbeck has reckoned that by 1339, 130,000 acres of farmland and a sizeable chunk of urban property had been given over to the *waqf* to support schools, fountains and hospitals. It was a figure that grew. 'By the end of the eighteenth century,' Rodenbeck calculated, 'a fifth of all Egypt's arable land – some 600,000 acres – was held in *waqf*, including one small property, endowed in the thirteenth century, which provided for the daily feeding of Cairo's stray cats.'

The street of al-Muizz li Din Allah, the heart of the old city, was lined with spectacular monuments, built by Mameluke sultans and emirs to the glory of God and their own good name. Sultan Qalawun's was typical. A Kipchak Turk from the Lower Volta and Mameluke to Saladin's great-nephew, Qalawun became sultan in 1280, ruled for ten years and was succeeded by two sons and three of his own Mamelukes. Qalawun also built one of the most imposing monuments in Cairo, a complex of tomb, mosque and hospital. The inscription on the facade is both long and revealing. First, the sultan blows his own trumpet:

'This noble dome,' the inscription starts, 'this magnificent college and blessed hospital was ordered by our Lord and Master, the August Sultan al-Malik al-Mansur, the Wise, Just, God-assisted, Victorious, Champion of the Faith, Conqueror, Sword of the World and the True Religion . . . Lord of Kings and of Sultans, the Sultan of the Length and Breadth of the Earth . . . King of the Two Continents and the Two Seas, King of Kings of Arabs and Non-Arabs, the Guardian of the Two Qiblas, the Servant of the Two Sanctuaries, Qalawun al-Salihi, the Associate of the Commander of the Believers – may God prolong his glory, glorify his victories, elevate his beacon and double his power . . .' Then he notes that 'the beginning of all this took place in one of the months of 1284 and its ending in one of the months of 1285.' Just over a year, when he had been on the throne for only four years. To build his complex, Qalawun is said to have plundered stone from the Pyramids at Giza and from older palaces on Roda island, and used all available labour, including slaves, prisoners and even passersby, himself standing whip in hand, like the pharaoh's slave drivers in front of the Pyramids, to see the work was done.

Beside Qalawun's complex on Sharia al-Muizz, his son al-Nasir Muhammad built his own tomb and mosque. Beyond that stood the tomb and mosque of Sultan Barquq, who reigned a century after Qalawun. One day as I was passing, an old man shouted, 'Come in! Come in!' and walked ahead of me up the stairs towards the black and white marble entrance. Through the great bronze doors, along the bright green matting, he asked, 'Want to see the tomb?'

I did.

'Good.' Now he turned round and showed his ravaged face, his sagging wrinkles, the loss of teeth. His narrow eyes were dead. 'I will show you, but first you will give me money. For the ticket.'

I gave the blind man a banknote which he flicked between his fingers with the ease of a bank teller. He nodded as though he knew just from the feel of the paper how much I had given him. It seemed petty to demand a ticket in return.

The blind man led me around the corner into the mosque, built towards the end of the fourteenth century. 'This one took two years to build . . . Where are your shoes?'

'In my hand.'

'Good.' We were on the edge of a large courtyard, surrounded by four soaring, vaulted recesses where the four different schools of Islamic law had once been taught. 'Nice, no?' the man said, as though he was seeing it all himself for the first time, as he may well have been doing in his memory.

The mosque was being restored, but the blind man walked around as though he could see each of the new obstacles in his way, warning me to watch out for the hose, to mind the ladder. 'Look at the ceiling.' We were in the eastern recess. 'Beautiful. See . . . See . . . It is carved. And the pillars here,' taking my hand to touch one of four red columns, 'made from porphyry, by the Phar-a-oun. Very old.'

'And the sultan's tomb?'

'Oh no,' the man explained, 'Sultan Barquq is not here. His family is here, but the sultan went to the *qarafa*, the cemetery. Why? Well it is not good to say these things of the dead, but I have heard a story that he killed many, many people in his palace, which was near here. With his hands. Yes, yes, and a knife of course.'

Late in his life, Barquq began to spend time with some sheikhs who lived in the cemetery outside the city walls. The cemetery had already become a place of refuge and there were several *khanqas*, monasteries, for mystical Sufi sects. They obviously had an effect on Barquq because although his tomb mosque on Sharia al-Muizz was already built, on his deathbed he announced that he wished to be buried in the cemetery. The story the old man had told me wasn't true – it was Barquq's son Farag who killed when he became sultan. And it was Farag who built his father's tomb complex which included funerary chambers for men and women, a school and a monastery. The intention was that people should live there all year round, as they were doing at the *khanqas*.

Cairo grew in density before it grew any further in size. The tenth century Fatimid palace-city gave way to a thirteenth century Mameluke world-city, a great commercial centre trading with India and Europe and doing good business with Venice. Saladin had moved the palace up on to the citadel, leaving the old city to the people. Spacious palaces were replaced by smaller, taller buildings, the dead risked becoming as cramped as the living and before long other sultans followed Barquq's lead and built their tombs out in the cemetery. With the extra space and cheaper land came the possibility of larger funerary complexes. When Sultan Qayt Bey, who died in 1496, began to think about his tomb, he recognized and exploited that possibility.

The sultan's tomb is another magnificent building, perfectly proportioned and with some extraordinary stonework. Qayt Bey had done much to encourage Egypt's links with Europe and the East and his policies had turned Cairo into a centre of world trade. One of the functions of his tomb complex was to provide safe accommodation outside Cairo's city walls for travellers and traders from Syria and the Levant, Italy and southern Europe, the Gulf, Sudan, the East African coast and India. As well as a *khanqa* and school, his tomb was surrounded by a *raba* or accommodation block for travellers, public fountain and all the amenities of a village, from bakery to blacksmith. The entire complex was surrounded by a wall and beyond that, the desert. With the sultan's mosque at its heart, it looked very similar to the great funerary temples of ancient Egypt.

Mrs Devonshire, whose guided tours of Cairo were legendary in the 1910s and 1920s, described the cemetery as 'a most remarkable place . . . it looks like a large town with innumerable houses and many half ruined domes and minarets, but it soon becomes obvious that this is a dead city, or rather a city of the dead.' Within this city, alongside the great monuments of Barquq and his successors, Cairo's less famous citizens were also buried, their graves 'enclosed by walls with large windows to them, within which are often found, besides the family vault, a dwelling for the keeper of the tombs, his wife and children, and a more or less luxurious room in which, on certain dates of the year, the female relatives of the dead come to spend the night . . .'

Beside the guardians, there were stone cutters and masons, grave diggers and chanters of the Koran, and as the number of burials increased, so did the number of people required to look after the existing tombs and to prepare new ones. Mystics and Sufis were moved on, but in their place, early in the twentieth century, came people who worked the lime kilns in the northern part of the cemetery and lime quarries in the south. Between 1937 and 1947, Cairo almost doubled its population. The City of Dead was growing too. Partly as a result of the 1948 Arab–Israeli war and the 1956 invasion of Suez by British and Israeli troops, which drove many people from eastern Egypt to the capital, and partly because of a national population explosion, between

1947 and 1960 the cemetery population also doubled, to 100,000 – the size of a significant city in Britain at the time. As there was not enough work for them in the cemetery, many people went into the living city during the day and returned home to the cemetery at night. The cemetery had become a strange, but workable suburb. By 1986, its population had risen to 180,000. And these days? There are no reliable statistics, but with the move away from the countryside into the city, with the growing population, estimates vary between a quarter of and half a million. Abduh had no idea.

'We are many,' he said, 'so many. But who is interested to count us?'

I laughed at the idea. Later we discovered there was someone with just such an interest.

I had been on my way to see Gomaa, the guardian of Burkhardt's tomb, when I met Abduh. I wanted to know more about the City of the Dead, about rumours of a living underworld that thrived among the dead. I was also certain that the more I learned about the way Egyptians went about burying and honouring their dead, the closer I would come to the surviving ancient customs.

I saw Abduh by a water tap, filling plastic jerry cans, or rather he spotted me. He was about sixty years old, with a strong, heavy frame, bold brown eyes and thick grey stubble. I asked if there was a café nearby. There was. 'But why are you thinking of going to a café when you know that my house is just here?'

I assumed he was being hospitable in the way that Egyptians often are, easily, genuinely, slightly excessively, and I followed him down another alley, past several tombs, round corners. Children and the old men we passed greeted him with respect.

Abduh lived in a tomb, a patched-up wooden shack built over a single grave. Slight frills around the edge of the wooden roof were Turkish in style, suggesting that the house was at least nineteenth century, maybe much older.

Abduh and his family had made the area around the tomb their own by putting out wooden benches, stringing an awning above them and hanging washing lines between the markers of other tombs. When we arrived, Abduh's wife, Attiyyat, was making tea on the raised bench of another grave.

She was a solid, fleshy, no-nonsense sort of woman, her hair up inside a scarf, her eyebrows plucked far apart, gold hoops on her ears. She sat me down and poured me a glass of black tea.

'So, Roberto, how are you?' Abduh began.

'Not Roberto, but Anthony. Antoon. Antonio.'

'Roberto,' he repeated emphatically. 'Roberto Cairo.' As he talked I realized that he thought I was an actor, that he had seen me in some movie. I explained again that my name was not Roberto and that I was not an actor.

Abduh was the guardian of this section of the cemetery. 'I used to live in a place called Hassaniyya, but then our house fell down and we moved to the tombs. I've been here forty years now, so it's part of my life.' Twenty-six years earlier, he had met Attiyyat. 'Before that, I was married twice. Or was it three times?'

'You don't remember?' I whispered, though Attiyyat was a couple of graves away.

'Let's talk about love,' he whispered back with a devilish sparkle in his eyes. 'This is the department of truth. Maybe there were more than three, I really can't remember.' He roared with laughter. 'What happened? One wife was scared to live in the cemetery, so I divorced her after a month. Another wife didn't want me to work. That's no problem – I was not going to object. But then someone else had to make the money and she didn't. This one,' he said, winking towards Attiyyat, 'bears with me. We have been through the sweet and the dark. One day we eat chicken, one day we eat bread and salt. She is prepared to live according to the wind.'

I had difficulty talking to Abduh that first time. In my experience, the dead were kept far from the living. How many corpses had I seen? Three or four at the most. And my family observed a tradition of staying out of the cemetery where relatives were buried if one's parents were still alive. Mine were, so I was unused to feeling at home in a cemetery. In Abdul's home, there were a fridge, beds, cupboards and some photographs on the wall, but I couldn't ignore the fact that someone was buried beneath me, another beneath Attiyyat's cooker. Macabre shadows – and that word echoes the Arabic *maqabir*, tombs – hung over my thoughts.

Abduh lived in a culture that had fewer taboos about the dead. He lived in the cemetery. He was understandably more pragmatic.

'The dead, may God protect them, they are finished. They don't want anything from us or the world. No matter what you offer – the wealth of the world – it is of no concern because they are with God. We respect the dead. They are under the ground now. People like us, who live in the tombs, must believe in God and live rightly, because we are living on sacred ground, but we don't worry about the dead.'

'Excuse me for asking, but isn't it a little bit scary living here?'

'If you are born in the cemetery you aren't scared, but if you are from the cities you are.'

Attiyyat, who had been listening to us as she cooked, said, 'If we invite someone at night, they are scared and we have to go and pick them up.'

'What are they scared of?'

'*Afarit*, *djinn*, the ghosts of dead people,' Attiyyat listed as easily, as though they were ingredients for the dish she was preparing.

'There aren't any *afarit*,' Abduh insisted, starting to laugh. 'None of that is true. It's just something we tell our children. Other people believe in *afarit*, though, and sometimes we make fun of them when they pass at night.'

'What do you do?'

'We put on masks of devils and appear out of the dark. It always scares them.'

Attiyyat laughed with him.

'I am surprised anyone wants to walk around the cemetery at night. Where are they going?'

'There are many people in the cemetery at night. Sometimes there are lovers looking for a quiet spot. We tell them to go away, because this is sacred ground. Sometimes there are thieves, but we always catch them. But once,' and suddenly he was serious, 'when I had been out working and I was coming home, I saw someone wearing a white suit. I ran after him and eventually chased him into an alley. The alley was blocked at the end, so I thought, "Aha, I've got you." I was going to find out who he was. But do you know what happened? He just disappeared. Gone . . . Vanished . . . I was scared after that.'

'Scared of what exactly?'

'I can't talk about it. The whole cemetery is full of secrets. There are angels and *zahera* [outward signs, phenomena], but I can't tell you about them because they belong to Our Lord.'

It occurred to me, while Abduh was talking, that although he had said the dead were beyond us, he appeared to believe they were very much alive and in some way a conduit between the living and the world beyond. This he had in common with his ancestors.

'Is your family here?' I asked.

'The tombs of my mother and father are here, yes. We are on top of them all the time.'

It took a moment for that one to sink in. 'What do you mean?'

'My brother Bulbul lives in a house over their grave. Sometimes we take things to them and read the Koran in their tomb during the *Eid*.'

'Do many people bring things for the dead?'

'Many. Especially during the *Eid*. It is a time to be with them.'

'What else do people do for the dead?'

'Sometimes they write letters to ask for their help. Many people do this with the sheikhs and holy ones.'

There was also a tradition of writing letters to the dead in ancient Egypt, which dated back to the Old Kingdom. This passage from a husband's message to his dead wife, inscribed on a stele in the First Intermediate Period (2181–040 BC), is typical: 'How are you? Is the West taking care of you [according to] your desire? Now since I am your beloved upon earth, fight on my behalf and intercede on behalf of my name.'

I asked Abduh how he got his job.

'The government appoints the *muallimin*, the bosses, and they appoint us, the guardians and tomb builders. Then there are the tomb diggers, the stone cutters, the Koran reciters and all the other people who make the cemetery work.'

The list was very similar to a head count one could have taken in an ancient Egyptian cemetery, even down to the people Abduh didn't mention, the outlaws, the draft dodgers and the people who hung around in the hope that the mourners' charitable instincts would provide them with a hand-out.

'My boss is an ambassador, so he is always out of the country. But the government doesn't pay me. I get paid by families when they come to visit their tombs and read the Koran. We have our quiet times and our busy times. During the *Eid* we were very busy making sure everything was clean and tidy and getting ready to receive our customers. We opened the tombs for them and when they left they paid us for our efforts. We ate well after that. We cooked rice, *kofta*, chicken and good things and instead of two kilos of meat we bought three or four.'

'And what about other people living in tombs? How do they get there?'

'There is a man who works here as a middleman, who can find you an empty tomb. But if you want to live quietly in the cemetery, like we do, then you must find the owners. Our house belongs to a family who haven't been to visit for twenty-five years. But they know I'm here and that the old man who died is under us. His son has been working in the East a long time and he considers us the guardians of the cemetery. He doesn't ask for any rent.' He thought about it for a moment. 'Nobody asks for rent here because we are all poor. In return we keep the place clean.'

The *muezzin* announced midday prayers from the mosque and, wanting to avoid putting Abduh and Attiyyat in a position of having to offer me food, I decided it was time to leave. Abduh objected, and pointed towards the grave where his wife was cooking. 'You must stay. Here you can eat real Egyptian food.' He ran through the menu again, as he had done when talking about the *Eid*, only now he started to salivate.

'Another time, *inshaallah*, but I must go. I am expected elsewhere.'

When I stood up, I noticed a photograph on the wall in which Abduh appeared alongside a famous Egyptian actress.

'That is my other work.'

'As what?'

'A *kombars*, an extra in the cinema. I've been doing it for years, since I was fifteen or sixteen.' That explained why he had thought I too was an actor. 'I got into it thanks to a man from the studios whose mother is buried here. He sat with me as you sit with me and he told me I was good to do cinema. So the next day I went to the studios and since then I have appeared in about fifty films and ten or fifteen plays and TV soap operas.' He went over to the cupboard and came back with a plastic album full of pictures of himself arm in arm with some of Egypt's most famous movie stars. 'Am I not famous?'

'You're a star, Abduh.'

'So now you know,' and he pulled a strong-man pose, flexing his considerable biceps, a hand on his head, which is how I left him.

'Come back soon, Roberto Cairo. Promise you won't leave it so long next time.'

On my way out of the cemetery, I passed a funeral procession, a huddle of men walking along bearing a dead man on a stretcher. Everyone took a turn to carry him a part of the way to the grave. People came hurrying out of the café and some houses, took the stretcher for a few metres and then returned to whatever they had been doing. The clothes of the mourners rustled as they hurried along; their prayers and murmurs were muted. Their feet made no noise across the mud and sand, in contrast to the noise made by a group of black-robed women, who walked a little way behind them. Among the women were professional – paid – mourners, who wailed, waved their hands and threw dust on their hair.

Edward Lane wrote in the 1830s that 'the wailing of women at funerals was forbidden by the Prophet; and so, also, was the celebration of the virtues of the deceased . . . It is astonishing to see how some of the precepts of the Prophet are every day violated by all classes of the modern Muslims . . .'

Winifred Blackman listed several analogies between ancient and modern funerary customs in the last chapter of *The Fellahin of Upper Egypt*. Among them were the use of holy water to wash the corpse, the carrying of palm branches in the funeral procession and the way tombs were built. A few seemed particularly significant to her. One was the *tala*, the weekly visit to the cemetery by family and friends bringing food. 'On more than one occasion,' she wrote, 'I have observed the widow of the man who is buried there squatting down and addressing her dead husband . . . This woman told me that she is happy to be able to go to her husband's grave on this day and meet him there, which shows how definite a belief it is that the dead return to their graves on the day of *et-Tala*.' Also of note was the behaviour of the female mourners. 'The utterly uncontrolled grief displayed by the women when a death occurs is still admirably illustrated by a relief in an Old Kingdom tomb-chapel at Sakkareh. The widow is depicted as having collapsed in a faint on hearing of her husband's sudden death . . . The various attitudes of grief of the women surrounding the widow are characteristic of modern female mourners. It is interesting to observe, too, that one of the attendants holds the widow's necklace, which has been taken off on receipt of the news . . . further proof that the modern Egyptian peasant women display their grief before and at a funeral by exactly the same gestures as did their ancestors – by dishevelling the hair, tearing the clothes, exposing the breasts, gathering up mud and with it plastering the head, breasts and arms.' All, as Lane had pointed out, contrary to the silence requested by the Prophet, but very much in keeping with a famous image of women mourners I had seen in the Valley of the Nobles.

Umm Seti also traced lamentations back to antiquity. 'When a death takes place in an Egyptian village, or in the more unsophisticated quarter of a town,' she wrote, 'the women of the household immediately start wailing and shrieking. Some of them rush out of the house, bare-headed and bare-footed and, snatching up dust or mud, with which to daub their heads and faces, go screaming and lamenting through the streets.' This was similar to what I had seen. Umm Seti pointed to the Old Kingdom Pyramid Texts for proof of the antiquity of the practice:

It is this that thou hast heard in the houses,
What thou hast learned from the walkers in the streets,
on that day when this Pepy [king] was summoned to life [i.e. died].

Herodotus, the fifth-century BC Greek historian, wrote that 'when a distinguished man dies all the women of the household plaster their heads and faces with mud, then, leaving the body indoors, perambulate the town with the dead man's female relatives, their dresses fastened with a girdle, and beat their bare breasts.' Some of this public grieving was performed by what Umm Seti called 'professional mourning women, who made their living by attending funerals'.

The anthropologist Elizabeth Wickett, who spent several years in Egypt in the 1980s recording funerary laments, discovered that many practices that had disappeared in Cairo were still common elsewhere in Egypt, where people were less exposed to foreign influences. Even in Luxor, regularly visited by tourists for centuries, women clung to old traditions. But there had also been significant changes. As a result of the law forbidding professional mourners, for instance, and perhaps more recently because of pressure from Islamist groups, women rarely went to the cemetery when a corpse was being buried. Instead, laments were performed in a funeral tent erected especially for women or in a separate room of the deceased's house.

Wickett gained access to these funerary tents and to several homes, and spent years recording, annotating and comparing lamentations, and analysing images and the language with which they were expressed. In her dense, two-volume doctoral thesis, Wickett made a distinction between the *sirah*, the 'high-pitched cries which echo throughout a village at the shocked discovery of a death', and the *idid*, the lamentations chanted during the three days of the funeral and at gatherings to honour the dead on the seventh, fifteenth and fortieth days after the death, as well as on the first anniversary. The later lamentations formed the core of a tradition passed on by word of mouth and it was on this that she had concentrated. When she asked one woman where she had learned her laments, she was told, somewhat cryptically, 'an abundance of sadness teaches one how to weep.'

Wickett felt sufficiently confident of her findings to make parallels between lamentations contained in the Pyramid Texts and other ancient sources and those she heard in Luxor. 'It is striking,' she wrote, 'that in Upper Egypt, where discussion of religious dogma and practice is pervasive, that the modern laments contain no reference to either Islamic or Christian theological ideas. They seldom invoke the name of God . . . and there is no allusion to heaven or hell.' If not Islam or Christianity, then what? There were, she realized, all sorts of similarities with ancient Egyptian thought and image. In Wickett's opinion, these laments were 'distillations over time of ancient fragments of Egyptian thought'.

There was something even more surprising. In her conclusion, Wickett suggested that after several millennia, having survived the passionate conversion from the pagan religion to Christianity and then Islam, attitudes to lament were only now undergoing a fundamental change. As a result, those 'distillations over time' were about to be transformed. The causes weren't hard to find.

One of the core images of both ancient and modern laments was the inundation, which washed away the debris of the old while promising fertility and renewal. Yet the Nile had not flooded for decades. For how much longer would Egyptians continue to use images that were no longer relevant? Throughout Egypt there was also an increasingly restrictive social order, driven by religious conservatism and encouraged

95

by the government. Fundamentalists pointed to the saying attributed to the Prophet Muhammad in the Hadith or tradition: 'The mourner and those who surround her – to hell.' The government had its own reason for restricting behaviour. When *Fortunes of War*, the television adaptation of Olivia Manning's *Balkan Trilogy*, was being filmed in Egypt in the 1980s, it included a funeral scene in Luxor. The director paid some local women to 'perform' their lamentations, throw dust on their hair and do whatever else they did when someone was buried. 'It was a fantastic shot,' he told me. 'We had them coming along the Nile, a row of them chanting in their black robes. They looked fantastic.' The Egyptian film censor thought otherwise. His brief was to safeguard the image of his country and in his view this sort of thing was demeaning. The scene was cut and the tape handed over to the authorities before the rest of the film was allowed out of the country.

The censor was echoing an attitude that I had run up against in print and heard often in the cities. It was fine to portray Egypt, in the words of its Ministry of Tourism, as 'the cradle of civilisation', but it was also necessary to stress that those primitive ways were in the past. Tombs and temples were all very well, but they belonged to another time and had nothing to do with the here and now. Modern Egypt, so the thinking went, was a forward-looking place of mobile phones, satellite dishes, new farm equipment, modern refuse systems, of suits and ties, jeans and T-shirts. And so it was, in parts. But in the other, larger parts, where most people were still without phones, dressed in *galabiyyas* and were proud of their traditions, it was its old self.

I returned to the City of the Dead several times – perhaps once every few months – and most times I bumped into Abduh before I reached his house. On the few occasions when this didn't happen, a child, assuming I was lost, would point the way down to Abduh's house. The last time, when I went to make sure that he and his family had survived an earthquake, I noticed a new sign at the entrance to the cemetery, but as I couldn't read Arabic I had no idea what it said. Also, fresh numbers had been painted on the side of each tomb and house.

Abduh was as welcoming as ever, but something in his attitude had changed. 'That's from the government,' he explained gloomily when I pointed out the new numbers. 'They are counting us. Maybe after the earthquake they think it is time for us to move.'

Abduh was careful about what he said to a stranger, to me.

'We have already moved into flats twice before, and both times we came back after two or three months.'

'What happened?'

'There was no water and no electricity.'

'So you don't want to go?'

'I would like to go. I want to live in the world. I want my children to grow up somewhere clean and decent, to work in a good job, to have their own children somewhere else. Only the dead should live with the dead.'

At this I protested. 'But there have always been people living with the dead here in Egypt.'

Abduh knew nothing of survivals and he responded with a shrug. 'People have always lived everywhere.'

'And your work is here?'

'Believe me, if I could find a nice place elsewhere you wouldn't see me here any more. At night there are insects, beetles, scorpions – we're fed up with them . . .'

I don't know why he stopped, but whatever the reason, he changed his tune and took back all he had said. 'We are happy here. We have water and electricity. Our lives are cheap and our kids are good and the vegetables are cheap and everything is cheap. Look at this bread,' he said, grabbing a disc Attiyyat had left on the kitchen-grave, 'all white and beautiful, hot from the oven. *Mashaallah*. What God wills. So sweet and good and clean that I could live off just that – and it is made in the cemetery. The ovens will go, the schools, the cafés, the markets – everything will go. And then the tombs will go.' He stunned both of us into silence.

The plan was dreamed up by a Franco-Italian team. The idea was to rehouse the people, referred to as 'squatters', on the far edge of the city – the sort of development Abduh already knew about, hours away by bus from his work, where the water and electricity seldom got connected – and to clear the cemetery outside the two remaining Fatimid gates of Bab an-Nasr and Bab al-Futuh. The graves were going to be opened, bones exhumed and reinterred far out in the desert, beyond the city's limits. There was a precedent for this. In the early twentieth century the cemetery immediately in front of the old walls had been cleared to make way for a new road. Mrs Devonshire in her

Rambles in Cairo noted that 'the part immediately close to the wall had been used for a number of graves, so long ago as to lose all trace of the names of individuals or families buried there; cheap wooden huts had been put up and refuse of all kinds had accumulated. Now the wall is visible, so impressive that no fortifications in the East or West can be compared with it.' The current situation wasn't an exact parallel. The names of the occupants were known – some were world famous – and in their place this time they were going to build a new hotel and tourist bazaar.

'And you will go.'

'Yes. But you know something? We are who we are wherever we go.' It was as close as he ever came to admitting that he understood the traditions with which he lived.

CHAPTER 5

Happy Birthday, Abu'l-Hajjaj

The observation of Herodotus, that the Egyptians could not live
without a King, might find a parallel in the impossibility of their
living without a pantheon of gods.

Sir Gardner Wilkinson

'Merry Christmas, Professor,' Ibrahim shouted across the street.

'It's not Christmas yet, Ibrahim.'

'Yes it is. Christmas for the Muslim people, the moulid of Sayyidna al-Husayn.'

I knew about this already, as did everyone in our building. Even if I had been able to ignore the extra sheep carcasses hanging outside the butchers, the blood dripping on to the pavement, there was no way to avoid the *zabaleen*, the refuse collectors, knocking on doors throughout the building to wish a merry Christmas and hanging around long enough for a gift to be forthcoming. Ibrahim, being more sophisticated, more subtle, his eyes on a greater prize, suggested that I should go to visit Husayn's tomb as a sign of respect and, a nice touch this, 'Because it will bring the *baraka* on your book. And your book is most important, ya *doctour*, because then the people in your country they will know everything about us.'

'Not everything, Ibrahim.'

I handed over the present he was expecting, and although I declined his offer to drive me to the mosque of Husayn – his price had been going up with each journey and the holiday surcharge he would spring on me at the end would have paid for a new front seat, or a couple of wheels – I was going to visit the festivities.

Ibrahim wasn't entirely wrong to call it Christmas for it was both a birthday celebration and a religious festival and the person whose birth was being celebrated was up there with Jesus in the eyes of some

Muslims. Husayn was the grandson of the Prophet Muhammad. When Muhammad died in AD 632, he was succeeded as leader of the faithful by his father-in-law, Abu Bakr. But the succession was disputed and the three caliphs, successors, who followed Abu Bakr were all assassinated: Omar, on whose orders Egypt was invaded, was stabbed at prayers; Uthman was stabbed over his Koran, and Ali, Muhammad's son-in-law, was murdered on his way to the mosque. Husayn was Ali's son, and according to legend he was killed doing battle with rival claimants in AD 680. The blow that severed his head from his body split Islam into the two factions that exist today, the Sunni and the Shia, or party, of Ali. According to legend, the head of Husayn was recovered on the battlefield at Kerbela in Iraq. Later it was kept in Damascus. Some reports have it brought to Egypt in a green silk bag in the tenth century, others say that it lingered in Syria for another two hundred years before arriving in its rightful home. Whether it really was the martyr's head is impossible to say, but lack of proof has never stopped Cairenes: they made Husayn the city's patron saint and the focus of a great cult.

Late in the afternoon I took a taxi to the Old City, crossing the Nile while the pleasure boats were out in force, avoiding the downtown jams and getting up on to the bridge over the markets at Ataba, the Threshold. That was where we hit the traffic and I had time to count the Old City's minarets, now outnumbered by neon signs, while the driver tempered his frustration with the knowledge that this was the feast of Husayn and that I would tip him generously.

On the street of al-Muizz li Din Allah, it was no easier to walk than it had been to drive. More than a million people pushed and stumbled together, shoulder to shoulder, hand to back, toe to heel, fumbling towards the mosque of Husayn. I had walked along this street often before, but this time it was unrecognizable. The shops were full and brilliantly lit by bulbs the size of dinosaur eggs. The facades of mosques were hidden by canvas stalls, their architraves covered with the banners of Sufi sects whose members had pitched their tents in the courtyards and prayer recesses. I tripped over guy ropes and the legs of people who had decided to sit with friends for tea and a chat. If I hadn't known better I might have thought these were refugees, forced from their homes and into the city by war or some natural disaster.

We passed through an alley, a corridor of savours and scents, of hot sweet potatoes, corn cobs, chickpeas, peanuts, yellow beans, *ful*, *kushari*, spaghetti, sweets, prunes, and then the junk, the perfumes, cassettes, gold conical moulid hats and little brass cymbals. The alley led out into the large square in front of Husayn's mosque, where there were more tents, more people, more food. Breathing was difficult in the crush, made worse by a group of Husayn's passionate supporters pushing past on their way to pay him their respects. I had no intention of following. I remembered how Khalid and I had fought to get near the mosque at the moulid of Sayyida Zaynab, Husayn's sister. Not today, ya Husayn.

From the square, I could see a row of men rocking from side to side and back and forth, swinging and rolling on the upper balcony of the Husayn Hotel. Following their leader, they chanted the same word again and again and again. *Allahu*. On the east side of the mosque, groups of women huddled in the hope of a blessing. Beside them a barber had set up a little wooden booth above which hung a graphic painting of a boy with a red ring round his penis and a smile on his face. The reality was different. When the curtains burst open, a screaming child was passed over the counter. Taken by his father, he was kissed and held up over the crowd, another boy circumcised in the name of the Prophet. The women nearby ululated with joy. 'May you bless him, ya Husayn.'

The crowd moved on as though this was an everyday sight, passing cafés that had spilled over on to the streets. We were entering the heart of the old city, Gamaliyya, one of the most densely populated places on earth, and a parallel to the crowds who lived around Kamak Temple in ancient Luxor. The street narrowed, twisted, became slippery with mud, spilled tea, animal blood. From open tents, men to one side, women and children to the other, came the smoke of waterpipes and steam from hissing pots. A brown cow blocked my way as it waited for slaughter, its calm eyes on me, its head wedged between two speakers from which came a shuddering, staccato chant. *Allahu! Allahu!*

The sight, through a doorway, of what looked like a calm courtyard presented an opportunity not to be missed of a rest and some tea. I pushed my way to the entrance, adjusted my clothes, went in and sat down.

A young man in white shirt and black trousers came over. I ordered tea and a waterpipe.

'Tea no problem. But maybe no waterpipe.'

I was about to tell him that his must be the only café in Cairo, perhaps in the whole of Egypt, that didn't have a *shisha*, when it occurred to me – something in the way the other men were looking at me, the way the women were preparing food – that this was not a café.

'No,' said Selim. 'Not a café. This is my house—'

'I'm so sorry—' I was on my feet.

'But you are welcome. Please, welcome. Sit down again and I will bring you tea.'

I hesitated, imagining the sort of reception an Egyptian would meet in London were he to walk into someone's open door on Christmas day, but then I was greeted by the other six men in the courtyard, all wearing suits. They offered their hands and best wishes. These were Selim's relatives. 'It is the feast of Husayn,' said the oldest of them, a wizened man in a zoot suit who was worried in case I thought the city always looked like this, 'and in Sayyidna's name, you are welcome wherever you come from.'

Selim brought tea. 'Tonight we will celebrate and you must stay to join us. We will eat. We will dance and sing. We are happy.'

After tea, Selim wanted to show me the house. Whatever I had been expecting, I was surprised. It was a fine building with walls of solid stone and details of delicate carving. The doorways were high, the corridors broader than some of the alleys I had seen that night.

'To live in a house like this you must be a pasha, no?'

'It is a museum,' Selim explained.

It was also a palace, built by wealthy businessmen from Fayoum in the eighteenth century and then bought by Muhammad Ali Pasha in 1820. It was here that Muhammad Ali's grandson, the future ruler Ismail, who drove Egypt to bankruptcy in his insistence on modernization, was born in 1829. Selim showed me the main reception room, a grand traditional hall decorated with elaborate, gilded paintwork and some exquisite carved wooden screens. 'My family are the caretakers, so I can say that I, like Ismail Pasha, grew up in a palace.'

In the courtyard, the men asked where I was from, what I was doing in Egypt. 'Are you a tourist? And where did you learn to speak Arabic?'

I explained that I was looking for traces of ancient Egypt, the shadows of the pharaohs and their people.

'Ah,' said Selim's uncle, a tall, fat, clean-shaven man, 'so you have been to the antiquities museum?'

'I have. But I am looking for living traces, for customs and beliefs that you keep but which began long ago.'

None of the men answered and I began to wonder whether I had overstepped the bounds of hospitality, when Selim said, 'We are Muslims. We are proud of our heritage, of the pyramids and Tutankhamun . . . All of those things are a part of us. But we do not have the same gods or the same beliefs as in the time of the pharaohs. The pharaohs had many gods, but we say, "There is no God but God and Muhammad is his prophet."'

'Selim,' I said quietly, 'I hope you won't be offended, but I have seen with my own eyes many things in your country which were here at the time of the pharaohs.'

'Oh, you mean like the *fellahin* in the fields? The mud houses?'

'In the city too.'

'Like what?' he asked with a touch of defiance.

I explained about the way tombs were used and how they had been used in antiquity. I pointed to similarities in visiting the dead, in the need for the dead to be remembered, but he remained unconvinced. 'And there are some people,' I went on, delicately, 'who say that moulids are not to do with Islam. That there were moulids before Islam, before the Prophet Muhammad, when Christian saints were celebrated, and even before with the old gods.'

'*Haram*. This is a sin. Who told you this? How could this be? In moulids we celebrate the birthdays of our sheikhs, our holy men, so how could we have them from the pharaohs?'

I reminded him of the split between the rival factions of Islam. 'Husayn was a Shia, not a Sunni like Egyptians.'

'Husayn,' he replied magnificently, 'was a Muslim.'

I told him I thought it significant that the date of the moulid of Ahmad al-Bedawi in Tanta, the biggest moulid of all, was fixed not by the Muslim calendar, like al-Husayn's, but by the Coptic calendar, which followed the old pharaonic calendar.

Selim began to laugh. 'No, no, ya An-toony. You have been listening to people without brain. They do not know what I know. Next you will tell me that Sayyidna al-Husayn, may peace be upon him, was really a Copt. Not possible.'

Our disagreement seemed to sour relations and although the old men still talked to me, and Selim offered more tea, I decided to leave before the food arrived.

I began to wonder whether Selim was right, whether these moulids, these festivals in honour of the birth of holy men and women were purely Muslim celebrations. After all, I had seen them across the Arab world, in Morocco and Tunisia, in Jordan and Syria and Yemen. If they were essentially Muslim, I wondered, then how were they viewed by the Muslim authorities? To find the answer I made an appointment with a sheikh at al-Azhar, Egypt's oldest and most important theological authority.

Al-Azhar is a university built around a mosque. The mosque was completed in AD 971, two years after the Fatimid caliphs from Tunisia conquered Egypt. The university was opened in AD 988. Both were at the heart of the palace-city built for the sultan, his court and army. Al-Azhar formed the south side of a square and the mosque of Husayn the north side. Al-Azhar's administrative building, an early twentieth-century block, sat between the two, so close to the road that the doorman had trouble hearing me over the noise of the traffic.

'I have come to see Sheikh Muhammad Mustafa Gemeiah,' I screamed.

Sheikh Muhammad handled enquiries from foreigners, more than that I didn't know, but he was on holiday the first time I went to see him, in spite of earlier calls to ensure he would be there. The sheikh's assistant pleaded with me to return. 'You will?' he asked, again and again. 'You really will?' I really, really would, I assured him, and promised by the Prophet, al-Sayyid al-Husayn and al-Sayyida Zaynab.

Some days later, Ibrahim drove me to al-Azhar. He was beaming, radiant, emitting light with pleasure at the idea that I, his friend, his pet foreigner, was going to meet a sheikh at al-Azhar. 'I will wait for you,' he announced. 'No need.' 'But I must.' He had that sparkle in his eye which meant that it was going to cost. 'Never mind, I'll make my own way back. I'll go for a walk. I'll make a pilgrimage to al-Husayn.' In the end I refused to go in until he left.

Sheikh Muhammad Mustafa Gemeiah was sitting in his spacious first-floor office, his back to a large window, and leaning over a heavy, glass-topped desk. On the desk: dictionaries, files, an empty coffee cup, a phone and a large register which he closed as I approached. In front of the desk: several chrome and brown plastic chairs, still wrapped in plastic covers. The place had all the utilitarian charm of a British registry office.

As soon as the sheikh ushered me into one of his chairs I thought I understood why foreigners were sent to him. His English was excellent, his manner charming, he smiled, he had a touch of humility and he cut a fine figure in his cleric's black gown and red and white hat. But there was another, more significant reason why foreigners went to see Sheikh Muhammad: he was the one who converted them to Islam. A conversation, a signing of the declaration, a recital of the formula and I too could be down on my knees being led to salvation in al-Azhar's thousand-year-old prayer hall. I hurried an explanation that I had come to ask about saints and moulids for my book.

'We both have something between us,' he replied, smiling his broad, knowing, unsettling smile, 'because like you I also write books. I have written many books. One about all the prophets, one about the Prophet Muhammad, may peace be upon him.'

I told Sheikh Muhammad about the things I had seen and heard connected to Muslim saints, to the sheikhs and their moulids. He replied by offering me tea, sitting back in his chair and placing the fingertips of his two hands together. He waited out the dramatic moment, then jumped right in.

'There are great differences between tradition and the essence . . . the law of religion. There is no such thing as a holy man in Islam.'

I thought of all the miracles and cures I had heard about, all the reverence paid, the blessings invoked, the stones touched, the cloths kissed and prayers recited. All for nothing?

'Even the Prophet Muhammad,' and he looked to the ceiling, 'may peace be upon him, is not a holy man. He is a Prophet and a Messenger, but I can say no more than that he is a man. This is what the Koran says.' He looked me straight in the eye, unblinking, and recited from a sura. ' "It is not suitable for the Most Beneficent, for Allah, that He should beget a son. There is none in the heavens and earth but comes unto Allah as a slave." This is where the Christians are wrong about Jesus. The prophets are only men.' And, smiling again, 'Abraham, Isaac, Jesus and even you – all are Muslims.'

I apologized. 'Really I am not.'

'Take a little time. Think about it. Who is Muhammad? What is he saying? What does he want us to do? To worship Allah and no one else. In India I find people worshipping cows. In Africa I find people worshipping snakes. What is that? God has tried to help us. He has sent His messengers, but instead of worshipping Him we worship cows and even trees.'

Sheikh Muhammad was flying. I imagined him in a pulpit roaring through the Friday sermon, leading towards some celestial light. But he saw that I wasn't flying with him and he turned on me. 'What are you doing here, my brother Anthony? Why this search for things that should have ended long ago? What is wrong with your life that you have come here to me? We have reached space. America and England send spacecraft into outer space. We know so much, yet we know so little about ourselves. Galileo was executed for saying that the world was round but this was not new. Allah affirmed 1417 years ago, long before Galileo, that the world is round. What do we know?

'Come. Come and read with me.' He held up a copy of the Koran. 'You are a Muslim, my brother Anthony. Let us read together.'

Sheikh Muhammad was ready for me to read the profession of faith – there is no God but God and Muhammad is His prophet – and I was ready to run for the door. There was a stand-off. He fingered the large book that had been open when I first arrived, the register of new converts, but knew that he had gone too far, that he had lost me. He backtracked seamlessly.

'There are no holy men in Islam,' he repeated. 'After finishing my work I will remove this hat, this robe, and I will be a respectable man. Like you. I will not even be like you, because for you there is a place in paradise, guaranteed, if you accept that you are a Muslim. For me it is much harder to reach paradise.'

I ignored his mission and kept to mine. 'Why do so many people in this country go to moulids and visit the tombs of sheikhs if it is forbidden?'

'The reason for this, my brother Anthony' – I had to admire his insistence – 'is ignorance. But you are not ignorant. So if you see someone behaving badly, don't say this is Islam. If he's good, say he's a good man who is a Muslim. Islam must be judged by the Koran. Some people believe they can control devils, but this is not Islam and Allah Almighty will not accept any prayer or any fasting from them and they

1. Winifred Blackman and Hideyb Abdel-Shafy, with whose family she stayed in Fayoum (see chapter 5).

2. Winifred Blackman taking tea with Mansour Bey and Colonel Sherif. Hideyb is standing behind her.

3. Men performing a *zikr* in a crowd at Dimishkin, 1924.

4. The 'servants' of Sheikh Haridi, 'who was originally believed to be a snake'; the Sheikh's tomb is in the background. Some of the servants are his relatives (see chapter 6).

5. A Muslim poet reciting while spinning a disk in the Coptic cemetery at Ezbet al-Muharraq during the Eid al-Ghutas, January 1921.

6. A woman rolling from the stone of Sheikh Habs al-Wehish, Fayoum, December 1925 (see chapter 5).

7. A woman jumping over charms in Winifred Blackman's garden in Fayoum, January 1926.

8. 'On the site of an ancient temple in Middle Egypt is a pool of water ...
believed to possess miraculous powers ... [Women] clamber over the stones
... three times, and going more or less in a circular direction. After this
they hope to conceive.' (see chapter 3).

9. A fertility rite involving a flour cake, a candle and a pottery jar, 1925.

10. Women wailing at a grave-side, Deir al-Muharraq. Contemporary funeral lamentations have been called 'distillations over time of ancient fragments of Egyptian thought'.

11. People sheltering for *baraka* in the shade of a tree believed to be inhabited by a saint, Fayoum, 1926. Modern Egyptians, like their ancestors, hope to find a shade tree waiting for them in paradise.

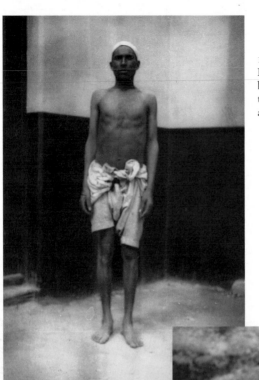

12. A youth near Badeh, Fayoum, who Miss Blackman believed showed 'physical features strongly resembling an ancient Egyptian'.

13. The 'servant' of Sheikha Khadra, near Kom Aushim, Fayoum, 1926.

will not see paradise. This again is ignorance. But to answer your question about moulids: if a good man dies, we can celebrate his life, his work, and one way we do this is to go to his tomb. What is happening nowadays in moulids is celebrating in a bad way. If I celebrate the birthday of Muhammad, is it *haram*? No. I cannot say that. But I must remember how he lived, what he did, what he said. I must remember by practising it. Not by banging drums and dancing. So the problem is how we are celebrating.'

'Who decides what sort of celebration is OK and what is not?'

'We do. Here at al-Azhar.'

'At the moulids I have seen, people in the *zikrs* seemed to be in a trance. Is that OK?'

'The *zikr* is OK. The *zikr* is to pray, to ask God for forgiveness. *Zikr* literally means "remember", remember the worshipping of God. But people have begun to do this in a bad way. They swing their body to the left and right.'

'Exactly.'

'These are ignorant people who don't know their religion well.' Then he turned on me again. 'I understand why you are searching, my brother Anthony. We must all take lessons from the past, and from the future. After all, the first revelation which was given to the Prophet Muhammad was sura ninety-six in which it is written: "Observe the man who rebukes Our servant when he prays. Think: does he follow the right guidance or enjoin true piety? Think: if he denies the Truth and pays no heed, does he not realize that God observes all?"'

Sheikh Muhammad had been talking for an hour and was no nearer converting me than he had been when I first walked in. He knew that, and he was winding down, running out of steam, a little downbeat. 'We in Egypt also have some searching to do. Life is not going well for us now because we are far from our religion.' He went silent for a moment and gazed into space, then got up and walked over to the bookcases.

'I want to give you this present. It is one of my books.' He handed me a heavy green volume with gilt calligraphy and decoration. *Stories of the Prophets by: Imam Ibn Kathis. Translated by: Sheikh Muhammad Mustafa Gemeiah, Office of the Grand Imam, Sheikh Al-Azhar.*

I wanted to offer him some consolation. I turned the pages and told him it looked very interesting.

'I wrote it so that the many Muslims who cannot read Arabic will know the lives of the Prophets.' To cheer him up, I told him that Islam was the fastest-growing religion in Britain. It gave him an idea. 'If there are so many Muslims, perhaps they too would like to read my book?'

'I'm sure they would.'

'But how can I find someone to sell my book in your country? It is very difficult to arrange these things from here with telephones and faxes . . . You are a writer – there must be people you know who will want to publish my book in England. When you go back to your country you must be my agent.'

I held up my hand to stop him. 'This is not my field. I don't know who might publish it.'

'But you can find out.'

I smiled. It was misleading, I admit, but I wanted to get away from him. As far as Sheikh Muhammad was concerned, when I arrived I was a possible convert to Islam. Now I was his agent and foreign rights were as good as sold.

On the threshold – a man carrying a tray of tea down the corridor, a veiled woman walking head down, the sound of traffic in the street – I turned, dramatically. 'Sheikh Muhammad, if moulids and saints are not Islam, what are they?'

He shrugged. For him it was enough that they were not part of his religion. But I needed to know more.

Husayn's early life was spent in the company of the Prophet, his later life in pursuit of his claim to the leadership of Islam. The fact that he lost his life in pursuit of his beliefs appealed to the Egyptian sense of persecution, an instinct honed by two thousand years of foreign occupation. The fact that they believed his head was buried in Cairo added to his appeal. It was just as easy to understand the appeal of the young Sheikh Alaa ad-Din whose shrine was built on to the wall of Medinet Habu temple. (Unlike Hamida, who had shown me the shrine and who believed the sheikh had moved on, an old man who lived nearby told me the sheikh was buried beneath the shrine.) But there were literally tens of thousands of sheikhs or saints all over Egypt and more moulids than days of the year. How had this come about? How were saints created?

One reason why the Prophet's message caught on in Egypt was that it told men and women that they could pray directly to God without intermediaries, without a priesthood. It was a dazzling, revolutionary move in a region where lay people were rarely allowed into temple sanctuaries. In Egypt, where Coptic rituals were almost as exclusive as their pagan predecessors, where the altar was hidden from all but the priests by a screen, the idea of direct communication with God was bound to be popular.

As well as direct communication through prayer, Muslims had the Koran and stories from the life of the Prophet to guide them. But there was also a hierarchy within the Islamic tradition which recognized that some people were closer to God than others. Muhammad, the messenger of God, and Moses, who talked to God, are obvious examples. Lower down the scale there were the *walis* and sheikhs. The problem with them was that there were no guidelines to explain how they were created or chosen and no ecclesiastical authority to perform the elevation, as the Pope does with saints. More important, there was no authority with the power to say who was not a *wali* or a sheikh. Even Sheikh Muhammad held back from making that sort of judgement, preferring instead to condemn the celebrations.

Nicolaas Biegman wrote in *Egypt: Moulids, Saints, Sufis* that, 'The main criteria for establishing sainthood are miracles (*karamat*) happening during or after the saint's lifetime, and his appearance in dreams and visions.' The proof of sainthood, he was saying, was in the performance, the implication being that saints were intermediaries for God. A lack of miracles reflected a lack of divine favour. But Egypt was a country full of miracles and, therefore, also full of saints.

In Winifred Blackman's notebooks from the 1920s, which I had seen in Liverpool, there were many accounts of sheikhs and their miracles which she had been told by villagers. Early on there was a 'note on Sheikhs' tombs': 'Every sheikh, at any rate all those of any standing, has some tombs associated with them. [I have since heard, *she wrote in the margin*, that a celebrated sheikh may have any number of tombs. One, whose tomb I visited, had 40 tombs erected to his memory in different parts of Egypt.] This does not mean that the body of the sheikh is buried in any of the tombs, or beneath any of the stones, though there are cases where this is so. The usual thing is that the sheikh appears to some man and tells him to build a tomb for him on such and such a spot. He usually appears in a dream. Sometimes a village which possesses the tomb of a venerated sheikh has inhabitants who are guilty of bad conduct. The dead sheikh may then appear to a man in a distant village and tell him to build a tomb on such and such a spot, sometimes leading him to the site.'

Of the many stories in Blackman's notebooks, this, concerning the sheikh of a place called Hawara, is typical: 'The Sheikh is buried under the floor of a small mosque, situated in a narrow street (or rather pathway) in the centre of the village. I visited the mosque and was shown the spot under which the Sheikh is buried, close to a pillar which differs slightly from the others which support the building. The people wanted to erect a special building to mark the Sheikh's burial place and to transfer his body thither, but the holy man intimated to one or more of his admirers that he preferred to remain in his original place inside the mosque. Outside the sacred building is the Sheikh's well. The water of this well is believed to have curative properties, so people who are ill, or who are possessed by an *afrit* or by the spirit of a dead sheikh, come to this well and are lowered into its depths. This is believed to effect an almost immediate cure.'

In the Blackman archive in Liverpool I also found a newscutting from the 1920s with the sensational headline: WOMAN PROBES EGYPT'S SECRETS. LONELY STRAW-HUT LIFE IN UNEXPLORED VILLAGES. 'HOLY' STRANGER. 'Living in straw huts,' the story began, 'quite alone except for two native servants, an Englishwoman, during the past four years, has sought, by patience and "the human touch", to lift a little higher the veil of haunting mystery and romance that enshrouds ancient Egypt.' I loved that 'mystery and romance'. There was no mistaking the tone, nor the timing: just a couple of years after Howard Carter opened Tutankhamun's tomb in Luxor and while the international press was still getting good mileage out of the 'pharaohs' curse' story. But that isn't to belittle Winifred Blackman's achievement. I was impressed that she had lived in the village.

A key to her relationship with the villagers was suggested elsewhere in the article: 'They [the villagers] regard her as a holy woman – a Sheikha – endowed with supernatural powers.' I had images of other intrepid women who had lived in the Middle East, of Lady Hester Stanhope, daughter of a British prime minister, who was treated as royalty by the Bedu of the Syrian desert; of Jane Digby, formerly Lady Ellenborough, married to the nomadic Sheikh Medjuel el-Mezreb; and particularly of the enigmatic Isabelle Eberhardt in the 1900s, dressed as a man, moving through Algeria in search of local customs, mystical enlightenment and adventure. Curious to see whether the tombs Winifred Blackman mentioned were still in use, and whether she was remembered in the village where she had lived, I decided to visit Fayoum.

Alan, the Scot I had met through Roman Marina, came with me to Fayoum and I was glad of his company. Ever since Islamist extremists had begun their campaign of violence against a government that refused to negotiate with them, foreigners had been a target. In an attempt to control the situation the Egyptian authorities had made it increasingly difficult for foreigners to travel without armed escort.

We had arranged to meet in a café on Tahrir Square. There was no mistaking Alan in the Egyptian crowd. His long brown hair hadn't been brushed for weeks and he looked as though he had spent the night in his clothes. Everyone else in the café was Egyptian and all wore neatly pressed shirts.

We took a minibus from the other side of the square up Pyramids Road and then caught the old blue village bus to Fayoum. After more than an hour of grey desert, Fayoum was an extraordinary sight. Its fields and trees were velvet green, the sun was shining, the heat was bearable and once we had got over the difficulty of finding a driver – Gomaa – and then of negotiating for him to take us around the villages, we felt as easy as only city people can when faced with the prospect of a day in the country.

Winifred Blackman mentioned a saint called Sheikh Muhammad Abu Atla – also known as Muhammad, the Father of Death – whose tomb, she wrote in her notebook, was a forty-five minute donkey ride from the village of Seleh. Near it, just in the desert, was a remarkable stone connected to the sheikh. 'People roll from it,' she wrote. 'They lie down close to the stone, putting the little fingers of either hand in a deep hollow worn into the stone, and then roll as far as they can in various directions. When I visited the stone,' she noted, 'some of the people were calling out, "*ya abui, ya abui*", [o father, father!] and screaming and groaning. This was caused by the *afarit* which possessed them. Many of the people were suffering from various ailments, some obviously had whooping cough . . . On the other side of the railway line are the Sheikh's trees – a *lebbakh* and several palms. There is also a small covered place (a *sabil*), like a well, which contains a *zir* which holds water from the stream which runs close by. After rolling, the people come and drink some of this water. Behind the tree stands the Sheikh's tomb, built of brick, but without the usual domed top.'

'You think we'll find those people still rolling down the rock?' Alan asked, rolling words over his thick Scottish accent. It was clear from his tone that he thought we'd be lucky to find the tomb, let alone the rollers. I nodded.

Gomaa, our driver, had never heard of the sheikh, but at the village of Seleh the first person we asked, a fruit seller, knew who he was. The vendor looked at us with suspicion. 'They want to pay their respects to the sheikh,' Gomaa told him. 'Came all the way from Cairo.'

'The sheikh will be glad of their visit,' he said, and gave directions.

The sheikh's tomb, a small single-storey building, was still surrounded by trees, as Winifred Blackman had described it. I ran the few metres from the car, thrilled to find myself in front of a building that I had read about in a seventy-year-old notebook. The tomb was surrounded by sand and stood between the single-track railway and a field of wheat and berseem. It had obviously been kept up and cracks had recently been plastered.

Alan tried to open the tomb's metal door, but it was locked. He banged loudly. 'Open up, Sheikh Muhammad Abu Atla,' he commanded and, as though in answer, an old man sat up in the sand behind the tomb and offered the usual welcome.

The man, who had been sleeping in the shade of the trees, now adjusted his baggy country trousers, vest and waistcoat. While he retied his turban, I went to look at the *sabil*, 'like a well', as Winifred Blackman had described it. The water jar was broken and the well filled with sand.

'You know how he got his nickname?' the old man asked when he reappeared. 'Because he killed ninety-nine people, all of them with his stick.' He saw me shake my head. 'By God it is true.'

'Sheikh Muhammad Abu Atla wanted to know if he was going to heaven or to hell when he died, so he went to see another sheikh. This sheikh was afraid to tell Sheikh Muhammad Abu Atla that he would go to hell, so instead he told him to go out to a field and plant his stick, the one with which he had killed those ninety-nine people. "You will know by what happens to the stick what will happen to you." On the way, Sheikh Muhammad Abu Atla came across a couple of lovers. They were lying down. As he got closer he saw that the girl was struggling. Whenever the man tried to enter the girl, she covered herself with her hands. So eventually the man cut off her hands, and then her legs. Sheikh Muhammad Abu Atla saw what was happening and he was outraged. He took his stick and killed the man – making one hundred men that he had killed – and then he planted the stick as he had been told. The next morning he returned and found his stick had sprouted leaves, so he knew he was going to heaven. Why? Because the last one was killed in the name of Allah.'

The old man nodded, as though he had told us all we could possibly want to know, but then I asked about the rolling stone.

'It's over the railway.' He started off across the raised single track and down a steep incline of rock and sand. What he showed us was the protruding part of a large rock worn smooth by wind and sand. Here were the holes Winifred Blackman had mentioned, where people placed their fingers as they rolled. 'Some days many people come, twenty or thirty, to do the rolling, and Sheikh Muhammad Abu Atla hears their problems and helps them. They come from all around, but only on a Thursday morning, between eight and eleven. No one will come today.'

'Have people always come to roll here?' I asked.

The old man nodded. 'For as long as Sheikh Muhammad Abu Atla has been in his tomb, people have been coming here. They need him and he is there to help.'

As we left, the old man said, 'It's the sheikh's moulid in five days.' And then he settled himself back to sleep in the shade, as though he was waiting out the time.

Gomaa drove us through the rich farmland where Alan and I pointed out other tombs, some freshly whitewashed, some decorated with a flag – a custom the ancient Egyptians also observed – while others, perhaps where the magic had failed, had begun to crumble. They reminded me of roadside shrines to Christian saints or the Madonna, of niches for the Indian gods Ganesh and Shiva and of Thai spirit-houses.

We found several other tombs Winifred Blackman had mentioned. The seventy years that separated us were but an instant in the long register of Egyptian history. It was impossible to tell the age of the tombs – some were definitely newly built when Blackman visited them – yet I was thrilled by the idea that they had survived, that their buildings were maintained, their stories told to passing strangers, their powers to help and heal still intact.

In an article in *Wide World* magazine, in January 1924, Blackman wrote a popular account of her life in the Egyptian countryside. In her preface to *The Fellahin of Upper Egypt* she wrote that she had 'purposely suppressed the names of people and villages in nearly every instance as I do not think it would be either desirable or fair to publish them in a semi-popular book of this kind'. In the article, however, she did mention that she lived in the village of Lahun, on the upper floor of the house of a man whom she employed as her assistant.

'His name,' I told Alan as we sat in a cloud of dust in the back of the pick-up, 'is Hideyb Abdel Safiy. This being Egypt, where nothing disappears, I'm sure we'll find his family.'

Alan smiled at my irony. 'Now this time it's me thinking you're mad.'

Lahun was a small village on the Bahr Youssef, the canal that feeds the Fayoum with Nile water. At the entrance to the village, we passed the sluice bridge which controls the flow of water into the Fayoum basin. Near the village, the Pyramid of Lahun, built in the 1880s BC by Pharaoh Senusret II, has survived. Here you can feel the physical presence of the ancients in their surviving buildings and their irrigation system, still in use.

Friday is a day of comparative rest in Egyptian villages, when the men work in their fields, look after the animals or work in their houses until midday. The Friday noon prayers are the most important, the best attended and the longest of the week; it is then that sermons are preached. After prayers, families eat together, then there is rest, and a congregation of men in the cafés.

It was at this café point of the day, plenty of people on the streets with nothing much to do, that Gomaa drove Alan and me into town. Lahun has grown from the 'unexplored village' where Winifred Blackman lived in her 'straw-hut life' to a large town of tens of thousands of people. Many of the two-storey mudbrick houses that would have been familiar to Blackman had been replaced by higher brick or breeze-block buildings. There were cars, trucks, tractors, TV aerials and satellite dishes. There was change, progress, T-shirts with American sports logos, baseball caps and bottles of Coke. We were mobbed before our feet touched the ground. We could have talked about Michael Jackson, Princess Diana and all the other names which have become global common property, yet the moment we mentioned that we wanted to see the tomb of the Sheikh Abu'l-Latif, whom Winifred Blackman had written about in her notebook, we were met with silence and then with a dozen contradictory directions.

The tomb, it turned out, was only a few steps away, but it took several minutes of pushing to reach it. It was a familiar single-storey brick building, nothing fancy here, and although it had probably originally stood on its own, it was now surrounded on three sides by houses. It was also locked.

The longer we stood by the tomb, the more men and boys wandered over to find out what the fuss was all about; there were now at least fifty of them and their mood wasn't entirely friendly. 'Why do they want to see our sheikh?' one of the men asked. 'Where are their papers?' 'It is forbidden for foreigners to come just like that.'

Alan, shorter in both height and temper, was getting nervous. 'Is it forbidden to pay a visit to the sheikh and ask him for the *baraka*? What way is this to treat people who have travelled so far to see the sheikh's tomb?'

An elderly man standing nearby told us to follow him. The crowd parted and we walked down the street. Where was he taking us? To the police? To find the man with the key? To his house? 'I'm in no hurry to find out,' Alan whispered, 'but then I'd go anywhere to get away from this lot.'

We entered an old mudbrick house off the main street and were ushered through the first room, filled with animals, into a large, dark, back room with benches round the sides that would easily seat twenty. Within a couple of minutes the room was full, but there was none of the aggression we had seen outside. The men were calm, quiet, above all curious. We were facing some sort of council.

Most of the men were elderly; the younger ones had been shut outside. It was obvious they weren't used to seeing foreigners and found our arrival suspicious. I thought of Winifred Blackman among them and wished that she had given more clues about her reception here.

Alan explained again that we had wanted to pay our respects to Sheikh Abu'l-Latif.

'But how do you know about our sheikh?' a fat old man in a grey, tattered *galabiyya* asked.

'His name is known far and wide,' Alan exaggerated, but that didn't seem to satisfy them. 'There is something else. A long time ago an Englishwoman lived here in your village. This man,' he pointed to me, 'wants to find the house where she lived and the family who looked after her.'

'Why does he want to know?'

Before I could explain about my work, Alan said, 'He is from her family.'

The tension eased.

'Look,' I said and held up a piece of paper, 'here is a photograph of the man from your village in whose house she stayed.'

It was a bright afternoon outside but the room was twilit; several men called for light and a boy appeared with a large, glass-topped oil lamp. The picture was of a man standing in front of a house. He had an archetypal Egyptian face, slightly heavy, with a flat jaw, long nose and short, dark, curling hair. They passed the page among themselves. 'This was taken a long time ago,' I explained. 'More than seventy years. His name was Hideyb—'

'I am Hideyb,' said one of the younger men near me.

'Hideyb Abdel Shafiy. Do you know him?'

He shook his head.

'Or did you hear about an Englishwoman coming to stay?'

Again he shook his head.

'There are other Hideybs,' someone else suggested.

'Send for them,' was the call of the crowd and within minutes other men appeared and were shown the page, but it meant nothing to them either.

When we had exhausted all the possible Hideybs and Abdel Shafiys, and drunk the tea that was brought to us, Alan asked again if we might visit the sheikh's tomb. The men said they would escort us. The boys were still in the street – where else would they go when the elders were in closed session with two foreigners? – and now there were more like a hundred of us, pushing and shoving through the street crowd towards the sheikh's tomb. A tractor drove through the crowd and the crush got worse. When a policeman appeared, radio in hand, the crowd eased off.

'Where are you going?'

We began our improbable story again.

'No,' he said emphatically, 'you cannot see the tomb. It is forbidden for foreigners to be here.' Alan pointed out that there was no law forbidding our visit, but the officer wasn't interested. 'You see these people?' he asked. 'You see how they are? Then you must go.'

Winifred Blackman lived happily in Lahun through several winters of the 1920s, but they chased us out of town. Boys ran after us and jumped on the tailboard, from where they insulted us, until we reached the sluice bridge again.

'See,' said Alan, when he had recovered his breath and humour. 'I said you were mad, but would you listen?'

Bimbashi McPherson, a Briton who worked in Egypt for 'more than half of a long life', published one of very few works dedicated to the phenomenon of moulids. His *Moulids of Egypt*, published in Cairo in the dark year of 1941, remains a useful source book.

'A moulid,' he wrote in his elaborate prose, 'is a popular religious feast in honour of some saint, – in Egypt, usually of Islam, corresponding to the Feasts and Fairs held in Europe, (and its colonies) to honour some Christian saints; and although moulids hardly became a national institution in Egypt till the seventh century of the Hegira, – the thirteenth AD, nor perhaps entirely recognized officially as such till two centuries later, they in many cases are a continuation of Feasts held hundreds or even thousands of years before the Prophet.' Moulids, McPherson was suggesting, are the modern equivalent of feasts in honour of local gods in ancient Egypt. McPherson then proceeded to cite several examples, some of them providing direct parallels, the most famous of which was a moulid held near Cairo where a young man was carried naked in the procession with a string tied round his penis. A man behind him would pull on the string to keep him erect. The ancient fertility god Min appears on many temple walls in procession with an erect member, and then there is this description from Herodotus of the feast of Dionysus, in which 'they have puppets, about eighteen inches high; the genitals of these figures are made almost as big as the rest of their bodies, and they are pulled up and down by strings as the women carry them round the villages.'

Every village in Egypt has its sheikh or saint, and some have many more than one; Aswan, for instance, has seventy-seven. No one has ever managed to calculate the number of saints in Cairo, though there are certainly hundreds of them, probably thousands and maybe even more. Some were buried in magnificent mosque tombs, which became the centre of their cults – the mosques of Husayn, Sayyida Zaynab and Imam esh-Shafei spring to mind. Others were buried under the Egyptian earth, which is itself made up of the dust of past saints, their graves marked with a simple slab of concrete topped with a basic dome. However they were interred, I found the parallels between these sheikhs and the ancient gods irresistible.

In ancient temples, statues of the gods were kept in the sanctuary and storerooms, away from the public eye. In theory only the pharaoh could officiate in the temples. 'Only he,' wrote the American Egyptologist William Murnane, 'could stand, as a son before his parents, in the presence of the gods, and yet act as the representative of mankind.' But in spite of his divine nature, the pharaoh couldn't be everywhere at once, so priests stood in for him and it was they who had daily contact with the gods. Lay people had less access and relied on priests to intercede for them when the gods left their sanctuaries. The priests did this often, appearing in the temple's outer courtyards where they were accessible to a larger number of people. But it was only at their annual feasts that the gods appeared in public.

From the images of these festivals on several temple walls it seems, as Bimbashi McPherson suggested, that they bore similarities to the popular Christian festivals of Europe and South America, and to Hindu celebrations in India. After a service in the temple, the god entered a boat – a model of the solar boat in which the sun god and his companions sailed across the sky each day, a fitting mode of transport for the god of river people – and was carried out of the sanctuary to other temples or shrines, in the same way that Christian cult figures of the Madonna or saints are paraded on floats today. The crowds were there, the petitioners, the lame and the sick, the troubled souls, the mourners and grievers, the blessed and the thankful, the devout, the relieved, the there-but-for-the-grace-of-the-gods-go-Is, and they would have shown their devotion as people do today, by joining the crowd, by praying, cheering and making offerings.

The festival calendar was a busy one. At Thebes under the New Kingdom pharaohs, for instance, there were some sixty annual festivals in honour of local and state or 'great' gods, seasonal feasts celebrating the New Year and the harvests as well as significant military moments. Most had their own characteristics and many survived the centuries to the Graeco-Roman period. Herodotus described the annual festival of the fun-loving cat-goddess Bastet, held at 'her' city of Bubastis in the Delta, as 'the most important and best attended' of the festivals. 'They come in barges,' he wrote, 'men and women together, a great number in each boat; on the way, some of the women keep up a continual clatter with castanets and some of the men play flutes, while the rest, both men and women, sing and clap their hands . . . When they reach Bubastis they celebrate the festival with elaborate sacrifices, and more wine is consumed than during all the rest of the year. The numbers that meet there, are, according to native report, as many as seven hundred thousand men and women – excluding children.'

Even more eloquent than Herodotus are the images which survive at Edfu and Dendera, two of the best-preserved Graeco-Roman temples, of the annual Feast of the Beautiful Meeting during which Hathor, the cow-headed guardian of women, also known for her sense of fun, went to visit the falcon-headed god Horus. Each year, priests at Dendera placed the goddess's statue in its carrying barque, which was in turn put in a real Nile boat and sailed up the river to the temple of Horus at Edfu. The images show Horus's barge towing the goddess, near the end of her journey, along the canal between the temple and the river. The two deities were then carried to the sanctuary at Edfu temple, where they were left alone to consummate their union. Later, they returned to their respective barges and Horus escorted Hathor to the frontier of his territory. On the banks, as they passed, men danced and women shook their rattles.

One of the most important festivals in the ceremonial year took place at the great state temple of Amun at Karnak and the Nile-side temple of Luxor. The festival was at the height of its reputation when Luxor was the centre of power in Egypt, when pharaohs lived and were buried there. In the early dynastic period Amun was a small-time god, worshipped only in his local cult centre. He didn't even warrant a mention in the twenty-fourth century BC Pyramid Texts. Early on, he was depicted as a goose or a ram but, as with modern politicians, when his power increased so his image became sharper, more defined. The goose was dropped (although among the many names by which he was later known, there was a hint of his past in 'the Great Cackler') and Amun was associated solely with the ram, an identification that survived to the end of pagan times.

During the Eleventh Dynasty, Montu, god of war, was the most significant god of Thebes. Egyptologists group the previous four dynasties together as the First Intermediate Period, an age of chaos and decentralization that followed the end of the Old Kingdom. In 2060 BC a Theban prince called Mentuhotep – his name meant 'Montu is content' – reunited the country and created the new capital at Thebes. Amun came to the fore in the next century with the accession of a pharaoh called Amenemhet I, 'Amun is at the heart'. Despite a setback during a period of foreign invasion, Amun's influence steadily increased for a thousand years until he was worshipped as the pre-eminent state god.

During the New Kingdom (1570–1070 BC), the temple complex at Karnak became a city in itself, enriched over the centuries by the generosity of pharaohs. One inscription at Karnak records that Tuthmosis III (he reigned 1504–1450 BC), one of the great warrior kings who created an empire across the Middle East, gave Amun fields and gardens, cattle, gold, silver, lapis lazuli, no less than 878 African and Asian captives and three captured cities, each of which paid an annual tribute to the god. Other New Kingdom pharaohs were just as generous, and just as eager to have their generosity recorded on temple walls for posterity. Another inscription at Karnak mentions that Seti I gave 'all the silver, gold, lapis-lazuli, malachite, and precious stones, which he carried off from the miserable country of Syria'.

Nothing succeeds like success; the richer and more powerful Amun became, the more he was given. Three-quarters of Ramses III's extensive gifts to Egyptian gods went to Amun – 86,486 slaves, half a million head of cattle, nearly nine hundred thousand plots of land, 2756 divine images in gold and silver. It was these and other gifts that created the glory of the 'hundred-gated Thebes' that Homer refers to, where 'heaps of precious ingots gleam'.

To run the business of the temple, Amun had a bureaucracy, a central office for the upkeep of the house of the god and others for the treasury, farming and personnel (slave management). There were scribes and there were maintenance teams, the masons and painters, porters and cleaners, as well as the god's own police force. All these people served the vast priesthood which was itself, like everything else, arranged into that quintessential Egyptian shape the pyramid, a strict hierarchy. The pharaoh here, as elsewhere, sat on top of the priestly pyramid. Below him, during the New Kingdom, there were the first, second and third prophets, the divine father, and the lowest priestly ranks. As Thebes's power grew, so the priests of Amun took authority over other temples. The first prophet of Amun controlled the priesthood throughout the country; Amun's second prophet is recorded as having also held the title of high priest of Heliopolis, the ancient cult centre. By 1080 BC the priesthood was strong enough to dispense with the pharaoh altogether and to annex the south of the country, establishing a dynasty that ruled Upper Egypt for 135 years and owned two-thirds of all temple land, 90 per cent of all ships and 80 per cent of all factories. Imagine, then, how many people – the priests and households of Karnak, of Luxor, of the necropolis across the river, as well as from towns and temples throughout the country – arrived in Thebes to celebrate the great feast of Opet.

A clue to the realities of Amun's feast is given in a series of inscriptions that have survived on the walls of the Temple of Luxor. Once again I packed my bag, my notebooks and pencils, and headed for the south.

'Where to this time, ya basha?' Ibrahim asked after I had woken him behind his wheel. Since my visit to the sheikh at al-Azhar and the moulid of Husayn, Ibrahim had regarded me as he would a distant member of his wife's family, with some affection. I told him I was going to the airport.

'Luxor? Again?' He asked how much my plane ticket cost and then offered to drive me to Luxor. 'We can go together. It will be cheaper and better.' I thought about the drive, the roadblocks, the security problems, and then about Ibrahim's driving. Looking for reassurance, I checked my ticket. Still there in my bag.

'Ibrahim,' I told him, 'I would rather fly to the moon than drive to Luxor.'

'Yes,' he replied, 'so would I,' but went no further, realizing he was spoiling his pitch.

It took half an hour to reach the airport and along the way, when he wasn't pointing out the sights, like a new mosque or the presidential residence – 'guide at no extra charge' – he continued his campaign.

'What would your wife say if you leave her for several days? How will she manage with the kids?' I countered.

'She will thank you for taking me away and then go to thank the Prophet for answering her prayers,' he said, and then laughed his deep resonant laugh.

'When I get to Luxor I will make an offering at the tomb of the Sheikh Abu'l-Hajjaj for your continuing marital happiness.'

'You know Abu'l-Hajjaj?' he asked, surprised.

'Who doesn't know of the great sheikh? I am going now to visit his moulid.'

'God's blessing on you and the sheikh, ya Antoony,' he said and this time I think he meant it for we hardly had to argue when it came to sorting out the fare.

'God's blessing on you, ya Sidi Abu'l-Hajjaj.'

Along the corniche, the morning light was soft and the wake sparkled behind the *Mecca*, the old iron-hulled ferry, as it made its short pilgrimage across the Nile. Villagers were huddled in family groups under the trees. There was more than the usual contingent of hustlers and hasslers, of shoe shines and bean sellers, of carriage drivers shouting 'hello, *calèche*' in mock-Sandhurst accents. Cake sellers, paper boys, men with trays of bread and twisted platsels. There was more on sale and therefore, by brilliant deduction, there had to be more people around to buy.

When I stopped to take in the riverside spectacle, busy for once with Egyptians, not foreigners, a young man approached me and introduced himself as Mahmoud. Following my eyes to the ancient temple and the mosque of Abu'l-Hajjaj that sits on top of its colonnades like a stork in a precarious nest, he offered the sheikh his blessing. 'Have you come for the moulid?' he asked.

'Yes, I'm here for the moulid, *alhamdulillah*.'

Mahmoud offered more blessings and while he did so I looked him over for signs of religious fanaticism, remembering my experience with

Khalid at the moulid of Sayyida Zaynab in Cairo. No 'raisin', the purplish callous that was appearing somewhat ostentatiously on an increasing number of foreheads to show that the bearer spent much of his life prostrated before God. No beard. No chip on his shoulder. It looked safe.

Mahmoud was born and bred in Luxor and had recently finished training as a *mohandis*, an engineer, at a Cairo university. He was back in Luxor for the sheikh's moulid. 'It doesn't matter where I am – I could go to the other side of the world – I would still come back for Sidi Abu'l-Hajjaj. Why? Because he was a good man. Because he saved our city, so they say. Also, many good things have happened to people who have needed help and who have asked Sidi Abu'l-Hajjaj. But we should not stand here, talking. We should go and say hello to the sheikh. Come, we can go now.'

But just then the sheikh's muezzin called the faithful to prayer and as the words *la illaha illa'allah*, there is no God but God, reverberated through the ancient columns in front of us, Mahmoud apologized. He had to leave. 'But perhaps we could meet here tomorrow. I would like to show you the procession.'

The great sheikh, al-Sayyid Youssef Abu'l-Hajjaj, would have protested at any parallels being made between himself and the unbelievers who lived in Egypt in the time before the Prophet Muhammad and the Prophet Eissa (Jesus). Youssef Abu'l-Hajjaj was born in Baghdad. A descendant of the Caliph Ali and therefore also of the Prophet, the good sheikh travelled first to Mecca, then to Egypt. Legend has it that when he crossed the Red Sea a storm blew up and sank the pilgrims' fleet, but that the sheikh, perhaps recalling Moses or Jonah, prayed to God and his boat alone was saved. The sheikh studied with various Sufi groups in Cairo before moving to Luxor.

At the time of his arrival, Luxor was a small village set among the grand ruins beside the Nile. It was ruled, so the legend goes, by a strong woman called Sitt Towzah. The *sitt* was far from pleased by the arrival of the foreigner, but Allah be praised, the sheikh walked around the outside of the village, which he bound with a single thread. After that he had the place sewn up and there was nothing the *sitt* could do to resist him.

Abu'l-Hajjaj lived for many years in Luxor and founded a *tariqa* (the word literally means a way or a path), a centre for prayer and teaching. After his death in AD 1243, his reputation was so thoroughly embroidered that it was soon a rich enough tapestry to be laid out upon a revered sheikh's tomb. Luxor became a place of pilgrimage as Muslims came to venerate the sheikh. A mosque was built around his tomb, which sat on top of the ancient temple of Luxor, buried by a centuries-old accumulation of Nile silt, desert sand and human debris.

Several Arab travellers recorded their visits to Abu'l-Hajjaj's mosque, but none mention the details of his moulid. After the decipherment of hieroglyphs many books were written about Luxor, but even then there was little mention of the sheikh. Gardner Wilkinson, whose 1843 *Modern Egypt and Thebes* was the first authoritative guidebook to Egypt, makes no mention of the Luxor sheikh, though elsewhere in his book he notes that 'the observation of Herodotus, that the Egyptians could not live without a king, might find a parallel in the impossibility of their living without a pantheon of gods or saints. And, notwithstanding the positive commands of Islam to allow no one to share any of the honours due to the Deity alone, no ancient or modern religion could produce a larger calendar of divine claimants.'

Lucie Duff Gordon attended the celebrations in 1864 when 'Sheykh Yussef took me into the tomb of his ancestor, Sheykh Abul Hajjaj, the great saint here, and all the company said a Fattah for my health. It was on the night of Friday, and during the moolid of the Sheykh.' The following year, when her health was worse, she was put under the protection of the saint. 'I was obliged to be wrapped in the green silk cover of his tomb, when it was taken off to be carried in procession, partly for my health and general welfare, and as a sort of adoption into the family.' In 1866 she arrived back in Luxor from Cairo just in time to celebrate the end of the moulid. That night there were lively scenes around the tomb, but 'the day after my arrival was the great and last day. The crowd was but little and not lively – times are too hard.' On the *layla kebira*, the last night of the moulid, things were otherwise.

This was the big night of Abu'l-Hajjaj's moulid, and by then the celebrations and religious observances had been going on for a week. It was also the night of the middle of the Islamic month of Shaaban, a moment of great significance for all Muslims because tonight, they believed, their fate would be decided for the coming year. While

Muslims around the world were observant, in Luxor they were ecstatic.

Approached from the river, Abu'l-Hajjaj's mosque looked even more perilous than I remembered, hanging above the courtyard of Luxor temple. Strings of coloured lights had been draped around the white-washed building, which stood like a beacon over the darkened pagan shrines.

The yellowed night throbbed with bass notes from music and with incantations and prayers. The corniche was crowded, the pavement slick with discarded bean husks and sunflower seeds. Children in shiny wizard hats came and pestered me – 'a foreigner! a foreigner!' – until their parents called them back.

Luxor's waterfront had been given a facelift, but once off the main street I was back into that more familiar Egypt of peeling paint and crumbling houses, of steps swept several times a day, of grit and dust, sagging electric cables, doors open on to cobblers' or carpenters' workshops. Most shops were still open and several cafés had spread along the streets to cater for the sudden influx of people from around the country. Unlike in Lucie Duff Gordon's time, the turnout was good and money was being spent on moulid toys, on food and drink and sugar dolls. The dolls were cast out of pink sugar and came in two shapes. One was a horseman with his sword raised, modelled perhaps on Antar of the Abu Zayd al-Hilali story, on Mir Girgis, the Coptic St George slaying the dragon, or on the god Horus avenging the death of his father Osiris. The other figure was a woman with a conical base, a tight waist, bulging breasts and hands on hips. She wore a crêpe skirt and a headdress of pleated paper, a disc that surrounded her like the moon or a halo. I picked up one of the women.

'Twenty-five pounds,' the trader said.

The sum was outrageous. 'Who is it?'

'The *arusa*, the bride of Abu'l-Hajjaj.'

'But who was she?'

'Twenty-five pounds.'

I offered a quarter of the price and we haggled until we were both able to part with dignity intact.

The crowd was thick and I had difficulty carrying the *arusa* without getting her broken. 'Look, *ummi*,' a child said to her mother, 'the foreigner has an *arusa*.' Her brother giggled, old men looked away.

Umm Seti had had similar difficulty getting an answer about who the *arusa* represented. 'No one seems to know the origin of these figures,' she wrote, 'on sale at moulids and no other time. As the representation of human and animal figures is forbidden by the Koran, the custom of making them would appear to be pre-Islamic while their forms strongly suggest an ancient Egyptian origin.' Rough-cast figures of the gods, she pointed out, particularly of Osiris, were sold at ancient religious festivals.

At a crossroads on Souq Street, a space had been cleared, a ring of sorts, defined by wooden benches. In the middle, two men in the long, flared *galabiyya* of the south were brandishing metre-and-a-half-long sticks above their heads, circling each other in a ritualistic, almost choreographed dance, although there was nothing playful about the way they hit each other's sticks.

I sat on a corner of one of the benches, opposite two reed pipers and a drummer who were providing the jousters with musical accompaniment. My neighbour was a young, well groomed, intense-looking man in his twenties who soon introduced himself. 'Christian?' he asked, not waiting for a reply. 'I am a Copt,' he said and, in case I required proof, he pulled back his sleeve in the manner of a purveyor of hardcore pornography to reveal a cross tattooed on the soft underside of his wrist.

'They are doing *tahtib*,' he explained. 'They are only playing at fighting.'

'Don't they get hurt?' I asked as they clashed sticks again.

'Sometimes. But not the good ones.'

Two other men stood up, smiling at each other, and entered the arena of dust to take over the dance, like relay runners. For a while they circled each other, swinging their sticks to get the weight, the balance, the rhythm right, changing direction from time to time, the music a slow, plaintive wail. After several minutes they picked up speed and the music with them, the sparring becoming more like a fight, the blows more threatening, the smiles gone. '*Yallah!*' cried a man from the benches. 'Praise the Prophet!' from another.

Faster they went and faster swung the sticks, the strike and its parry less exaggerated, until another pair of men stood up and the music dropped its tempo like an athlete catching his breath.

My well-trimmed neighbour, Girgis, was an archaeology graduate.

He was proud of the fact that he spoke English, and with reason: he spoke very well. I asked why, as a Christian, he was celebrating the moulid of a Muslim sheikh.

'We have our own moulids, of course,' and he reeled off a list of local Coptic saints. 'The biggest for us is Abu Sayfein at Gamoulah.'

I had already read about Abu Sayfein, the Father of Two Swords, otherwise known as St Macarius. Georges Legrain, a French Egyptologist who spent many years excavating at Karnak during the 1930s, described the moulid, held in August, as 'the occasion of a great pilgrimage similar to that of Abou el Hajjaj of Luxor: people come from all corners of Egypt because of the saint's great reputation'. Legrain noted that the moulid attracted Muslims as well as Copts; principally, he thought, because of the miraculous cures the saint performed – three or four each year. The martyr was particularly effective in curing the possessed and the mad. Legrain was told that the miracles happened because the devils possessing these people suddenly decided to leave when the saint appeared. 'What strikes me as interesting,' Legrain concluded, 'is that this belief is older than the saint . . . a hieroglyphic stela in the Bibliothèque Nationale in Paris records that the god Khonsu, more than three thousand years earlier, exorcised Bentresch, daughter of the prince of Bakhtan, and rid her of a devil called Shamaou, who had possessed her for many years.'

I told Girgis what I remembered of this. 'So then you understand why Muslims and Christians go to each other's moulids. The Jews too. Really. The saints are for all Egyptians, Copts and Muslims.' I nodded, fast realizing that most of these survivals touched on all religions.

He pointed to my *arusa*. 'I see you like sweets.'

'I was curious to know where she comes from and why they are selling sugar dolls at the moulid of Abu'l-Hajjaj.'

'They sell them at many moulids, but why I don't know.'

Another round of stick fighting was reaching its climax, with an older man showing how lithe he could be. He was clearly enjoying giving his younger opponent the run-around.

'And why the stick dancing?' Umm Seti mentioned inscriptions recording ritual fighting during the feast of Osiris at Abydos and Herodotus referred to a mock battle, fought with clubs, at the festival in Papremis. 'Do you think this is the same thing?'

'The fighting isn't ancient. It was introduced by the Mamelukes as

part of their display at moulids.' And then he showed what I understood to be his religious bias. 'How could this Muslim festival have any
links with the time of the pharaohs? Muslims came from Arabia after
the death of Muhammad. But the Copts have always been here. Even
our name, which comes from the Greek word for Egypt, ties us to the
land. So in the Coptic Church you will find many things from the
pharaohs. With the Muslims, not.'

From Souq Street, I went to pay my respects to the sheikh, having
first wrapped up my *arusa* and hidden her in a bag for fear of
upsetting the great man's feelings. A full moon hung over the
celebrations, various Sufi orders were still rocking and chanting in
their tents outside the mosque, children were still playing in the
gardens nearby. The crush became more painful as a town official –
the governor, perhaps, or one of his deputies – pushed through the
crowd in his blacked-out Peugeot on his way to visit one of the
ceremonial tents, his bodyguards and police escort forming a human
barrier around him.

The passing car pushed us together like sand into a bucket, forming
the crowd into a solid unit that moved as one towards the sheikh's
tomb. I was pushed along, up the steps, past the beggars and
petitioners, to our first stop in front of a door that didn't open. The
door of the soul, it was called, the secret door through which Abu'l-
Hajjaj and the celestial saints could pass. It reminded me of the false
doors of ancient tombs where offerings were made and through which
the soul of the dead person passed.

'God's blessing on you, ya Sidi Abu'l-Hajjaj.'

The chamber beside the saint's tomb was filled by a group of
worshippers, a Sufi brotherhood I assumed from their ritual chanting.
I watched them from the corridor, entranced by the rows of men and a
few women rocking and chanting in unison, calling on the sheikh,
extolling his virtues, recounting his deeds, recommending him to God,
the leader's voice high-pitched and strained, the reply from his
followers a deep, earthy, unified grunt. *Allahu.* I was reminded of
images I had seen on western television news reports, accompanying
stories of Muslim fanaticism. In a way it was fanatical, extreme, taken
to the limits. It also stirred me as few things in my life. Here was the
great sheikh Sayyid Youssef Abu'l-Hajjaj in all his glory. Beneath us
was part of the temple of Luxor, unexcavated out of respect for the

saint; between the end of paganism and the coming of Islam, Christians had used the temple as a church. I was in one of those places and experiencing one of those moments when religions merge. In the name of Allah and His Prophet Muhammad, in the name of the Father and His Son Jesus, in the name of the great divinity, of Amun, Mut and Khonsu, the trinity of Thebes, prayers had been offered there, bread broken, flowers and images brought, animals slaughtered and the sick carried in the hope of cure, for as long as we humans have recorded our actions. As I sat watching the Sufis, the crowd walking up to pray for the sheikh and to receive his blessing, I was certain that Sheikh Muhammad at al-Azhar was wrong: this was Islam, and Christianity, and Judaism, and all the pagan cults that came before them. This was some essential human response. And what it suggested was that throughout the millennia, whatever the creed, Egyptians had held on to the belief that they could call upon the spirits of dead holy men to improve their lives on earth.

I met Mahmoud before midday prayers. I wanted to visit Luxor Temple and I suggested that he came with me.

'You think I am tourist?' he asked, amused. 'This is my home.'

A hundred years ago, the temple was cleared of accumulated silt and debris and all the buildings that obscured the glory of the pharaohs were done away with. All except the mosque of Abu'l-Hajjaj. As Mahmoud and I walked towards the inner sanctuaries of the temple, we passed beneath the mosque which hung above the temple wall, above the roof, its old door opening now onto thin air. If I was a photographer I would have been shooting film just then because nothing I had seen in Egypt more perfectly expressed the way in which things are built over each other, the way cultures absorb traditions – the Bible written over Herodotus, and the Koran over that, as Lucie Duff Gordon, whose house had also stood here, put it.

I found what I was looking for on the processional colonnade built in honour of Amun in the fourteenth century BC by the strong pharaoh Amenhotep III.

'What are they doing?' Mahmoud asked.

'You haven't been here before?'

'Of course I have. But no one has ever explained what this was.'

'This is a description of the great feast of Opet.' He had clearly never heard of it. 'Opet was one of the most important feasts for the pharaohs, when the god Amun, his wife Mut and their child Khonsu – the three gods of Thebes – left Karnak to visit Luxor Temple.'

The carved reliefs were added a couple of decades after Amenhotep's death, during the reign of Tutankhamun. They showed the boy-king at Karnak temple praying in front of the gods' ceremonial boats. The boats were then raised on poles and carried, with much singing and clapping, to the temple gate. At that time Karnak was linked to the Nile by a canal and the ceremonial boats were put on river boats and towed to Luxor by sailing boats, helped by a crowd who pulled ropes along the shore. From the riverbank at Luxor, not far from where Mahmoud and I were standing, the gods in their ceremonial boats were again carried by priests. Dancing girls led the way. It was a festival of renewal, celebrated halfway through the Nile's flood, a celebration of fertility. Amun in Luxor temple had a different character to the Amun of Karnak. This Amun, as Egyptologist William Murnane put it, 'was a dynamic entity, who may originally have represented the inexhaustible fertility of the earth'. The festival took its name from the innermost chamber of the temple, the Opet, or private apartments, where the gods were left to celebrate and where, it is believed, the pharaoh and his wife performed a ritual marriage during which the pharaoh's virility was renewed. And although they couldn't possibly have known it at the time it was built, Abu'l-Hajjaj's tomb was built over the shrine where the gods Amun, Mut and Khonsu rested on their way to the temple's Opet sanctuary.

Mahmoud was open-mouthed in front of the carvings.

'What are you looking so surprised about?' I asked.

'I have just realized what this reminds me of.'

As he said it, I remembered that the previous evening I had seen a small model of a boat hanging from the ceiling of the sheikh's tomb and that Umm Seti had mentioned seeing similar boats in the tombs of other saints, hung there to ferry them along the celestial Nile. There was, she pointed out, even a chapter called 'Bringing Along a Boat in the Underworld' in the Book of the Dead, the essential manual to making it to a happy afterlife in antiquity.

'No,' said Mahmoud, 'that's not exactly what I meant.'

'What?' I replied, a little gruff, unhappy at having what looked like a neat connection broken.

He did not know how much I wanted there to be a connection, how strongly I had felt the power of continuity as I watched the Sufi rituals the previous evening. He knew nothing of my search, my need to make these connections between past and present. What was any of that to him? Mere tourist talk.

'Let's go to the procession,' he said, 'and you will understand why I am surprised by what I see here.'

A crowd of Egyptians, eight or ten deep, lined the streets around the mosque and temple.

'Where are all the foreigners?' Mahmoud asked. 'Don't they care about Sidi Abu'l-Hajjaj?'

'Maybe not. Or maybe it has something to do with the tourist office telling them that the festivity would start at four o'clock.'

'Why would they do that?'

'Security?'

'There are no terrorists here.'

'How do you know? They have said that they think moulids should be stopped.'

'Let them try,' he said angrily. 'We will always honour Sidi Abu'l-Hajjaj. No one can stop that.'

After midday prayers the crowd filled out and spilled into the street. People had come from as far away as Aswan and Alexandria to honour Abu'l-Hajjaj. 'Because we love him,' as someone near me explained.

The security forces soon lost control of the proceedings, and as the crowd of devotees swarmed down from the mosque they blocked the processional route. 'We will be late starting, of course, but the sheikh will forgive us for that, I am sure.'

Then there was an even greater noise and a pushing from behind. 'Quick,' Mahmoud said, as if I had somewhere to go, 'here they come.'

The crowd pushed forward, the black-uniformed police blew their whistles, the crowd blew theirs, voices were raised, there were cheers, and the procession began to move, floats and tractors, trucks and jeeps, all decked out in honour of the town's patron saint. Then a tractor turned the corner pulling something with a sail.

'Look,' Mahmoud said triumphantly. 'There they are. The boats we carry around the town. Just like in those drawings you showed me in the temple.'

He was pointing to a wooden boat, complete with sail, a slightly scaled-down version of the lateen-rigged Nile boat which has been in use since the time of the pharaohs. Raised up on wheels, it was being towed towards us. Behind it I could see two more boats. In them, in the place of the Theban trinity of Amun, Mut and Khonsu, there rode children from Luxor. Sweets were thrown. There was cheering and much blessing of Abu'l-Hajjaj.

In 1925, a photographer from the Metropolitan Museum in New York by the name of Harry Burton was in Luxor taking photographs of the newly opened Tutankhamun's tomb for Howard Carter. Taking advantage of the opportunity it presented, he also made a film of the procession in honour of Abu'l-Hajjaj. In it, three full-size feluccas were dragged around the temple in honour of the sheikh.

An article in the anthropological journal *MAN*, in 1938, stated the belief of Egyptologists that the procession of boats was 'a shadowy survival of the great water festival of Opet'.

The boats turned the corner on to the corniche. In order to make a circuit of the mosque, they would also have to be carried around the ancient temple. Mahmoud was ecstatic as he pointed out the analogy with the ancient festival.

In a film she made on the moulid, anthropologist Elizabeth Wickett referred to the divine energy released through the act of 'going round'. 'He is the one who makes us feel renewed,' said one of the sheikh's devotees. Mahmoud and the crowd around us appeared to feel that sense of renewal. There was, of course, no conscious copying of the procession that carried the pagan triad round the temple three and a half thousand years ago, and no way of knowing whether there was any continuity in the act of going round. But there was no doubt that the sheikh's followers were there for the same reason as the devotees of Amun: to be released for a moment from their inhibitions, their problems, for their lives to be blessed, to have a glimpse, a reminder, of something sacred. They lost themselves in the celebration and they left with a sense of having been uplifted and renewed.

The next float to pass carried a transvestite, a man in a dress and bad make-up who pouted and preened, pulled up his skirt and juggled enormous breasts. He was trying to stir up the crowd: forget Islamic decency, I was reminded of Amun of Luxor, the fertility god with his enormous penis. The transvestite called out to people in the crowd, ground his hips and thrust out his groin. Some of the girls responded.

One near me forgot herself for long enough to follow his lead. She plumped up her breasts, pouted, even shouted back at him until her friends laughed her back home.

Just as I was putting the sheikh's procession down on my list of confirmed survivals – as convincing, I thought, as the fertility rites and as people living in the cemetery – another tractor came round the corner pulling another boat. That made four. No one ever mentioned four boats in the sheikh's procession. Did this call into question whether this was a surviving pharaonic practice? Even Mahmoud was beginning to have his doubts.

'Ya Anthony,' he announced almost apologetically, 'I can see another boat.'

'Five boats, Mahmoud? How can this be?'

He thought about it for a moment and then, somewhat stoically, he reached his conclusion. 'This is Egypt. We are growing, always growing, so nothing stays the same. Last year there were three boats. This year five. And Allah alone knows how many boats will honour Sidi Abu'l-Hajjaj next year. But of one thing – and only one thing – I am sure. That there will be boats, as there always have been, and that there will be people to cheer them in honour of the sheikh.'

CHAPTER 6

Mr Magic

So flourishing was the practice of magic in the Egypt of about
3000 BC, that the very name of the land has passed into our
language as a synonym for it.

Idries Shah

'Many people here can tell you stories about wonderful things,' Gamal
explained, 'because many wonderful things have happened here. And
they are still happening. All Egypt is known for its magical powers, but
here in this area, in Luxor, Tot, Armant, Esna, we are very famous for
it.'

Gamal al-Hajjaji, descended in a more or less direct line from Sheikh
Youssef Abu'l-Hajjaj, was a man of many parts. Greying, tall, thin and
upright – both in stature and character – he sold cigarettes, sweets,
drinks, shampoo and some of life's other essentials from a corner shop
near Luxor station. He also collected what was left of the region's
folklore. I told him about the unpublished papers of Winifred Blackman and Umm Seti and in return he confided that he had made
hundreds of recordings of storytellers reciting the old epics. When I
asked about the magical powers of sheikhs, he assured me that magic
wasn't just the preserve of the holy men of Islam. I swear I didn't
prompt him in any way, but he then said, 'This is something that goes
back to the time of the pharaohs.' Another survival, then? 'Certainly.

'It is written in the Koran that Sayyidra Mousa (Moses) was able to
practise magic. This Sayyidra Mousa was born near Cairo and left by
his mother in the plants beside the Nile. The pharaoh's daughter found
him and brought him up to be her own son. Later, he led the Jews
across the Red Sea, which he was able to do because of his magic. But
the interesting part for you happened before this, when he was called
before the pharaoh to test his magic.'

The story Gamal referred to is recorded in the Book of Exodus, in a scene in which Moses and his brother Aaron confront the pharaoh and his magicians. 'When Pharaoh speaks to you,' the story goes,

> saying, Shew a miracle for you: then thou shalt say unto Aaron, Take thy rod, and cast it before Pharaoh, and it shall become a serpent.
>
> Then Pharaoh also called the wise men and sorcerers: now the magicians of Egypt, they also did in like manner with their enchantments.
>
> For they cast down every man his rod, and they became serpents: but Aaron's rod swallowed up their rods.

'Do you believe in the people who live beneath the earth?' Gamal asked, lighting another cigarette in his mannered way.

'Like the *afarit*?' I asked.

'No, that is something else. You know if you have seen an *afrit*. Your hair will stand up and your hands will tremble. Even if you think you are just looking at another person like you or me, when the *afrit* opens its eyes they will be red and you will know.'

'So what do you call the other people?'

'I told you,' he said with slight irritation, as though I was being slow. 'They are the people who live under the earth.'

I thought of a story I had been told in the City of the Dead in Cairo about a city beneath the city, but I thought it best not to try Gamal's patience by mentioning it. 'No,' I told him, 'I've never heard of them.'

'A boy just passed who has been down there and stayed with them. Then he came back. If he passes again I will ask him about it for you. But the *afarit* are another sort of magic. I know a man in Esna who can bring up the *djinn* and *afarit* and make them work for him. He is a very great man and many people go to him.'

'For what?'

'To help with a woman. To help if something has been stolen. To curse someone who has done them wrong. To make them happy if they are troubled. To help with important things.'

'And does it work?'

Gamal looked at me as though I was simple. 'Anthony, there is no point in my telling you, now is there? You must see it for yourself, with your own eyes, or else you won't believe it. But it is difficult to meet these people. They do not welcome outsiders. However, I have an idea. I will tell them that you are in love with a girl who has left you, that you have a broken heart, are too sad and that nothing and no one can help you. You look somehow sad, you know. Then they will help you in this case.'

He broke off to serve a boy and then came back to the chairs in front of his shop. 'All this will take time. For now, I can show you something else. We will go to visit a sheikh.'

One of Gamal's many virtues was that he was as happy to promote Coptic saints as Muslim sheikhs. In fact he decided that we should start with a Copt. 'We have here a very known sheikh called Anba Younus. "Anba" is like a doctor, one who has studied a lot. Usually it takes many years to become an anba, but this Younus was only six or seven years old. How can this be?'

Until this point, it hadn't been clear whether the prodigy Gamal was talking about was dead or alive, but now I realized I was on my way to visit another tomb.

'In the church there is some oil which has magical properties. It has healed many people. I myself know someone who was helped by it.'

Gamal pulled down the shutter on his shop and walked me through the centre of Luxor to the Coptic enclave, where he was also known. This, I realized, was unusual, as the two communities generally stayed away from each other. 'As a boy,' he explained, 'I used to live near here. I grew up with these people. At that time there was no problem here between Copts and Muslims. Now it's terrible, people being killed, like a war. And for what? We both worship the same God.'

Not all Muslims shared Gamal's enlightenment and the Coptic church, school and administrative buildings were all under guard, their doors locked and their walls fringed with barbed wire. An elderly priest appeared at the gate and Gamal explained why we had come. The priest returned some minutes later, clearly embarrassed, and apologized. The man with the key to the church and the shrine could not be found, so the anba could not be visited.

'Then we must go to the Mosque.' Allah had intervened and Gamal was not one to resist divine direction.

We crossed back through town towards the Nile. I thought I knew this part of Luxor quite well, recognized some of the shopkeepers, the telephone exchange, the tax-free shop, but Gamal pointed out things that made me feel I had never been there before. How had I missed that old cannon on the side of the road? Had the man selling rough country pottery always been squatting on the pavement nearby? Gamal told me so much about his town that by the time we reached the mosque he wanted me to see, I was suffering from information overload. I didn't even manage to take in the name of the venerable sheikh whose powers extended to endowing the oil that seeped from a niche near his tomb with healing properties.

Gamal had noticed that I had several scabs on my elbow and asked if I had fallen down. I explained that it was a skin condition I had lived with since childhood. 'The sheikh will cure it,' he assured me and began to reel off the names of people who had benefited from the sheikh's oil. 'We can visit them, if you want, so that you will see.'

I was prepared to settle for oily patches on my arms as proof of the efficacy of the sheikh's powers and was duly annointed.

I left Gamal at his shop. 'Come tomorrow, and I will have news about the magician in Esna.'

Before I went I had one more question. Did he, by any chance, know how I could speak to a Rifai?

'A Hawi?' he asked.

'No.' I was quite specific. 'A Rifai.'

'I will make enquiries.'

The black-robed, gold-toothed, hennaed women sitting at my feet on the floor of the ferry back to the west bank at Luxor could have been waiting for their props to start the incantations from Shakespeare's *Macbeth*, eye of newt and toe of frog, gall of goat, liver of blaspheming Jew and all the rest of their terrible prescription. The old man opposite me, tucking a large studded wallet into the breast pocket of his inner vest, might have been secreting his book of charms and spells. Egyptian magic is older than history. Third-century Clement of Alexandria called his country 'the mother of magic'. In ancient Egypt, magic was ubiquitous, a central and integral part of everyday religious rites and habits. It was no more bizarre than a European, washed, groomed and ready for bed, kneeling on the floor, eyes closed, palms of hands placed together, chanting a request for the divine protection of family and friends.

Magic has left its legacy as well: two of our most common terms for magic refer to Egypt. As Sayyed Idries Shah put it: 'So flourishing was the practice of magic in the Egypt of about 3000 BC, that the very name of the land has passed into our language as a synonym for it . . . one of the oldest names for Egypt (*Kemt* – dark, black) came to be translated Black, in place of Egyptian, Magic. Egypt, of course, was called "The Black" not because of the diabolism of its magic, but from the colour of its earth when flooded by Nile water. A second term, alchemy (Arabic *al-kimiyya*), also stems from this same name.'

The Oxford English Dictionary defines magic as 'the pretended art of influencing the course of events by compelling the agency of spiritual beings, or by bringing into operation some occult controlling principle of nature; sorcery, witchcraft'. There is an anomaly, an unevenness, in that explanation, as there is in the way we use the word, because *magic* derives from *magus* and, as we are taught from an early age, the Magi, the three wise men, the kings of the Orient, were the first – apart from the shepherds – to know the Truth.

We tend to overlook the presence of the magician's tools – the incense, the ritual, the mysteries or secrets, unique clothing, the distance from the audience or congregation and often the use of a foreign language and obscure symbols – in our own religious activities, yet they are there. In the same way, it is easy to misunderstand the relationship between magic and religion in ancient Egypt. In the sense implied by the dictionary – that of 'influencing the course of events' – magic was at the heart of religious ritual.

Snakes were central to this part of ancient Egyptian religion and there isn't a tomb or a temple which doesn't carry a representation of them. Cobras wrapped themselves around doorways, the night barque of the sun-god Ra was made in the shape of a two-headed serpent and it was through the coils of the snake-god Mehn that the spirits of the dead had to travel to reach eternity. A bronze magician's wand, found in a Theban grave of the sixteenth century BC, is fashioned in the shape of a cobra, believed to represent the goddess Weret Hekau, 'the great of magic'. A rearing Egyptian cobra took centre place on the pharaoh's crown. And it was tempting to see symbolism rather than opportunism in the preferred method of suicide of the last independent ruler of ancient Egypt – Cleopatra died of a snake bite. It wasn't by chance that the God of Moses chose to reveal his power through a snake.

The old world gave way to the new but the Egyptians preserved their religious tendencies. It seemed likely that both Christians and Muslims maintained the memory of this snake worship. Difficult to prove, though. Neither Umm Seti nor Winifred Blackman paid much attention to snakes, but the writer Paul Brunton, who specialized in the esoteric, devoted a chapter of his 1936 bestseller *A Search in Secret Egypt* to snake charming, though not of the sort seen in India and Morocco, where dozy snakes are charmed out of a basket by the sound of a reed pipe. Brunton's charming relied on incantations and could, he claimed, be traced at least as far back as the twelfth century and the life of Sheikh Ahmad ar-Rifai.

Little is known of the life of Sheikh ar-Rifai and even his ending is disputed: as Bimbashi McPherson pointed out in his *Moulids of Egypt*, the sheikh's burial is disputed between Cairo, where he is said to have been buried in the mosque that bears his name, and Basra in Iraq. In the 1940s, when McPherson did his research, the moulid of Rifai was described as 'quite extinct'. A century earlier, when Edward Lane lived in Cairo, the followers of Rifai were amongst the most celebrated of Sufis or 'darwishes'. Lane describes the Rifai as divided into several orders, among which were the Ilwaniyya (who 'pretend to thrust iron spikes into their eyes and bodies without sustaining any injury') and the Saadiyya ('who handle with impunity live, venomous serpents, and scorpions, and partly devour them'). Lane then cast doubt on their skill by suggesting that the snakes are 'doctored'. 'The serpents, however, they render incapable of doing any injury by extracting their venomous fangs; and doubtless they also deprive the scorpions of their poison.' On certain important occasions, the Saadiyya performed another miraculous feat: the head of the order rode over the bodies of the devotees on a horse without causing any harm. 'Many Rifá'ee and Saadee darweeshes,' Lane concludes, 'obtain their livelihood by going about to charm away serpents from houses.'

Later in his book, Lane gives a more detailed description of the snake charmers, admitting that although his learned friends all condemned them as fakes, none were able to explain how the Rifai did what they did. Lane himself also appeared to be convinced by their snake-hunting skills. 'I have often heard it asserted that the serpent-charmer, before he enters a house in which he is to try his skill, always employs a servant of that house to introduce one or more serpents; but I have known instances in which this could not be the case; and am inclined to believe that the darweeshes above mentioned are generally acquainted with some real physical means of discovering the presence of serpents without seeing them, and of attracting them from their lurking-places.'

Winifred Blackman made no mention of snake worship or snake charming, but she did record her visit to the tomb of one Sheikh Haridi. The sheikh was buried in the limestone hills near the Nile between Asyout and Sohag. Haridi was one of the most unusual Egyptian saints. In her notebook, Blackman recorded that 'the Sheikh Haridi was originally believed to be a snake, but this belief seems to have died out.' Had it continued, I would have been on the trail of another survival.

The sheikh was buried 'in a hollow some way up the Gebel [mountain] Haridi, in a most romantic situation. It is approached by a rough, rocky, steep gorge, with giant rocks, like mountains, standing up on either side.' Blackman climbed up and was rewarded for her efforts. Several villagers were at the tomb and 'I was told that I was the first English person to visit the tomb . . . and that no Christian had ever been permitted to enter the sacred building before.' She knew this wasn't the case, of course. Several people had already published accounts of visiting the tomb. The eighteenth-century traveller C. E. Savary left a full account of the sheikh. 'Upwards of a century ago,' he explained in his 1786 Letters on Egypt, 'a religious Turk called Scheilk Haridi died here. He passed for a saint among the Mahometans. They raised a monument to him, covered with a cupola, at the foot of the mountain.' All very familiar. Then, 'one of their priests . . . persuaded them that God had made the soul of Scheilk Haridi pass into the body of a serpent. Many of these are found in the Thebais, which are harmless. He had taught one to obey his voice. He appeared with his serpent, dazzled the vulgar by his surprising tricks, and pretended to cure all disorders . . . The successors of this priest . . . added to the general persuasion of his virtue, that of his immortality. They had the boldness even to make a public proof of it. The serpent was cut in pieces in presence of the Emir, and placed for two hours under a vase. At the instant of lifting up the vase, the priests, no doubt, had the address to substitute one exactly resembling it. A miracle was proclaimed, and the immortal Haridi acquired a fresh degree of consideration.' Savary, good child of the Enlightenment, couldn't comprehend this lack of proof and reason. 'They believe in the serpent Haridi,' he mocked, 'as firmly as in the prophet. The Christians of the country have no more doubts of his virtue, than the Turks.' He then showed off his reading: 'The serpent has played a very astonishing part in the history of mankind. He seduced Eve. By the order of Moses, he devoured those of the Egyptians. He made Alexander of Abonotica pass for a god. He cured at this day the inhabitants of Achmim. This serpent is of the kind described by Herodotus, and which was held sacred in ancient Egypt. They were called *Agatho daimon*, Good Genius.'

In 1843, Gardner Wilkinson mentioned 'the superstitious belief attached to a serpent, reputed to have lived there for ages, and to have the power of removing every kind of complaint: and many miraculous cures, that might have offended Jupiter, are attributed to this worthy successor of the emblem of Aesculapius. It is, perhaps, to the asp, the symbol of Kneph, or of the good genius, that this serpent has succeeded.' In the 1850s, Bayle St John noted that 'the story of the serpent of Sheikh Hereedi seems better known to travellers than it is to Egyptians. At any rate we did not find anyone willing to talk knowingly on the subject.'

Seventy years later, Winifred Blackman had no such problem. 'I removed my riding boots, for I had ridden up this way on a donkey, and was received by the recitation of the *fatheh* as I entered the tomb, chanted by the "sons" of the sheikh who had all assembled there to greet me. Some of their female relations, who were standing together in the corner of the building, greeted me with the *zagharit*.' Coming to the point, she explained, 'The Sheikh Haridi still exercises great power over snakes, for, in the summer when they come out in great numbers, any that come within the vicinity of the sheikh's tomb become quite harmless, and anyone can pick them up without fear of being bitten, however venomous they might be.'

I wanted to visit Sheikh Haridi's tomb and from Gamal's shop I went to the Luxor bus station to ask about tickets to Sohag. The clerk was apologetic but firm. 'There has been a problem near Sohag. Our problem,' he was quick to clarify, 'not your problem.' And then with brilliant logic: 'So you cannot go now.'

'How about Asyout?'

'Same same.'

A group of fanatics were active in the region with guns and knives. They had shot at trains, killed policemen at roadblocks and attacked Coptic businesses and churches. Until they were caught, foreigners without the right ID or police protection would never get through the roadblocks. As there was no point in going with a police escort, which would never allow me to visit the sheikh's tomb, I went looking for a Rifai.

I decided Zeitoun might help. I got to his house late in the afternoon. Medinet Habu temple was closed and the guards had retreated to their shack inside the massive gateway. The last of the tourists were having a drink at the café in front of the entrance, and village kids played football on the asphalt parking. Girls were filling plastic containers at the water tap, the animals were being led home, some women were cutting feed for them in the fields. Zeitoun's neighbour Muhammad, home from his work rebuilding the mortuary temple of Ramses II, was in his field clearing the ground ready for planting.

David, with whom Zeitoun had built the house, was on the upper terrace with some friends, including Dr Boutros, enjoying the view over Muhammad's field to Medinet Habu. In the course of conversation, someone mentioned that there had been a scare at Muhammad's house a few days earlier, where one of the women thought they had seen a snake.

'But it's OK now,' David assured me. 'Nothing to worry about. The Rifai came this morning, so now there's no problem.'

'The Rifai?'

'The snake catcher.'

'He was a Rifai? What did he do?'

'Rifai. *Hawi*,' David scoffed, 'they're all charlatans. I reckon they put the snakes there in the first place.'

'And I wouldn't believe any of those things they say about the Rifai,' Dr Boutros warned. 'It's all a load of hocus-pocus.'

'How can you be sure?' I asked.

'I can be sure . . . because I'm the one who has to treat them for snake bite.'

'Never mind – can we get him back?'

'Not a chance,' David said, 'because we all know that there aren't any snakes here now.'

*

During the days I spent in Luxor waiting for Gamal to make contact with the magician of Esna, I reread the chapter on magic in Winifred Blackman's *Fellahin of Upper Egypt*. Blackman listed several sorts of magicians of either sex. There were some who used magical formulae, others who used spells and charms, some who were possessed by sheikhs, through whom the sheikhs exercised their power, and others who consulted 'familiars'. There were Coptic and Muslim magicians, the Copts enjoying a reputation for finding hidden treasure. There were black magicians who knew how to inflict injuries and bring about sudden death, magicians who knew the *afarit* and the *djinn*, as well as the names of the seven kings and the others who live beneath the earth, magicians with the power of divination and others who knew the hidden truths, including the whereabouts of stolen goods and the identities of perpetrators of crimes. Others were skilled at modelling wax or clay, at writing charms on little scraps of paper that were then secreted on the body as a protection against evil, and many more knew how to use herbs and chants to cure ailments which the village doctor's remedies had not removed.

'Nonsense,' Dr Boutros insisted again. 'All nonsense. Even the sheikhs come to see me in the end.'

Richard Critchfield, describing Shahhat's mother Umm Muhammad's attempts to provide a healthy heir for her increasingly impatient husband, mentioned that after getting nowhere with her doctor and her prayers to Allah, she went to consult a woman in a nearby village who was credited with having special powers. Critchfield calls her a sorcerer. It was she who advised Shahhat's mother to make that nocturnal visit to the sacred lake at Medinet Habu.

The sheikha lived in a village not far from the house. Zeitoun's neighbour Muhammad knew her and showed her great respect, and he agreed to take Zeitoun and me to visit her. The next day, he appeared washed, closely shaved and wearing his best, neatly pressed *galabiyya* and thin white scarf. He sat in the front seat of Zeitoun's old Russian four-wheel-drive as excited as a schoolboy on an outing and told a few stories about the efficacy of the sheikha's powers.

The sheikha was an old, bent woman with an unusually dour expression for an Egyptian. She held her audiences in the courtyard of her mudbrick house, in the centre of a fast-growing village where breeze block was gradually replacing mudbrick. A couple of black-gowned women were talking to her, but when we entered they stood up and left. The sheikha was immovable. So much so that although the wall against which she was leaning was of concrete, her head had worn its imprint into it. I wondered whether she had been sitting there all her life, but discovered that she had inherited the role from her father. They were a dynasty of sheikhs – Sheikh Ali, her father, had been the village seer before her and his father before him.

In a time of social tension, the sheikha was wary of foreigners. She knew Muhammad and gestured that he should sit near her. Zeitoun and I sat across the small yard, though it soon turned out that she knew Zeitoun, for he had built a dome over Sheikh Ali's tomb. 'They came and asked, so I went with my form and built a dome for the sheikh. Here in the cemetery.' But that had been many years before, and he grinned with pleasure that she had remembered.

'Ya Anthony,' Muhammad told me, 'the sheikha also knows of you.'

Several years before, I had rented the house beside Muhammad's and we had been neighbours for some months. Our doors were always open. His wife brought us the dense loaves of sour-bread she baked in her outside oven in the same way as the ancient Egyptians had baked, his children came to play and occasionally he would come and knock to see if I was writing or if there was time for tea and talk. One day while we were out, there was a break-in and things were stolen. Such a thing had never happened there before and Muhammad was scandalized. He blamed it on the *majnoun*, the madman who lived in the mountain, the fool on the hill, a legendary character whom no one had actually seen. Although it wasn't his responsibility, Muhammad was ashamed. He felt he should have protected me. In his troubles, he went to see the sheikha, in search of a clarity of vision. And now, years later, after all the troubles that had been poured out to her in that courtyard, she still remembered his visit. And now here was the foreign writer. 'Everybody comes to see the sheikha in the end,' Muhammad said, nodding at the truth.

'But not all are the same,' she corrected. 'There are people with integrity, honest people, and others without. People who don't have integrity, there's nothing to be done for them.' While talking, she had pulled a long thread from a bag beside her and had begun to fiddle with it. Her thin, withered fingers pulled it taut, smoothed it out, felt it, tested it for tension and then began to fold and wind it. She kept this up for the time that she spoke directly to me, for the minutes she was thinking of me. 'It's a two-way thing,' she was explaining, those fingers working. 'I can help you, but only if you will help yourself.'

People visited the sheikha for all sorts of reasons. Mostly it was because of village business such as missing donkeys, infertile cows, that sort of thing. But occasionally someone brought an affair of the heart, financial problems or a criminal confession. And while the worries and sins of the village, the west bank of Luxor, of Upper Egypt were laid out before her – people came from as far away as Qena and Aswan, a day's journey, to consult her – the diminutive woman sat on the ground, her head slowly wearing away the concrete wall behind her, spinning out her skeins, weaving charms, keeping the countryside on the straight and narrow.

She held out her hand and in it was the charm she had woven from the thick green thread as we had talked. It was a couple of inches long and made in the shape of a key. It reminded me of an *ankh*, the ancient symbol of life.

We stood up when our audience was over, but the sheikha remained in her place. Zeitoun squatted down near her to say goodbye, but the old woman wasn't finished with him yet. She had recognized his integrity and saw, in that moment, an opportunity to say something about herself.

'When I was a young girl,' she said apropos of nothing, 'I was married to a man in Cairo. A doctor. My life was there. But then he died and I came back. I didn't want to, but I had to. My father wanted me to continue his work. I didn't want to do that but I had no choice. What could I do? When my father died, I didn't want to continue. This was my chance – I thought I could stop and I went to hide myself. I had had another life. Listen, Zeitoun – twenty-two years you've been here and for twenty-two years I was in Cairo. Imagine. But when my father died and I hid, the people came and found me. They insisted. Perhaps I was weak then, but what could I do? People need someone to sort out the problems. Always have, always will.'

Two women and a man were waiting, sombre-faced, in the outer yard of the sheikha's house.

'It's like a sort of therapy,' Zeitoun decided as we stood outside among the sand and chickens. 'She works as a sort of psychoanalyst.'

'She works better at night,' Muhammad said, now wreathed in the aura of a pilgrimage fulfilled. 'She's more powerful then.'

'You know?' Zeitoun said as we drove away. 'When she dies it will be a big thing. They'll build a tomb for her – maybe I'll build it, even – and everyone will come. Even though she will die, the magic will live on.'

Gamal had no good news. His welcome at the shop near the station was muted in the way I had come to recognize amongst Egyptians when they think they are letting you down. 'This thing you want is very difficult. You need time.'

'Gamal, I have been on the trail for years and there are only so many of those in a lifetime.'

'But you must see the magicians in Esna. The things they do, the power they have, the knowledge from the old times . . .'

'How will I get to see this?'

'I will arrange it for you,' he said with renewed confidence.

'And I will come back to Luxor when you do.'

But whether because I wasn't there, because he had other things to do, because the fabled magicians of Esna, heirs of Aaron, able to turn sticks into snakes, didn't want to reveal their secrets to a curious foreigner with a broken heart, or because they had divined that my heart was far from broken, Gamal never did make those arrangements.

'I could not help recurrently thinking,' Paul Brunton wrote in the 1930s, 'that underneath the doctrines and practices of the Rifa-ee Dervishes there lay a remnant of some ancient serpent-worshipping cult, that went back, perhaps, to immeasurable antiquity.'

Brunton wrote a sensational account of his travels – and an account of his sensational travels – in search of the esoteric side of Egypt. He was thorough in his research. He had slept alone inside the Great Pyramid, had tracked down memory men and magicians across the country and gone to great lengths to become a snake charmer. Brunton had been initiated by one Sheikh Mousa el-Hawi, the head of Luxor's snake catchers. This was a privilege the sheikh had not bestowed before, except on his own son who had subsequently died from a snakebite. Sheikh Mousa's grandfather had also been killed by a snake.

'It was apparent,' Brunton observed in his desiccated tone, 'that snake-charming in Egypt was hardly a vocation to attract numerous recruits.'

Sheikh Mousa, who claimed to be a Rifai, said that his power over snakes came from God but was exercised through the power of words and of talismen. After Brunton had lived alone for a week on little food, devoting himself to prayer, the sheikh brought him his own talisman – 'a sheet of paper covered with Arabic writing, mostly magical spells and verses from the *Quran*' – which he had to wear close to his skin. Then there were the long incantations which, he claimed, possessed the power to stop a snake in its tracks and which started: 'O thou snake! Come forth! I adjure thee by Allah, if thou art above or if thou art below, that ye come forth!', invoked the Holy Place, the Holy Book, Sheikh Ahmad av-Rifai and ended: 'In the name of Solomon the Wise, who holds dominion over all reptiles. Hear! Allah ordereth thee.' Over a period of two years, which the sheikh had warned was as long as the protection would last, he caught several poisonous snakes and scorpions without being hurt.

In the spring of 1924, Winifred Blackman recorded in her notebook the following instruction given her by one Sheikh Muhanni:

How to Become a Good Snake-Charmer

If a man wishes to become a really good snake-charmer he must go through the following ritual. He must go to another man who is a good snake-charmer, and this man will pour some water into a plate, then he makes a snake drink this. After this he puts a piece of salt in the plate with a little more water, and then makes the snake vomit the water he has drunk back into the plate. The would-be snake-charmer must then drink this water. After he has done this he can handle any snake, none will hurt him.

Umm Seti made the following connections regarding the eating or drinking of magic:

Some modern magicians, wishing to learn a new spell, write it in ink on paper. They then wash off the writing in water, and drink the water, the magic then being supposed to stay in their bodies.

This method of learning is also mentioned in an ancient story about Prince Khamwise, one of the many sons of Ramses II. The prince lived in the thirteenth century BC, but the oldest-known papyrus containing the story is from a thousand years later:

'He put the book [of magic] in my hand. I recited one spell from it; I enchanted the sky, the earth, the underworld, the hills and the waters. I found out what all the birds in the sky, the fish of the river and the beasts were saying. I recited another spell; I saw the Sun-god shining in the sky with his Nine Gods; I saw the Moon rising, and all the stars of the sky with their (true) forms; I saw the fish of the river, with Divine Power resting in the water over them.

'As I could not write I was speaking to Neferkaptah, my elder brother, who was a good scribe and a very wise man. He had a sheet of new papyrus brought to him, and he wrote on it every word that was in the book before him; he burned it, and dissolved the ashes in water; when he knew that it had dissolved he drank it and knew what had been in it.'

Abu Rawash is one of several villages lining the border between the desert and farmland north of Cairo. It is the site of the most northerly of the pyramids, including the pyramid of Djedefre (c. 2566–58 BC), the king who succeeded Khufu, builder of the Great Pyramid at Giza. It is also known as a centre for snake catchers.

I arrived by pick-up one warm weekday morning and did a quick tour of the town. There has been a settlement at Abu Rawash for thousands of years, but most of what I saw was modern, a jumble of brick and breeze-block houses, separated from the farmland by a main road and stagnant canal. Then I noticed a small sandstone hill behind the village. It was a strange place of caves and niches and as I climbed to the top I was tempted to imagine that the path I was following had been worn by the passage of people over millennia going to perform some strange snake-oriented ritual in the furthest cave, whose roof was clearly fire-blackened. The facts were probably more prosaic: apart from an ox in a distant field, it was hard to imagine a landscape more devoid of animal life. Nothing stirred and not even a dog barked in the distance, though I was at least rewarded with a view from the worn and slippery top over the rich farmland towards the Nile.

As I had seen no obvious signs of snake catchers, no skins hanging outside shops, no snakeskin shoes, no snake meat simmering beside the beans in the café, I went to have a look at the domed mosque which lay at the heart of the village.

The mosque was empty, but an old man living in a nineteenth-century house beside it was pointed out as the keeper. Any hope I had of finding another Sheikh Haridi disappeared when I saw him. From the trouble on his face it was clear that he didn't see too many foreigners and that in his mind they were confused with extremists, bloodshed and the probings of secret police. He wanted none of it.

I asked if he knew who was buried in the mosque. 'Sheikh Abu Rawash.' Did he know anything about the sheikh or his life? 'No. All I do is go from here to work and from work to here.' He was already sounding paranoid and I was sounding like the secret police. Did anything special happen at the sheikh's moulid? 'Nothing.' No *zikr*, even? 'We don't do the *zikr*. The *zikr* is *haram*.'

I went back to what might have been the main street if Abu Rawash had been planned, stopped under an awning beside the canal – an impromptu café – and ordered tea. 'No *shisha*?' I asked the pretty, provocative girl. No *shisha*. The young man who was obviously her husband soon appeared and sat down to talk. He was intense and quick with his confidences and after a few minutes he explained that he wanted to open a restaurant selling *ful* and *taamiyya*, but that he needed 1500LE (Egyptian pounds), about £300, to set it up. Did I want to be his partner? There were already two places selling the same dishes in a small town and I wasn't an entrepreneur, so I declined the offer.

'Do you want to buy a snake?'

'Why?'

'Because I have. They are 30LE (£6) a metre.'

We talked about football, money, the beauties of Egypt and then he came back to the snakes. 'Well, what about it then?'

The snakes weren't his. Had I had my eyes open on arrival I too would have known about them, because there on the main street, at the roundabout and the junction with the Cairo road, there was a sign – EXPORT. REPTILES AND ANIMALS. And to make the point, a stuffed and weathered crocodile hung under the sign.

Unlike the keeper of the mosque or the café-owner, Sheikh Tolba, whose business venture this was, was not surprised to see me. He had had many foreign visitors before. A snake? Sure, no problem. Step this way. And as we passed through several rooms, he handed me his business card.

Sheikh Tolba dealt in animals. In the first room he showed me hedgehogs and tortoises, slipping his hand into one of many cases and pulling out a hedgehog. 'Here,' he said, handing it to his boy. 'It is dead.'

We passed through the room where he had been eating when we arrived; flies topped the tin food dishes. Beyond was his strongroom, filled with sacks and crates and the fetid stink of caged, neglected wildlife. In contrast to the view from the sandstone hill above the village, Tolba's strongroom was an ark, a zoo, a seething, limping, wriggling, whinging mass of animals for shipment round the world.

He started by showing me lizards of various sizes and colours, one of which, from Borg al-Arab near Alexandria, he was particularly proud of. In another stacked crate I saw a small fox-like creature with large, nervous ears.

The snakes were kept in tall barrels closed with weighted lids. The boy reached into one and pulled out a white cloth bag which he handed to Tolba. 'No, this isn't the one. Get the big ones.'

This time he untied the string round the white bag and took out a snake by the tail. It was a metre and a half long and out of some forgotten instinct – for my life has not been spent in the company of reptiles – I backed towards the door as the snake arched up towards Tolba's hand. At this point it looked to me like any other large, nasty, fork-tongued snake. Then Tolba hit it with his stick and it reared and puffed up and then there could be no mistaking it. This was the Egyptian cobra, the ancient uraeus, symbol of royalty. In spite of its being deadly, and able to spit venom over several metres, the cobra was a victim in modern Egypt.

While I waited near the door, Tolba put the snake down and held it against the floor with his stick. The cobra became increasingly angry, its long ribs flattening out its neck until not even the great catcher was prepared to play games. He tossed it back into the wriggling bag, which went back into the barrel.

'I didn't hypnotize that one,' he said and then offered tea on his woven plastic mat, in a room soiled with animal faeces.

'I was going to ask you about that. In England some years ago I saw a television programme about a snake catcher who claimed that he stopped snakes biting him by the power of words.'

'Perhaps it was me,' he said, blasé. 'I have appeared on television many times. I and my family are all known for catching animals. This is my profession, which I learned from my father and he from his father. I catch them in the *gebel*,' he gesticulated, referring to the hills behind the village. 'And I sell them to collectors. People have come from zoos and bought fine cobras from me – 1500LE a time, and sometimes more.' The man from the café, who had been with us, silent, all this time, let out an *Allah!* – that was just the sum he needed for his restaurant.

I mentioned what I had learnt from Winifred Blackman and others about snakes, and also that the television documentary mentioned the use of spells which go back to the time of the pharaohs.

'Certainly these words have always been known, have always been used.'

'How do you know?'

'Because they were handed down and because they work.'

When I asked him to give me more details, he refused. 'This is my business and I need money. If you want to know more then you will have to pay me.' He mentioned 400LE.

'But your best cobras only cost 1500LE.'

He became dramatic. 'How will I eat? Where will I get my clothes from if I tell you what I know?'

By now the price had gone up, the door was closing. 'Can you just tell me if you think there are similarities between what you do and the Rifai?'

In reply, he handed me another business card. 'For when you want to buy.'

In the end it was serendipity rather than research or intuition that led me to a Rifai. I was in Luxor in one of those summer days when the tarmac goes soft and brains go softer. I was standing near the neo-Pharaonic train station, trapped in a small patch of shade, when the drivers on the nearby taxi rank spotted me. One of them, a young man named Wael, came over and started to bend my ear about how cheap the ride would be.

'How can you tell me the price when you don't know where I'm going?' I asked.

And then it occurred to me. 'I'll take your taxi if you can bring me to a Rifai.' And to make my point, I stressed, 'Not a hawi or anything else. Just a Rifai.'

He held the passenger door open. 'Sure. No problem,' and he called over the roofs of the parked taxis to the drivers: 'Anyone know where the Rifai lives?'

Wael racked up the fully reclined driver's seat, where he appeared to have spent the day and perhaps also the night, and drove me alongside the Nile.

The river was slow and soupy, the country beyond it a rich green velvet. We stopped a couple of times on the twenty minute ride to make sure we were on the right track and I smiled at the irony, at the dazzling simplicity of the thing: everyone we asked knew where to find the Rifai. The man lived in a one-street village to the north of Luxor, in a mudbrick house that, from the outside at least, was no different from his neighbours'.

Inside, Wael and I were invited to sit and drink tea while we waited for the master to return. I looked around the large room – several wooden benches with cushions or mats on them, an inscription from the Koran, a black and white photograph, but nothing to suggest the occupation of the owner. Then his adult son appeared and placed a white cloth bag in front of us on the beaten earth floor. From the rope tied across its opening and the way it was wriggling I knew what was inside.

The Rifai was an elderly man with a tightly-clipped moustache, impeccable manners and a slight hardness of hearing. He wore the fellah's uniform of gallabiya and white turban. He was amused by my curiosity. Not that he didn't take his occupation seriously, but, as I realized, he was more matter-of-fact about it than I had expected. He also appeared happy to talk about it, which surprised me, and after tea and cigarettes, he asked his son to fetch another bag, out of which he produced a large, thick cobra.

'Look,' he explained, 'when I find a cobra, or another snake like it, I take out its venom.' He walked the snake over to a table on the other side of the room where he showed me how to make it "safe" by milking its poison. 'And after that, there is no problem.' To prove the point he suggested that I play with the reptile. But I was less than confident about its docility – and was hardly encouraged by Wael heading for the safety of the open door.

So instead he laid it on his son's shoulders and I watched, mouth wide open, as the cobra wrapped itself around his neck and arranged itself around his head in the sort of pose made famous by the pharaohs. This wasn't the only trick he could do: among his repertoire was the ability to make a snake wrap itself around a stick, in the manner of Moses' snake at the court of the pharaoh.

'You should go on the stage,' I suggested.

'I do. I perform for tourists at the hotels here in Luxor.'

'But I thought you were a Rifai?'

'I am. But I still have to work.'

His work included catching the snakes, which he did when people called him to their house, though sometimes at night he went out into the fields and lit a fire, which always attracted snakes.

'But don't you worry about being bitten?' I asked, to steer the conversation my way. He shook his head. 'Because of your being a Rifai?'

He explained that he had inherited the skill from his father and that he was passing it on to his son. And then he smiled, somewhat sphinx-like, making it clear that there was no chance I was going to find out any more about it from him.

Strange goings-on in Egypt: an invasion of Satanists. Some days after I met the Rifai, the local press reported that more than a hundred people were arrested by the Egyptian police on Satanism charges. Several things were unusual about this. First, many of the people detained were young and from wealthy families. Second, the evidence against them was as follows: they had been listening to heavy metal music. Schools banned the wearing of Bob Marley and Nirvana T-shirts, legal action was started to strip 'the accused servants of Satan' of their nationality, and in Cairo University a group calling themselves the Students for Intellectual Freedom Movement began a protest – not at the authorities' actions but to denounce both Satanists and terrorists. Their proposed rally was banned by the university's president.

Around that time, an Egyptian newspaper carried the following report: 'Police in Asyout last week arrested 11 sorcerers misleading people with their uncanny power to cure them of diseases and drive out evil spirits haunting them.'

Satanism and sorcery seemed extreme labels. Many people in the country were nervous, and magicians, understandably, tried to make themselves invisible, which didn't help my search. Then Alan took me to meet Munir Fayed, a friend of his who lived at the foot of the pyramids.

Munir had spent all his life in the shadow of the monuments, his family had been there for generations and his brother lived in the house next door. He was an old man, with just a couple of teeth left in his lower jaw, his grey hair thin, but his thoughts still clear.

'There's someone here in the village,' Munir said, while Alan got down on the floor to fix the video machine, 'who you go to if you're ill.'

Attiyyat, Munir's wife, interrupted. 'He either gives you advice or writes something down for you. With a pen.'

'A red pen,' Munir elaborated.

'Not just any red pen, ya Sheikh, but a special one.'

'And he makes his ink from saffron. When he has written something down for you, you burn it, drink it or wash with it, rubbing it over your body.'

I remembered the story Umm Seti recorded of a prince of ancient Egypt doing just that. 'But what is it that he writes?' I asked. 'Letters? Numbers?'

'Words. Words from the Koran.'

'My daughter was ill,' Attiyyat took over, in case I doubted the efficacy of all this, 'but now she is better thanks to the sheikh.' She went off, adjusting her blue flowery scarf over the black voluminous dress, and came back with a photograph of her healthy daughter in her hennaed hands.

'And do people go to him with other problems, not just medical?'

'Sure,' Attiyyat replied. 'He'll write something for you and then you'll be safe.' This was just what Gamal al-Hajjaji had claimed for the magicians of Esna. 'We'll ask him to come one day soon.'

Ahmad turned out to be a pragmatist. A quiet and unassuming man in his fifties, with greying, wiry hair, he combined the practice of the healing arts with work as a house painter. He was cagey, a little nervous, which I put down to the 'Satanist' and sorcery arrests. He declined to give his full name and he smoked throughout the meeting. He was under the impression that I wanted to consult him profession-ally, so when he had settled down in Munir's antechamber, I showed him the elbow I had anointed with a sheikh's oil in Luxor but which still hadn't healed. Before he started talking, he wanted to know how much I understood of what he did. I told him that I knew there were two different ways of healing, one using physical objects like charms and amulets and cures, the other using the word, whether written or spoken.

He sat on the bench across the room and told me there were three ways. 'The third involves *shaytan*, the devil.' I understood why he was nervous. I was going to get worried if he carried on like that.

'In what way does this involve the devil?'

'How many chapters are there in your New Testament? How many in the Koran? One hundred and fifty. In the Black Book there are 366.'

I told him he had jumped way ahead of me and asked him to start with traditional medicine.

He learned his trade from his father and he knew that at least seven generations of men in his family had followed the same line. 'You can't learn this sort of thing at university. Maybe in China or Japan, because there all studies are herbal.' He called it Arab medicine. 'What I do is complementary medicine. Like your homeopathy. I can't do something for someone with an appendix, but I can help with cancer, by getting to its sources and working with diet. There are books, but you also have to have experience.'

He was calmer now. I asked him which books he used. The first he mentioned was Ibn Sina (980–1037) – Avicenna as he was known in Europe – a tenth-century scholar from Bokhara. Ibn Sina's *Al-Qanun fi- 't-Tibb*, The Law of Medicine, a million words long, was an attempt to codify medical knowledge as it existed at the end of the first millennium. Through the Law, a visionary work which summed up not only past beliefs but also current knowledge on both sides of the Indian Ocean, we can reach back to antiquity. Ibn Sina also included a catalogue of 760 medicinal plants and their uses, but in the west his writings are the preserve of scholars, so I was surprised to hear they were part of Ahmad's small library.

'I use two other books. One is a book that the Prophet Muhammad wrote on the subject. This is mentioned in the Hadith and is called Prophetic Medicine. The other is called Spiritual Medicine in Human Bodies, which was written about three hundred years ago.'

I asked how he used Ibn Sina.

'In the book of Ibn Sina there are descriptions of different trees and plants and their properties. I don't usually collect the ingredients myself. Usually I tell people to go to the Attar, the herbalist in the souq and bring them to me. But some things aren't available in the souq.'

'In England,' I explained by way of encouragement, 'scientists are taking herbal medicine increasingly seriously. Many now recognize the need to rediscover this old knowledge.'

'The government here sees it as a form of deviation,' and, as if to show why, he began to explain about what he called the spiritual side of his work. 'One of the most common problems I see is that people start speaking in a language that isn't understood, like Coptic, Surrealiyya and Roman.'

'Surrealiyya? A surrealistic language?' I tried not to smile.

'I myself speak surrealiyya,' he said matter-of-factly, as if he had been talking about French or English, 'so I speak to them and tell them what has happened and that they must now speak in Arabic.'

Alan said, 'But surely these people are possessed, troubled by spirits?'

'Not by spirits but by their qarin.'

Alan had never heard the word before and rolled it round with his thick Scots accent. 'A qarin, you say?'

Winifred Blackman wrote in The Fellahin of Upper Egypt: 'Every human being is said to be born with a double, which is quite distinct from the afrit, and it is called, in the case of a man, the qarin (colleague or companion), in the case of a woman qarina . . . The ginn, or afarit, are often called "our brothers and sisters beneath the earth," but they are separate beings from the aqran (plural of qarin) though the two communities are in touch with each other.' The word translates literally as 'associate', 'companion', 'spouse', 'consort', the female version translates as 'demon', while the root of the word is 'to compare'.

'The aqran are believed to be of different colours,' Blackman continued, 'some being white, some black; their looks also vary, as some are beautiful and some are ugly. This belief is easily accounted for, as each person's qarin is a facsimile of himself or herself, and doubtless the colours are racial distinctions. The aqran are not, I believe, always malevolent, though stories of their mischief-making propensities are commoner than accounts of their good deeds.'

'A qarin is what we would call a soul or spirit,' Alan decided. 'So how do you help a troubled soul?'

'For a troubled qarin,' Ahmad explained, 'I encourage the use of amulets, verses from the Torah and the New Testament. The Koran itself tells how to use them.'

It was getting dark outside and the evening call to prayer shuddered out of a speaker near Munir's house and across the empty desert. Attiyyat brought more tea and Ahmad, realizing time was short, spoke more quickly.

'There are things I use which come from the beginning of time because there was magic even before the pharaohs.'

For a moment no one spoke. Then Alan said quietly, in English, so only I would understand, 'I hope the police aren't bugging us here or we're in big trouble.'

'You say this knowledge has come from the beginning of time,' I asked, 'but how do you know?'

'Because it is written in the old books and on papyrus.'

I wondered whether the government crackdown was going to affect people like him. 'Aren't you worried this will disappear?'

'Not at all. More and more people are using this sort of medicine, so now you can find some of the cures in the chemists. And at least three-quarters of the information that anyone needs is written in the Koran, if only we knew how to understand it, so I don't think it will disappear. There is a verse in the Koran, the sura Yassin, which the Prophet Muhammad used when he went off on pilgrimage and didn't want non-believers to know that he was going. We can use this sura to make people forget they saw us.'

'Oh,' said Alan in English again, 'I wonder if there's one to help people forget they ever heard all this stuff.'

Ahmad didn't understand. 'Other verses are for medicine – about forty of them give cures for various ailments.'

'And what do you call this sort of work?' I asked him.

'There is no name for it now. When people come to me they just say, "Open the book," because it's a secret, a closed book, what I do. It's illegal. Sometimes, in Cairo, people open offices for this sort of medicine and thirty or forty people will go each day. Then the police hear about it and arrest the man.'

'I heard about that,' I told him.

'It is forbidden not because it is wrong but because the government wants people to go to doctors, clinics, hospitals. But that doesn't stop us, or stop people coming to us.'

It was late and the village was now as quiet as the desert. 'Is there anything else you want to know before I go?' Ahmad asked.

There was something. Until then, Ahmad had assumed that I was only interested in finding a cure for my skin problem. Now I explained that I was looking for customs that had survived from the time of the pharaohs and that I was sure some of the herbal remedies he prescribed had been in use for thousands of years. I told him I was struck by the way he had talked about the *qarin*. 'A little way from here, out in the desert below the pyramids, archaeologists have found the village where the construction workers lived. They also believed in their *qarin*, which they called their *ka*. It wasn't a soul or a spirit, but a double, just as you described. On the temples there are pictures of men being modelled by the gods and alongside them are their doubles and here you are talking about it in the same way. This is an enduring thing, a survival, a glimpse of eternity.'

Ahmad lit another cigarette and considered me for a moment while he smoked. He said he was unhappy about the parallel, unhappy, I guess, with my unIslamic way of thinking. Perhaps he was also angry that I hadn't told him what I wanted from the start. 'You won't find eternity in other people or other places. Don't hope to find it in these things you call survivals. You must look within yourself. That's where you'll find it. There is no eternity on the face of the earth. Eternity is the face of God.' I glimpsed again the fundamental difference between my rational, humanistic approach and that of Ahmad, between my desire to explain these things away and his conviction that no explanations were needed because he understood that we were living in a world of spirits – even in the Koran, *djinn* are recognized as being as much a part of the world as humans. Perhaps I was glimpsing also the gulf created by his religious certainties and my serious doubts. 'As for your skin,' he said without pausing for breath, 'I suggest you go to the cemetery just here and take some *laban*, some sap, from the *gemmeza*, the sycamore tree. This you should rub on to your elbows. It will form a scab and when it falls off you will see the skin will be better.'

I remembered Gamal's insistence that I should see a magician with my own eyes, that seeing would bring about the believing. Munir had heard that a levitationalist would be performing at a moulid in

Dahshur, another pyramid-town south of Cairo. 'He isn't one of those fairground people. Go on the *layla al-kebira* and you will see magic.'

Many moulids included some sort of magic or illusion show as part of the celebrations. During the moulid of Husayn in Cairo a large area was given over to a series of tents and arenas for this sort of thing. Elsewhere I had seen men with lightbulbs on their heads, performing sleights of hand and all kinds of other illusions. 'At Dahshur,' Munir promised, 'the magician is said to be the best.'

Alan came – he felt he had a stake in my search for a magician – though later he wished he hadn't. We took a pick-up from Pyramids Road and followed the canal south through farmland along a road that may well have existed four and a half thousand years ago, since the Pharaoh Snefru built his pyramid at Dahshur. It was already dark, cool, damp. As we moved further from the city the sky turned from orange to black and in the new darkness lights glowed in a galaxy of villages. I had no idea which one was Dahshur, but it didn't matter because everyone crowded on to the pick-up was going there too.

The sheikh whose life and death were being celebrated was not among the pantheon whose moulids were written about and no one I knew had heard of this one. It was a country affair, *baladi* as Cairenes would say dismissively. This was the last night and it was well attended; the pick-up driver couldn't get anywhere near the centre of town.

We jumped off among the first buildings into a shoulder-to-shoulder and heel-to-toe crowd. Most of them were young, from the nearby villages we had seen sparkling in the night. They had a few notes in their pockets and were out for some fun. Two foreigners presented them with a great opportunity, and everything we stopped to look at, every gesture, each sound we made was noted and mocked by a hundred boys. When we walked, they pushed. When we stopped they crowded in on us, hands reaching into our pockets and over our bodies. Alan is the only person I know who enjoys the crush of a Cairo rush-hour bus, but as the boys got rougher, his face turned red.

I have never been so happy to see a policeman; when we saw an officer surrounded by his men, installed in a café, we forced our way off the street to join them. 'Perhaps we'll be arrested and escorted back to Cairo,' Alan hoped. The boys followed us into the café, but the *ahwagi* chased them out and apologized. 'You are welcome.'

'Yeah,' Alan said after he had brought us bitter tea, 'but we can't stay here all night, now can we.'

The magic show wasn't due to start till later, so we left the café, paid our respects at the sheikh's tomb and then went to join a crowd performing a *zikr* outside the house of a venerable old man, under strings of multicoloured lights slung between palms and beside a refuse-strewn canal. Even there, where prayers and praise were being offered to the sheikh, the Prophet and Allah, a few boys came to ask for cigarettes and to mimic the way we were standing. One of them then joined the *zikr*, but was pulled away by an old man who explained that this was not a disco.

The magician had set up his auditorium along the moulid's main drag which might also have been Dahshur's main street, though it was impossible to tell what lay behind the stalls of Chinese plastic toys, the pyramids of beans and peanuts, the mountains of fluorescent pink sweets. Among this movable bazaar there was a four-metre-high hoarding with a gaudy painting of the magician raising a woman with exaggerated breasts and red, red lips. Here the crowd was thicker, the pushing heavier. A small entrance cut into the hoarding was guarded by two policemen with long, thin whipping canes. This was the only attraction at the moulid you had to pay to enter, and beside the policemen, a man collected money. Occasionally the policemen brought their canes down on the heads nearest them.

'What are we waiting for?' I asked the man collecting money, screaming to be heard above the surging crowd.

'For others to come out.'

'Has the *sihr*, the magic started?'

'Oh yes,' he assured me.

We got past the guards in the next wave, without being beaten, and came out into a high-walled enclosure at the other end of which was a stage. Two, maybe three hundred people were let in and then a rough, tough-looking man appeared on stage and started muttering provocations into his microphone, more like the warm-up for a prize fight than a magician's front man.

Behind the man there was a screen and from behind the screen two girls appeared dressed in heavy sequin bikinis and gauzy skirts, their lips painted glowing neon-red. There was a rush for the stage. One of the girls, with a thick waist, a thicker bottom and enormous bust, began to swing her hips. Music was played loud, the girl provoked and the men responded, shouting obscenities, threats and promises.

To calm things down, a crooner appeared and sang a couple of numbers, long enough for the girls to smoke a few cigarettes. When they got to their feet again the crowd went into a testosterone-driven frenzy, climbing the fence in front of the stage, reaching out for the girls, offering the world. When the police appeared, as wound up as the crowd, they didn't wait to take in the situation, they issued no warnings, but rushed at us, slashing with their canes in the manner of an old-fashioned cavalry charge, raising welts rather than severing heads. After the noise from the stage there was an eerie silence, the tramp of feet on sand, a ssswishing of canes, and the grunts of men squeezing themselves back out through the single gap in the hoarding, the odd unfortunate taking a thrashing. Alan and I had kept on the fringes – we were foreigners, after all – but the police made no distinction, the place had to be cleared and that included us, so we joined that huddle at the exit. On the street side of the hoarding, other policemen standing above us were lashing out. It was one of the few moments when I wished I wasn't so tall. As I raised my hand to protect my head, the thin strip of wood cut into me and red welts grew across my wrist.

'I think we should ask for our money back.'

'Are you mad?' Instead, Alan had spotted a boy selling drinks from a cart. He ordered two and the boy dipped deep into the barrel and produced a thin grey liquid with a tall head of froth. It tasted of the desert, of dirty glasses, unstirred sugar and somewhere far, far in the back, a vegetal beginning.

'What is it?'

'*Booza*,' Alan said, a moustache of froth over his mouth. 'Fermented palm drink.'

'It's disgusting.'

'It's the only bloody alcohol they sell at moulids. Come on – let's have another.'

As we stood in the road, drinking, another crowd was being let into the arena we had just left.

'Come on, Anthony. There's no magician here tonight. It's a scam and it looks like the police are in on it. They must all be earning their month's wages tonight.'

No magic, then, just illusion.

Depending on your beliefs, you will say it was either fate or coincidence that I happened to be sitting on that particular smashed-up bus at that particular moment and that I happened to have Winifred Blackman's book open at that particular page, number 191, just as my neighbour turned round. It had to be that particular man (more or less) and that particular page. Another man might have ignored it, or kept his thoughts to himself.

My neighbour's name was Muhammad Abdel-Wanis and most of the page I was reading was unintelligible to him because he neither read nor spoke English. But on the page there was an illustration of a magic square, divided into sixteen sections, in which were written various numbers and squiggles. According to Blackman, the square was part of a murder ritual. 'If a man wishes to procure the death of a man whom he regards as his enemy he will go to a magician, who acts in the following way. He takes a hen and kills it, keeping the blood in some vessel. He then obtains an egg laid by a hen that has black feathers only, and on it he writes this magic square with the blood of the hen.' Incense must be burned, various formulae chanted and the egg hidden in a tomb. Death will follow.

It was this magic square that Muhammad Abdel-Wanis recognized. He did a double-take when he saw what I was reading on the bus, looked more closely at the page and said, 'I've got one of those.'

'What?'

'That square. And many others like it.'

'Where?'

'At home.'

'What are they doing at your home?' Was he trying to have someone killed? And if so, why was he telling me?

'I have books where I have written them. I do that sort of thing. Come to my house and I will show you.'

We made a date before he got off the bus. He lived in the village beneath the pyramids, a mile or two from Munir's house.

This time Alan wouldn't come with me. I thought maybe the memory of the Dahshur moulid had put him off, but it was more straightforward than that. He didn't like the sound of this man or his magic. 'When it comes to things like that, I'm just scared.'

His reluctance heightened my own tension, yet the scene in the village when I arrived at sundown couldn't have been more normal. A dozen men were chasing a ball across the old square, a couple of adolescent hawkers were counting money on top of a urinating camel and the sun was still above the pyramids. Some kids came running up to me. 'Sphinxes there,' they shouted, pointing away from the alley. 'You can't go that way – it's closed,' the elder continued, becoming more insistent. I carried on, although I was far from sure if I was in the right alley. Some of the facades were late nineteenth century, some late twentieth. As I passed a group of women sitting in a doorway, exchanging news at the end of the day, a girl, an elf-like beauty, jumped up and signalled down an even smaller alley. '*Itfaddal*, welcome.'

'Is Muhammad at home?'

'Baba? No. I will go and get him.'

A boy appeared and ushered me in. 'Please sit down.' Muhammad arrived almost immediately, a heavy man, 1.9 metres tall with a huge chest and thick neck. His white *galabiyya* bore evidence of a dusty day. He welcomed me warmly.

'How are you, Tony?' he asked. He was one of the very few Egyptians who thought of using the diminutive of my name. We went through the traditional exchange – how are you? Praise be to God, and you? Praise God. So what news? 'Please sit down,' and he indicated a bench with a cover and cushions. He didn't ask why I had come.

I asked about his day.

'Thanks to God it has been a good one. Yesterday I was at the pyramids in the evening and met some tourists, Americans, who wanted to climb the pyramids.'

There had been a ban on climbing the pyramids for several years, since a couple had died while coming down, so I was surprised.

He kicked off his flip-flops and folded his large frame on the plastic mat. 'It is no problem. They paid me $200 for the two of them to go up and down. They came at 5 a.m. and we went together. I made them wait out of sight and went to talk to the guards. I paid them three dollars each, which is a lot for them because you know how much money they get from the government each month? About sixty dollars. So I'm giving them more than a day's pay. When the Americans came, the guards looked the other way. Just one minute, that's all. It takes half an hour to go up and they stayed some time, taking pictures.'

'And today?'

'Today I have been lying around, not doing very much.'

After the young girl had been sent to buy Pepsi, Muhammad asked a few more times how I was feeling, then came to the point without introduction, reached under the cover on the bench and pulled out a desk-size diary. From the back he produced some yellowed manuscripts and handed them to me. They contained writing, symbols and boxed characters.

'What are these?'

'They are charms, and spells. Look, this is written in Arabic. But this,' and he turned the page, 'is from the Copts.' I began turning the pages, one by one, first the printed pages and then the diary which was also filled with charms and incantations. Muhammad leaned over and pointed out 'the star of Solomon' (the pentangle), 'the pictures of the pharaohs' (what looked like demotic script and some pictograms) and 'the writing of the Copts'. What lay in my lap could have been a condensed version of all that I had been looking for. This was the sort of secret text Herodotus had been told about, which had ensured Egypt's fame among the Arabs, sent Europeans across the Mediterranean in the medieval period looking for the wisdom of the past, which underpinned much of the mystique of the Enlightenment and nineteenth-century interest in Egypt, and which some believed was still lurking in the deeper recesses of storerooms in Coptic monasteries.

While there was no doubting the authenticity of the papers, I wasn't sure that Muhammad knew what to do with them. 'So what can you do with this?'

Muhammad looked at me hard. The whites of his eyes were the colour of rotten eggs. 'Anything. You can do anything. You want to see *afarit*? Then you must bring a frog for me to kill and I will put blood from the frog over your eyes and read the words on this page here, and you will see the *afarit* come here and here and here.' As he pointed to the corners of the blue room I remembered what Gamal in Luxor had told me about rigid hair and trembling hands. 'With these pages,' Muhammad continued, 'you can call the *djinns* and the people who live under the ground. You can also call the *Malayka*, the angels.'

'Down from heaven?'

'There are in heaven and there are also many down below.'

Muhammad's house was at the edge of the village, hard up against the bottom of the pyramid plateau. As soon as the sun dropped behind the pyramids, even with the door open, the room became gloomy. I still wasn't convinced that he knew what to do with the papers.

'Do people come to you because of these books?'

'Many.'

'And are there other people in the village who have pages like these?'

'Some.'

'And use them?'

'Not everyone knows what to do. I was given these pages by a sheikh a long time ago and for me they work very well.'

'So what else can you do?'

'You are missing a girl, perhaps? You would like to see her here? If we write this charm and follow the instructions then tomorrow when you come back you will find her here. Or maybe there is one who has been bad with you and who you want to punish. We write her name with this,' he shook a bottle of red ink, 'and some words from this book and then we burn it. And as it burns, so she will break.'

In ancient Egypt, as Umm Seti pointed out, 'magicians were men of high rank and education, and . . . many of them were princes, as was the case of Kha-em-Wast, the son of Ramses II, . . . whereas their modern descendants are usually poor and uneducated.' If Muhammad possessed such power through his magic, I reasoned, how come he lived in this small house with its simple furniture? How come his good-looking children were running bare-footed and ragged in the streets? How come his wife was always working and he was making arrangements for American tourists to climb the pyramids? If he had power, he should be able to create wealth for himself, just as he was offering to do for me. If he had power, I realized, watching his dark mask of a face watching me, then he must be able to read my thoughts. Hello, Muhammad, I thought. If you can read my thoughts then maybe you'll use your magic to help my book.

Muhammad looked around the room, went to the other divan and brought back another book of spells. 'These are for other things.'

'Such as?'

'If you want we can make it so your wife will always love and desire you, or so that your book is a big success so everyone will want to read it.'

I'm not superstitious and apart from ouijah boards as a teenager, I've had no experience of this sort of thing. I had arrived as a cynic, a sceptic, an unbeliever, but I must admit that by this stage I was terrified by the possibility of what he might be able to do. As a rationalist I was way out of my depth there, lured into this by my need to know and to understand. It occurred to me then that this was a key difference between him and me, between Egyptians and westerners (as far as generalizations can be applied), between people who have lost their traditions and those who live with their survivals. Just then it felt to me that my own survival was in question.

Fate or chance stepped in again on my behalf in the shapely form of Muhammad's wife. They had things to do, people to see. Had he forgotten?

'Think about what you would like me to do. My house is your house, so please come again.'

We stood up. It was customary for villagers to pay for this sort of session, so I offered a generous amount. Muhammad refused it the four times I tried to give it to him. 'You are my guest,' he said each time.

'Then let me impose one more time: if you can perform your magic and have such power, is there nothing more that you would wish for yourself?'

He smiled at last, and with indulgence. 'Look at me. I have a house, my wife, children, my health. All this. And in the end, it is all due to the will of Allah. Only sometimes we can get help. I will pray for your book.'

I didn't go back to see Muhammad and nor did I find a Rifai who was prepared to talk to me, but by then it didn't matter. I knew that the magical element of ancient Egyptian religious practices lived on in the dark arts, in the 'sorcery' of the herbalist and maybe even in the secrets of the Rifai. What remained to be seen was whether Muhammad's prayers and incantations would help me find the survivals I wanted.

CHAPTER 7

The Original Egyptians

Nothing is more striking to me than the way in which one is constantly reminded of Herodotus. The Christianity and the Islam of this country are full of the ancient worship.

Lucie Duff Gordon

The Pyramids rose out of the fug of the Cairo dawn like the first land emerging from the Sea of Chaos, their three peaks standing up above the smog, the desert haze and the mists of time. I had been standing before them in the darkness, watching them slowly come into focus, pale beige limestone on a pale grey morning. The guards marched off. New ones appeared. Behind me was the village of Nezlet es-Semaan and its neighbours. Somewhere down there were the houses of the sheikha whom Marina had consulted for fertility, of Munir and the herbalist-decorator, of the magician Muhammad Abdel-Wanis. The cocks crowed, dawn prayer was called and across the valley came the constant rumble of traffic. Cairo wound itself up for the day.

I wanted to see who visited at dawn, who came to watch the sunrise, the villagers in search of the blessing of fertility, foreigners looking to get a kick out of climbing the Great Pyramid, New Agers ready with prayers and incense to greet the coming of a new day with blessings for Isis and Osiris.

Two guards stood nearby. One had attached a small radio to his ear and was listening to the morning sermon. The other eyed me suspiciously. After a while he called me over, brandishing his machine-gun. A few years ago I would have laughed at him, confident that he was all mouth and no bullets. But when the terrorist campaign started, the Ministry of Interior levelled the playing field by issuing their guards with live ammunition. So when the guard waved his weapon at me, I went over, but as slowly as I could.

'What are you doing?' he asked, almost angry with incomprehension. 'It is forbidden to enter at night.'

'It's not night any longer.'

'You need a ticket to enter. Where is your ticket?'

'I don't want to go in. I just want to look, from here.'

He knew he had no right to move me on. 'OK then, give me a cigarette.' I didn't have any, but even if I had I wouldn't have given him one. This thought didn't occur to him. 'OK then, give me one pound.' No wonder Muhammad the magician had had no problem getting these guys to turn their backs on foreigners who wanted to climb the pyramid.

I had intended to stay around for the morning, but the wind suddenly picked up and performed its own sort of magic by conjuring a sandstorm out of the desert and making the Pyramids disappear. Even though I was little more than a hundred metres away from them, I was now unable to define even their outlines through the orange-brown air. This might have explained why there were no other dawn visitors. Perhaps the New Agers had had divine premonition, or the good sense to check the weather forecast.

The taxi driver who took me back to town had a flashy seducer's smile. At that time of the morning, as part of a solid belt of metal clattering into the city, it was going to take an hour to get to the centre. I replied to his few pleasantries in as brief a manner as I could manage, then took out my notebook and started to write.

The driver's name was Sayyed but he clearly wished it was Steve McQueen. In spite of the lack of sun – the air was so thick we could only see a couple of cars ahead – he put on his metal-framed Ray-Ban sunglasses and lurched and jumped and wove across lanes in the hope of sneaking around the car ahead. Each time we stopped, Sayyed stared at me with a mixture of fascination, amazement and unease. Finally he nodded at my notebook and asked, 'Why are you doing this?' There was an edge to his voice, as though I was doing the strangest thing in the world and he was feeling threatened. 'Are you writing about my car?'

I began to wonder how many people he knew with pen and paper. Magicians who could write spells that would bring his engine to a halt? Traffic police who had a habit of picking on young taxi drivers whenever they needed a little extra cash in their pockets? I put the notebook away.

Pyramids Road used to be one of those idyllic country tracks where landscape, ancient monuments (in this case the Pyramids) and villagers happily co-existed. It created the sort of scene Orientalist painters loved. A long straight road lined with shade trees, it was surrounded by farmland in the 1860s when Edward Lear painted it. It was raised, too, to keep it above the waterline when the Nile flooded, making it a dry causeway connecting the city with the Pyramid plateau.

You can still get a sense of how it must have been on the road to Saqqara. But when Cairo started spreading, wealthier citizens built villas in the suburbs and the land between the city and the Pyramids became their playground. Nightclubs, garden restaurants and casinos opened, frequented by foreigners, rich Egyptians, big-name belly dancers, girls with a certain reputation and, in the 1940s, by the last king, Farouk.

A few of those grand neo-classical villas survived with their functions intact – the homes of foreign ambassadors, the Mubarak Library, some ministries and a few seriously wealthy Egyptians – but most of the miles between the Nile and the Pyramids were filled with concrete blocks, mid-range hotels, massive hospitals, rows of shops and fast-food outlets, clubs, theatres and the sorts of discos where Sudanese and Ethiopian girls went to earn their rent. While I looked out at all this tatty new glitter and, behind it, at some of the city's poorest housing, Sayyed began to make strange gestures, turning his hand over and holding it towards me in an awkward way. He was hoping I would notice the tattoo on his wrist. I had spotted it as soon as I saw him but the last thing I felt like doing was having a discussion about it. Now there was no avoiding one.

'Yes, I saw your tattoo. Very nice.'

'Do you know what it's for?'

'Yes.'

He pretended not to hear. 'Copt,' he explained, holding up his arm to show me a dark blue cross incised on his wrist. I noticed the seam of his green shirtsleeve had been clumsily stitched with red thread.

'I know.'

'Copt,' as if I was supposed to pat him on the back. 'And you Christian?' he asked hopefully.

'Not Copt.'

'Never mind.'

Of all the trite claims made in Egypt – Egypt, land of beauty and culture; Alexandria, pearl of the Mediterranean; Cairo, Mother of the World – the one about the Copts being the true descendants of the pharaohs almost rang true. I took a closer look at Sayyed, replaced his shirt and trousers with the loose robes of the ancients – he'd look convincing – and then asked what he thought about his pedigree.

He was immediately cheered. 'Of course we are the real Egyptians. We were here before the Muslims. When St Mark came to Alexandria . . .'

He made the familiar claim about Christianity having been brought to Egypt in AD 45 by the evangelist St Mark. I knew that there wasn't a shred of evidence to support the claim, and also that that made not the slightest difference to Sayyed. And anyway, using that sort of argument, the Jews I had met in Alexandria could claim to be 'the real Egyptians' because they could trace their tenure back even further than the Christians, to the reign of Ptolemy I and perhaps long before.

At the next set of lights, we sat beside a pick-up carrying three camels to the slaughterhouse. The beasts eyed the passengers in a crowded bus with magnificent disdain. We were to be there for a few minutes, because Sayyed switched off the engine. I made a note about the flimsiness of Sayyed's claim in my book. When I looked up, I saw he once more had about him that look of fear and deep-rooted persecution. I wrote a last note: 'Ironic that a descendant of the people who created paper and writing should show such fear of my notebook.'

Sayyed dropped me off in front of the compound of the Coptic Patriarch, not far from Ramses Station. At the gate the state security people didn't give me a second look, but the patriarchal guard raised his hand, palm up, inquisitive rather than challenging. 'Shenouda,' I shouted and the guard assumed I was referring to His Holiness Pope Shenouda III, 117th successor to St Mark as Patriarch of Alexandria. Still, he hesitated. Few of the pope's visitors walk through the gate. Then he waved me in.

The patriarchal compound had much in common with ancient temple compounds. Just as ancient temples stood in the centre of a large walled-in area, so the concrete mass of the new cathedral towered over a clutter of other buildings. As in antiquity, there were lesser shrines, storerooms, accommodation for priests, the residence of the patriarch/pharaoh, schools, a guard house, a shop. ('You can take that analogy a little further,' a Coptic friend mentioned later in London. 'and say that the Coptic pope is a reincarnation of the pharaoh. At the open meetings he holds in the cathedral, he is treated like a god, people kiss his hand, his robe, hang on his every word. There are miraculous healings, people faint. And he is autocratic like a pharaoh.')

I had come to see another Shenouda, Professor Chancellor Dr Zaki Shenouda, a warm and welcoming man, who had been director of the Institute of Coptic Studies for longer than his assistant could remember. When I arrived, he was drinking tea in his large office with several elderly male friends. He was elegant in spite of his short stature and his skin yellowed by age and sickness. Eighty years old at least, his manner was insistent. He sat me next to him on the sofa and held the sleeve of my shirt as though he was afraid I would run away.

'To understand what is a Copt, you have to sit here with me for three years.' He was only partly joking – there was a sense of a final confession about what he had to tell me, and he wanted to be sure that he said it all. 'The Copts are the heirs of the pharaohs. When the Arabs and Amr Ibn al-As arrived in Egypt, they understood nothing of the language of the Copts. In the matter of religion and of *civique*,' he said, breaking into French, 'they understood nothing. When they saw the statues and monuments that the pharaohs worshipped, they didn't understand that these were religious symbols. Nor did they understand that the pharaohs, like the Copts, worshipped one single god with one single name. And it was for that that they didn't write anything about ancient Egypt. End of story – and it would have been the end of the culture of the pharaohs had not the Copts kept alive the music and art of the pharaohs, both of which continue to survive in the Coptic Orthodox Church. In many other ways as well the pharaohs have survived. We can know how they prayed and acted in their temples by looking at the way Copts behave today.'

'But so many factors have changed, how is it possible to make parallels between yourselves and the ancients?'

He smiled benignly and nodded at his silent friends as if to say, Can you believe this jerk?

'I too am an author,' he offered, although it didn't answer my question. 'I have written many books, including one about your subject. The pharaohs said that the body took forty days to be prepared for mummification. The Copts take forty days to complete the burial.

Christian women do many things which we know pharaonic women did. They take dirt and put it on their faces, wear black and cover their faces with a scarf. You can also see this in ancient tombs.

'*Chez les pharaons*,' he said, 'there were prophesies that the Messiah would come. Osiris is the Christ and Isis is his mother, the Virgin. There are other things we've taken. Christians talk about the fallen angel, while in ancient Egypt there was the god Seth who killed Osiris and went on to become god of Evil. The pharaonic temple resembles our churches. In the construction of the temple and church we find high walls and no windows, because life inside is supposed to be like heaven. Even the clothes of the priests are similar to before. In ancient times the monasteries were very rich.'

'And today?'

He winked. 'Very. And in our church the patriarch is king, while for the ancients the pharaoh was also the chief priest.'

'But how has this survived?'

'Two important reasons. First, Egyptians are conservative and Copts especially so. Second, because the Copts have been separated from the rest of Christianity ever since the disagreement over the nature of Jesus at the Council of Chalcedon, in 451. Since then, without interference from anyone else, and with that Egyptian conservatism, we have preserved the original and I would say the true spirit of Christianity.'

Fresh tea was brought in on a small metal tray. Light flooded through the office's many windows. Prof. Shenouda's secretary and more visitors passed through. When he turned to me again, he gave me the books his secretary had brought, two of the three volumes of his *History of the Copts*, in which he laid out his claims for Coptic heritage.

'But just because we have guarded and furthered the pharaonic heritage does not guarantee our survival. This is a very difficult time for us. The government is against us. Before we had to stay and suffer, but now the pope has given his blessing for Copts to leave Egypt. Many have gone. Others stay. I have written books about Nasser, about the other one . . . Sadat . . . about government ministers. Some people didn't like what I wrote, I was going to be in trouble, but I am still here. And as one who suffers from cancer I can tell you that there is a cancer here in our country.' In spite of Prof. Shenouda's obvious distress, I felt there was something exaggerated in his view. The Coptic Church had been born and nurtured under Roman repression and had remained strong under continuous persecution. I could see no reason to believe it would give up the fight now.

Prof. Shenouda didn't know what would happen to the Copts. The bright sun seemed a mockery. There was no bright future. Maybe some would hang on. 'Last week someone tried to burn our church. Not the first time, either. He was lighting it, but we found him and he ran away.'

Professor Shenouda seemed happier with the past and in his round-about way had just come to the point of answering my earlier question about Copts. 'The Copt is both a pharaoh and a slave.' I looked puzzled by this, so he attempted to clarify: 'Outside we are slaves, but inside we are pharaohs.' Then several more men arrived and interrupted him. One was a younger lecturer eager for attention, who handed me a collection of his short paperbacks and suggested that we meet after I had had a chance to read them. They were called *The Anti Christ, The Coming Danger, The Number of the Beast 666, Cast Out Devils* and *Unidentified Flying Objects: Are They the Chariots of the Cherubim?* The message was clear: the Devil was on the loose and had the Copts, the living embodiment of ancient Egypt, in his sights. I slipped the books into my bag and slipped away. When he said goodbye, Professor Shenouda suggested, 'If I were you I would look at three elements of our religion: art, music and monasteries.'

It wasn't just the Copts themselves who believed they were the heirs of the pharaohs. Lucie Duff Gordon wrote in the 1860s, 'The Copts are evidently the ancient Egyptians. The slightly aquiline nose and long eye are the very same as the profiles of the tombs and temples, and also the very earliest Byzantine pictures; *du reste*, the face is handsome but generally sallow and rather inclined to puffiness, and the figure wants the grace of the Arabs . . . Their feet are the long-toed, flattish foot of the Egyptian statue . . .'

Edward Lane, writing several decades earlier, had sounded a note of caution. 'The Copts are undoubtedly descendants of the ancient Egyptians,' he wrote in *The Manners and Customs of the Modern Egyptians*, 'but not an unmixed race; their ancestors in the earlier ages of Christianity having intermarried with Greeks, Nubians, Abyssinians, and other foreigners . . . The Copts,' he continued, 'are, generally speaking, somewhat under the middle size; and so, as it appears from the mummies, were the ancient Egyptians . . . Most of the Copts circumcise their sons; another practice which prevailed among their pagan ancestors.'

Lane thought the Copts had taken their name from the town of Coptos, where many sought refuge during the Roman persecutions. Others suggest, as did Girgis at the moulid of Abu'l-Hajjaj, that it was derived from the ancient Greek name Aigyptios, which was in turn a Greek corruption of the ancient Egyptian name Ha-ka-Ptah, the house of the god Ptah.

It is impossible to trace the roots of Christians in Egypt back to St Mark's mission to Alexandria, although the legend is convincingly detailed: as St Mark walked into the city from the port, the strap of his sandal broke. Happily there was a cobbler's shop just by the city gate. The cobbler injured himself while he was mending the sandal, but St Mark miraculously healed the wound. The cobbler invited him home to meet his wife and Christianity made its first Egyptian convert. His name was Annianus and he became head of the Christian community in Alexandria.

On a more factual basis, the earliest New Testament text found in Egypt was written in the mid-second century AD. There were certainly Christians in Egypt by that time, perhaps initially converts from Alexandria's Jewish community. Some of the early claims of martyrdom are difficult to verify but persecutions were real enough in the third century, for there are documents recording them: Christians were forced to provide proof that they had, in the words of one affidavit of the time, 'sacrificed and made libations [to the pagan gods] and tasted the offerings with my wife, my sons and my daughter'. Then came the Emperor Diocletian's massacre of Copts which put the new religionists firmly on the map and led to the creation of the current Coptic calendar, the Era of Martyrs.

Even after two centuries of continuous research, it is still difficult to reach back to that time in Egypt and form a clear picture of Christianity as it evolved. Early texts are too obscure, too vague to help clarify the picture, while later accounts had an interest in altering the picture to fit their version of the way things had been. What seems certain is this: just as Christians converted pagan temples and defaced the images of the old gods to conduct their own services in them – or built over the past as the Church of John the Baptist was built over the Serapeum in Alexandria – so Christianity absorbed some of the basic theology and rituals of the pagan cults.

It is still impossible to know whether this was a conscious act on the part of the early Christians or merely a form of religious osmosis, but a merging of ideas and influences from the old cult to the new certainly occurred. It is epitomized by a fifth- or sixth-century invocation found on a papyrus fragment at Oxyrhynchus: 'Hor, Hor, Phor, Eloei, Adonai, Iao, Sabaoth, Michael, Jesus Christ', it reads, calling on pagan, Jewish and Christian divinities. 'Help us and this house. Amen.'

Dr Isaac Fanous received me in his studio, a huge airy room, the light cut down by blinds. There was something raffish about him, an air of the swinger, probably acquired when he studied in Paris in the 1960s, which was in conflict with the absolute seriousness of his work.

He had suggested I visit him in his studio because he wanted me to see what his class were doing. On a raised platform, several students were composing a large-scale mosaic. On one of the long benches, others were at work painting icons.

Dr Fanous is credited with having more or less single-handedly revived the art of iconography in Egypt. 'You would have seen the same activities in a workshop here some fifteen hundred years ago, but before the 1960s we just didn't have such a school. All this sort of work had stopped and no one was making icons. But then we thought we should have our own identity for our own church, so for my inspiration I went to see what had gone before.' Fanous looked back to that golden age of early Coptic icons – between the decline of Rome and the arrival of the Arabs – and consciously recreated their style and technique. 'The materials we are using here, the tempura, the wooden boards, are the same as were being used fifteen hundred years ago.'

Fanous suggested I speak to one of his former pupils, Dr Stephane René, whose thesis was on the table between us. 'Stephanos,' Fanous said, overflowing with emotion, 'was my best student.'

Since completing his postgraduate thesis with Fanous in Cairo, Dr René had been dividing his time between London, where he worked for the Prince of Wales Institute for Architecture, and California, where he painted icons for the growing Coptic community. I told him what I had been unwilling to tell Fanous: that if the tradition of Coptic iconography had lapsed, then they could not claim continuity. When he reinvented the tradition, Fanous had made all sorts of assumptions about the ways ancient painters had worked, assumptions that were impossible to verify.

Dr René was more eloquent than his master. 'In one way you're right. For fifteen hundred years, they were living with these things hanging on their walls or in their storerooms without being aware of them, of what they represented. But I believe that traditions survive, latent, inside us all. Fanous carries within himself the heritage of his people, whether he is aware of it or not. You could say it's in his DNA, his subconscious. Of course with Fanous it is different – he wanted to look at what had gone before. That was his conscious decision. He was working in Paris, so there were all sorts of other traditions and influences he could have called on, but he didn't. And don't forget that it was also Fanous who made the decision to move away from Byzantine art and to purge Egyptian icons of foreign influence. That was impossible, of course, but it was a valuable experiment because in the process he identified what was essentially Egyptian about these images.'

'And what was that?'

'The contours, the hieratic style, the absence of any extra decoration. So now when you look at modern Coptic icons, you are looking at a tradition – whether continuous or not – that you can trace back to the fourth century, when Coptic iconographers made the political decision to turn their back on the Byzantine style.'

'And before that?'

'Have you seen the Fayoum Portraits? Their painted faces were Graeco-Roman, but they were created to replace ancient Egyptian mummy covers, which also had painted faces. The Fayoum Portraits are the connection between pagan and Christian art, both in technique and form.'

'And before that?'

'Well, it's obvious. The technique came from ancient Egypt. There's a continuity in material because they used what they had to hand – natural pigments, chalk and ochres from the land.' I remembered the lumps of pigment-encrusted rock I had found while walking around Deir al-Medina, the workers' village in Luxor. 'And they painted on gesso, which has hardly changed since antiquity – calcium carbonate mixed with glue, usually gelatin which the ancient Egyptians got from cows.'

'And what about the subject of the paintings?'

'Well there are differences, but there are strong parallels too. When you look at an icon of the Virgin and Child and then see images of Isis suckling Horus you'd be blind to miss the connection. They are very similar in style and message. In Coptic art Mary, with the infant on her knee, is referred to as the throne of heaven, which has a direct parallel in ancient Egypt where the goddess Isis, with the infant Horus on her knee, was always portrayed with a throne on her head. There are popular early images of Jesus as a shepherd and as a winnower. The shepherd has a hooked stick, the winnower a flail – the crook and the flail—'

'—and the crook and flail just happen to be what Osiris carried in his hands.'

'Quite right. Like Jesus, he was killed young and through his death offered the promise of resurrection and eternal life. Take a look at the icon of Mari Girgis [St George] killing the dragon and ancient paintings of Horus killing the monster hippo in the marshes of the Delta.'

'It sounds like we could go on all day making parallels between now and then.'

'We could. But one thing we can't do is imagine what all this meant to a fifth-century Copt – or a pagan, for that matter. If we knew that, perhaps we would also know a little more about why the whole thing stopped in the eighth century.'

Another survival: I took the metro south to Mari Girgis station in what is known as Coptic Cairo. Within the site of a Roman bastion, several early Coptic churches have survived, though most have been rebuilt. There is also a Coptic museum.

I had visited the museum before, but after speaking to Dr René, I wanted to look again. On my way in, I was approached by an official guide, a man with an earnest and intelligent face. I liked the way he spoke and as it wasn't too difficult to fix a price with him, we went together to visit the museum. Inside, I realized I had made a mistake. Just as the Greek traveller Herodotus was told sheer fabrications by his guides – including one about the pharaoh's daughter prostituting herself to pay for one of the Giza pyramids – so my guide allowed his imagination to roam free. From gold hidden inside stone pillars to woven fabric under which Mary had laid the infant Jesus, he invented a story for each item I stopped to see. By the end, I was beginning to wonder whether he had also faked his official guide's badge. When we parted company, he asked for my address. 'What for?' 'Because you are my good friend,' he replied straight-faced, 'and I will miss you when you have gone.' 'But I live here in Cairo.' 'Very good. So then I can come to visit.' I left him with an address I thought he would find more useful than my own, that of the Institute for Coptic Studies.

Some years ago I bought a book entitled *Our Lord's Mother Visits Egypt*, written by one Pearl Zaki and published in Cairo in 1977. Chapter One opens like this: 'In the land of Egypt at Zeitun, the Mother of Our Lord came to earth in April, 1968.' This bold and somewhat bald style is kept up throughout long descriptions of the apparition of the Virgin on the roof of a church in a Cairo suburb. The apparition, descibed as 'a luminous body of a golden colour' by one eyewitness, recurred for many nights. Thousands of Egyptians and foreigners witnessed it. The Director of the governmental General Information and Complaints Department concluded that it was an 'undeniable fact'. The Coptic patriarch sent a Papal Committee to investigate, who reported that the rumours were indeed true. Even Muslims went along and were convinced. Invalids were cured, the damned saved, confessions made and photographs taken. Some of those images were reproduced in Ms Zaki's book. I studied them carefully. To me they looked less than convincing. White spots in the black night were said to be 'spiritual beings in the shape of big pigeons, bright fluorescent and white or sparkling from every direction', but they looked to me like holes in the negative. Another, supposed to be the Virgin herself, looked more like a wad of cotton wool. But a Coptic friend to whom I showed the photographs said, 'You see.'

'See what?'

'See it's true. What a fantastic book. Where did you get it?'

Whether the photographs were genuine or not, thousands of people believed the Virgin was there and were filled with joy. Very few were surprised. There was a general acceptance that such things happen in Egypt. The Coptic Church is built on miracles, on saints whose bodies have not decomposed and who still smell sweet, on priests who have the reputation for being able to command the *djinns* and *afarit* of magic. It was built on the ruins of the pagan religion – sometimes literally so – which it was instrumental in destroying.

Ibrahim was agitated to the point that I thought he might crick his neck peering round at me. 'But ya missiou, why the desert? And if you must go to the desert, why to a Christian monastery?'

'Are you worried for me, Ibrahim? What could possibly happen in a monastery?'

'Not possible! Do you read the newspaper? Do you know what the terrorists are doing? Do you know that they are shooting Copts and shooting foreigners and you will be a foreigner surrounded by Copts. God willing, nothing will happen. But sometimes that is not enough.'

'What do you mean?' I mocked, 'God not enough?'

'You are not a Muslim. How do we know that Allah is watching over you as he does over me? Anything could happen.'

Recent news reports had been gloomy. A series of attacks on Copts, government officials and tourists had culminated in the massacre of tourists at the Deir al-Bahari temple in Luxor. There was no denying Ibrahim's assertion that neither Copts nor foreigners were exempt. And I can't pretend that I wasn't terrified by the prospect of being caught up in some random act of violence. But I was on my way to visit a desert monastery, as Professor Shenouda had suggested, on the trail of another, spectacular survival.

If you were an ancient Egyptian looking for a place to get away from it all then Wadi Natroun would have done very nicely. It was so far off the map that it didn't even feature in Herodotus's description of Egypt. The ancient Egyptians knew about it, of course, and gave it the name it carries now, *Inti Hsmn*, or the natron valley. A twenty-first-century BC story refers to plants imported from the Wadi to Egypt proper, while a later, Middle Kingdom papyrus mentions it as a stop-off point on a trade route between the western oases and the Nile delta. And archaeological fragments and ancient statues found in the valley led Dr Otto Meinardus, who has spent most of his working life studying early Christian Egypt, to suggest that 'even in the year 2000 BC this region was held sacred'.

One hundred and five kilometres from Cairo, on the Alexandria road, Wadi Natroun was a perfect location for ascetics. Strabo, who travelled through the area in 25 BC, wrote of 'two nitre-beds, which contain very large quantities of nitre . . . Here Serapis is held in honour.' Nitre, as his readers would have known, was a key ingredient for mummification, and Serapis, appropriately, was a god of resurrection. Wadi Natroun's assocations with dying made it the perfect place for Coptic hermits to live through the symbolic 'death' of their retreat, and the desert hills were riddled with the caves and hollows of hermits. A cluster of monasteries also grew across the valley.

Copts point to monasticism as one of their most important 'contributions' to Christianity. In response to constant persecution by Roman emperors and the wild decadence of Alexandria's pagans and Jews, many devout Christians sought a place removed from society, where they could devote themselves to prayer and meditation. According to tradition – in this case, almost supported by fact – the oldest desert communities were in the mountains of the Eastern Desert between the Nile and the Red Sea, where St Antony and St Paul retreated in the third centuries, inspiring a generation of Christians to follow their lead. Desert monasteries sprang up the length of the Nile from outside Alexandria to beyond Aswan, rules were established to govern the lives of the inhabitants, farms were established in the Nile valley to support them, and occasionally a monk, a hermit, if sufficiently well prepared, went out into the desert, to nooks and crannies, old caves and rock fissures, where they lived as little a physical life as was possible for a human to endure.

'Egypt,' wrote Sir John Gardner Wilkinson in 1843, 'which once swarmed with monks, and was not less prolific in nuns, has now only seven monasteries.' Four of those seven were in the Wadi Natroun. Wilkinson would be surprised were he to see Egypt today, for whether as a result of Pope Shenouda's attempts to revive old traditions or because of the threat of Islamic extremists, there has been a monastic revival. Wilkinson quoted the historian Gibbon as saying there were some 5000 'anachorets' and the ruins of fifty monasteries in the valley. Wilkinson himself was told there were seventy-seven monks in the valley. In 1960 there were seventy. By 1986 that number had risen to 358 and it is still rising.

The lay population in the valley has also risen dramatically. I saw the signs as Ibrahim drove the eleven kilometres from the Cairo–Alex road to the monastery – the new housing, the trees, the seven children who climbed on to the back seat when we stopped to give two a lift and the greening of the desert which modern farming methods has made possible around the monasteries.

Deir Anba Bishoi looked more like a fortress than a monastery. High mudbrick walls with few openings on the lower levels, bell towers showing above the walls. After the noise of the children, when Ibrahim's taxi had disappeared back to Cairo, the silence of the desert almost had a weight to it.

Deir Anba Bishoi, the monastery of St Bishoi, was dedicated to a fourth-century Christian who had had visions that he was called upon to wash Jesus's feet and then received the *baraka* by drinking the water. It seemed an appropriate image for a thirsty man left on his own in the desert. Doubly appropriate, in fact – Umm Seti in her manuscript points to the purifying qualities of natron: 'Natron and water is . . . used in the villages . . . for bathing when a person is unusually dirty, especially from contact with oil or grease . . . Modern village women also use natron and water as a vaginal douche.' References in the Pyramid Texts suggest that from an early age ancient Egyptians also recognized its properties: 'Thou doest purify thyself with natron amongst the followers of Horus.'

Abuna Sidrak, the father in charge of visitors to the monastery, was waiting for me. 'I will show you the monastery and then you will see the Father.' Abuna Sidrak was a tall, thin, elderly man, elegant in his movements and in his long black habit. Coptic monks wear black cowls on their heads, the seam of which they embroider themselves, a dash of colour and individuality in what otherwise is an anonymous uniform.

From its foundation in the fourth century, the monastery came under attack from nomadic Berber tribes. But by the end of the eighth century, Arab rulers in Cairo were powerful enough to put an end to that and the Wadi Natroun monasteries avoided many of the persecutions later suffered by Christians in the Nile valley. However, not even the significant power of the sultan could hold back the Black Death, which decimated the monks as it had depopulated Egyptian towns. When Lord George Curzon visited Anba Bishoi in 1837 he found only three or four monks left. 'But since then many things have changed,' Abuna Sidrak explained. 'The old churches and buildings have been restored and the number of monks has grown, mostly thanks to His Holiness, our Pope Shenouda.'

Within the walls, there were five churches or chapels, accommodation for the monks, what remained of the library (much of it had been bought or 'borrowed' by nineteenth-century European travellers) and the *qasr*, or keep, a twelfth-century tower. The tower was built before the walls went up and was a place for the monks to hide during Bedouin raids. The entrance was on the first floor, which we reached across a drawbridge from the gatehouse.

It was hot and bright outside, and sunlight merged the colours of the tower and the desert. Abuna Sidrak led me into the cool, shady and quiet interior. 'I feel like I am stepping into the past when I come in here,' he said.

'Funny you should say that, because I have a similar feeling wherever I go in Egypt.'

Part of the tower had become a museum and the abuna showed me the refectory where monks and hermits used to eat after their weekly prayer meeting. 'But don't think they just talked to each other: meals were conducted in silence, while someone read passages from the *Paradise of Monks*.' The museum had acquired all sorts of things that had fallen out of use, including the old grain mill – 'we stopped grinding our flour with these stones in 1950' – and a winnowing fork. All very interesting, but I thought it was time to explain my quest.

Abuna Sidrak understood immediately. 'You have come to the right place. There are many things to show you, especially in the church.' We walked down to the Church of Anba Bishoi, originally built in the ninth century and altered many times since. The father pointed out the door to the church, which had no hinges but was attached to a swinging post 'pharaonic style'.

'You will see that even the structure of the church reflects something of the ancient temples. We have the *haikal*, the altar, which is hidden behind the screen here as the ancient altars were hidden. Here in the church of Anba Bishoi we have three *haikals*, as they often had before.'

The screen that hid the altar was heavily decorated and hung with many icons of the Apostles and the desert fathers, all painted by Dr

Isaac Fanous. Above the iconostasis, a row of oil lamps and ostrich eggs hung from chains. 'The symbol of resurrection,' the abuna said, pointing to the eggs. 'The ancient Egyptians believed in resurrection and the afterlife, just like us.'

'Why ostrich, Abuna?'

'The ostrich is big, it buries its eggs in the sand to hatch, and watches over them as God watches over us.'

The main 'sight' of the church was the remains of the monastery's founding saint. Abuna Sidrak mouthed a prayer as he ran his hand over the edge of the feretory. When new monks are ordained, they lie down beside the reliquary and have the relic cover put over them as a sign of their having 'died' with the saint and, like him, been reborn.

'The remains of Anba Bishoi are as they were when he died.'

'They haven't decomposed?'

'Not at all. And when we open the cover, there is a very beautiful smell.'

'How do you explain that?'

'You know, when we dig here in Egypt we find many bodies that have not perished. This is not unusual.'

Yet again I saw the differences between my own and the Egyptian view of the world. Mine had no place for such miraculous healings, for saints who don't decompose in death. I sought a logical, rational or cultural explanation for what I saw in the world. I remembered that ancient Egyptians came to this valley to collect its minerals, which were considered the essential ingredients for mummification. Perhaps the same qualities were keeping the saint's remains intact. I suggested this to the father.

He smiled indulgently. 'There is only one explanation for these things. They are God's will.'

When tensions between the Coptic Church and the government increased in the 1980s, Pope Shenounda, who had been a hermit before assuming the mantle of St Mark, retreated to Deir Anba Bishoi for a symbolic forty months of purification and isolation. ('House arrest' is another way of understanding his retreat.) Since then an elaborate 'papal compound' has evolved with accommodation blocks, refectory, workshop and clinic. Abuna Sidrak directed me along the imposing walls to the monastery's modern side-gate, the guarded entrance to this self-sufficient community.

A young novice called Peter, a Bulgarian from Sofia, acted as my minder. I was surprised to be met by a foreigner – most monks are Egyptian, and many of them well-educated professionals – but the story of how Peter arrived in Wadi Natroun was illustrative of Pope Shenouda's magnetism. Peter had got himself out of Sofia and was working in Johannesburg. 'But I was lost,' he confessed. 'I was wild, wasting myself. I just didn't know what to do with my life. Then by chance I met the pope – he just walked past me – and I knew that I had to follow. When I heard him talk, I knew what he was saying was right. I told him this and he arranged for me to come here.'

Peter took me into the inner compound where the pope himself stayed and where everything from domes to walls to lamp posts was topped with crosses. The terrace outside the papal suite was lit by lamps in the distinctive shape of the papal hat. We found my room in the accommodation block nearby and then went for a walk around the grounds. The monastery had greened the desert and the monks were growing a range of food from tomatoes and citrus fruits to wheat and potatoes. Or rather, the monks were supervising farm workers, Copts from the Nile valley who wanted to live in a Christian environment, and who worked on the monastery in return for their housing and upkeep and what Peter called 'moral training'.

'They are happy to be here. And we understand their difficulties, living in Muslim towns. The monks used to have to travel when they needed medical or dental treatment, but it has become too difficult for them outside.' For 'too difficult' I understood that he meant 'too dangerous'. 'So now we bring doctors from Cairo on Fridays and Sundays and we have a surgery where they can operate.'

I told Peter it seemed a long way from St Antony's vision of men retreating to the desert to shed the world and find God.

He replied with the passion of a new convert and with one of the many stock phrases he had recently been taught: 'You must find the desert in yourself before you can go to the desert.' It echoed what Ahmad, the herbalist, had said about finding eternity in myself.

Peter's timing was impeccable. We were at the edge of the monastic grounds, near the papal ponds, a small manmade lake where the pope raised trout. Beyond the perimeter fence there were rock hills and sand dunes and a series of what looked like concrete huts.

'This is where some of the hermits live,' Peter explained.

'So close to the monastery? I expected them to be far out in the desert.'

'It's not important to them where they are. Some go on from there into the desert where they find a cave to live in, but they still rely on us to feed them and once a week they come back to pray with the monks in the monastery.' It was late afternoon and the sun was low, the light soft, the desert at its most seductive. Easy to understand its attraction. But Peter pulled me back. 'Come, you will have your meal now.'

Peter described the monastic routine as one of work and prayer. Prayers start at midnight and continue until after three, when the liturgy starts. At eight, the monks go to work on the farm, in the hospital or in the workshops. And what about food, I wondered. Copts fast or refrain from eating meat and certain other foods during Lent, of course, but also on Wednesdays and Fridays, the forty-three days before Christmas, the fifteen days before Ascension – more than half the year in all. Happily I had arrived during an eating period and in the refectory a table had been laid for me with a familiar Egyptian spread of hummus and bread, pickles, beans in tomato sauce . . .

'Are you not joining me?' I asked Peter as he sat me down.

'Thank you, but I already ate. During non-fast periods we eat our meal at one o'clock.'

There were two others in the refectory, however, men with long beards and the ragged faces of refugees. Each time I looked up, they were smiling at me. They also appeared not to be eating their food, identical to mine. As soon as I had finished, Peter reappeared and took me through to another room. I asked him about the men. 'They are brothers who live in the desert. They have been there for many years. We are very happy to see them again.'

'They look happy to be here too.'

Before I could ask any more questions, the head of the monastery arrived. A tall, vigorous man with an intense gaze, he had a manner which suggested that he had long been used to ordering people. He also had a sense of humour which, in my experience, was a rare quality in monks. 'Ah, so you saw some of our hermits. They must have heard you were coming.'

I asked what they did all day when they were out in the desert.

'The idea is that they have as few distractions as possible so they can pray and read the holy texts without hindrance. Part of our job is to make sure they can do that, but it is becoming increasingly difficult.'

'Why?'

'Because more and more people disturb them as they go driving through the wadi in their four-wheel-drive cars.'

'I imagine that might disturb their concentration.'

'Most of the time the brothers don't even notice them.'

'We say that prayer,' Peter elaborated, 'is like a rope that ties us to God. Sometimes through prayer the monks before were able to heal the sick, stop the sun in the sky, find water.'

'Oh really?'

The Father saw the look on my face. 'No, no, people don't think we do that sort of thing now. The brothers in the desert now aren't tying their hair to the ceiling to keep awake.' His manner became absolutely serious. 'But we do suffer in our own way. The persecution we are subjected to is like a form of crucifixion.' His sadness reminded me of Prof. Shenouda at the Coptic Institute. 'Perhaps as a result of the persecution we find more and more people wanting to join us, wanting to go into the desert and emulate the early fathers.'

I explained my belief that the tradition was even older. There is graffiti in the Theban hills recording people who went there in search of isolation, who stayed for days, weeks, months in prayer and were rewarded with a vision of Amon. And that was in the Nineteenth Dynasty, in the time of Ramses and Seti, more than three thousand years ago.

The Father was unsurprised. 'We have preserved many ancient traditions. Think of our months, like Tut and Hatur – those names are from the gods of the pharaohs, Thoth and Hathor. Our cross appears to have developed from the ancient *ankh*, the symbol of life. Have you been to the monastery of St Shenuti, in the Nile valley near Sohag?'

I explained that foreigners now found it difficult to travel in that part of Egypt.

'From the outside the monastery looks like an old temple. There are many many similarities we have with the pharaonic people. During the Holy Liturgy, the priests, deacon and the novices all wear white as a sign of purity and we know from paintings on the old temples that the priests used to do the same.'

'But why not change?'

'Why?' he replied as easily. 'Our rituals exist, they are there, they are ancient. And some things do change. We used to have over thirteen liturgies, but today we only use St Basil. So that is something that is breaking down. But look at the Catholics. They changed everything and now they are in trouble. We have things changing around us, the technology, the fact that you can drive here from Cairo in a couple of hours – and we try to respond to that. It's not as if we ignore the outside world. But we are traditional and religious people. Things are passed from grandfather to father to son. We can bear some change, but the basics must stay the same.'

As the monks rose early for morning prayers, they went to bed in good time. I thanked the Father for his help and hospitality – in the morning he would be in church – and strolled back through the papal compound. The night was alive with cicadas, moths, mosquitoes, a distant television set. Above me, the sky was peppered with stars. I sat on the wall by the edge of the compound and felt the dry chill of the desert. I was intrigued by the Father's easy acceptance of the parallels between past and present, the ancient legacy which Copts appeared to have preserved so successfully. I was surprised, too, for I had been expecting him to distance himself, and orthodox thinking, from the pagan past just as Sheikh Muhammad Mustafa Gemeiah had done at Al-Azhar and as the Christian Church had done in Europe.

Back in my room, I looked through the Umm Seti manuscript for some pages I had earmarked earlier. In a section entitled 'Wanton Damage to the Egyptian Sculptures', she wrote: 'Much of the mutilation of the ancient figures has been correctly blamed onto the Early Christians. But for what reason did these people take such pains to work their destruction? It is said that some of the Coptic hermits who were dwelling in the painted tombs of Western Thebes, deliberately mutilated all the female figures on the walls, lest their beauty should put carnal thoughts into their heads, and put them off their prayers.' But Umm Seti had a more extraordinary explanation of this vandalism than a fear of mere imaginings. 'In the light of other evidence it is more likely that they feared that the lovely Theban ladies would come to life and "make passes" at them ... We must remember that to the Ancient Egyptians the representations of any living creatures, from Gods down to humble insects, could, after having had the rite of "Opening the Mouth" performed over them, receive a portion of the spirit of the being represented, and assume a kind of magical life, and be capable of playing an active role in this world . . . This belief seems to be the basis of the systematic disfigurement of tomb and temple reliefs by the early Copts. They feared that their ancient Gods and rulers would take vengeance upon them for their base desertion of their old religion, and (no doubt!) their plundering of the despoiled and desecrated temples.'

Umm Seti was suggesting that, although the Copts had turned their backs on the ancient religion, they had not abandoned ancient beliefs, that both pagans and Copts believed in divine judgement, in the weighing of the soul and the existence of a book or register in which our deeds are recorded, with St Michael taking the place of the ancient Thoth. Even the idea of the king being a son of God was thousands of years old by the time Jesus was born. As Jesus was to be, so had Osiris been killed, and through his resurrection guaranteed an afterlife for mankind.

In our time, Copts have had very little influence over the rest of the Christian Church. In the early centuries of Christianity, certainly by the fourth century, when much of Europe was still making sacrifices to their pagan gods, Egyptians embraced the new creed with all their considerable fervour and left their imprint on it, an imprint that still survives. Separated from the mainstream of Christianity, Coptic literature, art and liturgy has preserved fossilized elements of early Church beliefs and practices. The monastery was also part of that 'fossil' and there I had found many parallels, analogies or survivals from that early Christian era and beyond into the time of the pharaohs.

I couldn't sleep. I had too many thoughts splashing around in my head and I was making too many connections. Time disappeared as it has a way of doing in Egypt, and I thought of the men in the desert nearby (were they sleeping? already at prayer?) as there had been men in the desert here thousands of years ago. Late in the night I pushed open the shutters and stood out on the balcony. The monastic village was quiet, though occasionally the breeze carried the sound of men's voices, low, insistent, repetitive, the monks already at their morning devotions, reciting prayers. The Coptic language, the one the monks were using for their devotions, was the one element of the Coptic heritage that I had not considered, yet several people, including

Professor Shenouda at the Coptic Institute, had pointed me towards it. That afternoon, back in Cairo, I began to make enquiries.

Coptic is described by Andrew Dalby in his *Dictionary of Languages* as 'a new form of Egyptian . . . a language with an increasing number of Greek loanwords, and one that was no longer written in the hieroglyphic or demotic scripts, but in an alphabet based on Greek'. Used by pagans in sacred texts, it was adopted by Christians for their holy books and the Divine Liturgy. Coptic was the official language of Egypt during the Greek occupation, but the arrival of the Arabs in 641 changed all that. In 705, a law was passed in Cairo making Arabic the national language and, although there are medieval manuscripts in which Coptic is written in an Arabic script, and in spite of the great chronicler al-Maqrizi recording that the language was still being spoken in the south of the country in the fifteenth century, the Coptic tongue died just as travellers began to bring Coptic manuscripts back to Europe. 'Although religious texts in Bohairic [Lower Egyptian] Coptic are still used by the Christians of Egypt,' Dalby explains, 'they no longer understand the language. Arabic is now their spoken tongue.' It wasn't difficult to see what had happened.

The 705 legislation in favour of Arabic had little immediate effect on the use of Coptic. Egyptians had long administered in a foreign language. But it marked, as the Arab invasion had marked in so many ways, the beginning of a slow decline. Much more important were the large number of Arabs who migrated to Egypt, lured by its agricultural wealth and impressive reputation, and the gradual conversion of Egyptians to Islam, with its reliance on the Koran, the word of God delivered in Arabic.

Very few Coptic words live on in the new language of Islam. And apart from common and place names, most of those are agricultural terms, like *barseem*, clover (*bersim* in Coptic) and *damira*, the time of the Nile flood (*t-emere* in Coptic). There is also *tuba*, mud brick (*tobe* in Coptic and *djob'et* in ancient Egyptian), which as *al-tuba* entered Spanish via north Africa as *adobe*. Effectively, however, Coptic was a dead language.

None of that, though, was a deterrent to Dr Ragheb Moftah.

Dr Moftah was himself something of a survival. He was born towards the end of 1898, which made him ninety-nine years old. He had had time to form his opinions and he told me emphatically, and in English, that 'the Coptic language is still like the demotic language of the pharaohs. All the rituals and all our hymns are in this language. When the Apostle Mark came to Alexandria to preach Christianity, we were a pharaonic people and that is what we remain.'

I found it hard to concentrate on what he was saying. Not that it wasn't exactly what I wanted to hear, but how often does one get to sit beside someone so old? The Suez Canal was young when he was born, Khedive Abbas II Hilmi nominally ruled Egypt and Kitchener had just won the Battle of Omdurman. He was in good shape too, his hair neatly combed, his face clean-shaven, and although his shoulders drooped like a pair of wilted tulips, his thick brown eyes were still sharp. He was wearing a check jacket, braces pulling his beige trousers halfway up his chest, his tie held down with a silver clip. I thought he was a great advertisement for the health-giving qualities of hard work and obsession. He still had his office in the Coptic Institute, which was where we met, and he was still in the process of recording his favourite cantors chanting the liturgy and service for the holy days.

'We have three liturgies,' he explained, 'St Basil, St George and St Cyril. Cyril and Basil are still used and for the past sixty years I have been studying them. The liturgy always used to be passed on from mouth to mouth, but long ago,' he said, uncharacteristically vague, 'I transcribed it with Ernest Newlandsmith from the Royal Academy of Music in London. Then I began working with Mrs Toth.' The Hungarian musicologist Margit Toth had been working with him since 1970, which, over the span of his years, seemed like yesterday. 'Of these three liturgies, we used only one before the end of the sixth century, and that is the one that has interested me. The liturgy of St Basil, from the fourth century, is used in our Church throughout the year, though not during the festivals, when we use the liturgy of St Gregory.

A member of the Institute's board came to pay his respects and Dr Moftah rose shakily to his feet with a wry smile, an outstretched hand. When he continued it was with a different thought.

'You see, about Coptic music . . . it is sung in seven musical letters. That is significant. Someone in Alexandria in the third or fourth century BC said that the priests in the temple sang their chants in just seven letters. And Philo [in the first century AD] said that all the Christians did was to change the words of the ancient Egyptians. Because of this, and because we know that the method was passed from mouth to mouth through the centuries, usually by blind cantors, we know that Coptic chanting has come down to us from the ancient Egyptians, just like the language.'

'But isn't there a possibility that this technique you have identified came from somewhere else?'

'But where? Coptic music is not Turkish, not Arab or European. There are perhaps some Greek, some Jewish influences. But there is no relation between the principles of Coptic music and the principles of any other musical tradition, except ancient Egyptian. You must hear for yourself what I am talking about and then perhaps you will understand.'

One of his assistants went to a table on the far side of the room and with the manner of a magician's apprentice removed a cotton cover from a tape machine. She searched through a large box of cassettes, checked again with Dr Moftah and found the one she wanted.

The point the great musicologist wanted me to grasp was that the Coptic and ancient Egyptian traditions were the only two to involve what he described as 'the prolongation of a single vowel over many phrases of music that vary in complication'. Later on I was able to identify that technique in the prayer. But at first, with the sound low, the recording a little muffled, I was struck to hear that the cantor was chanting in a language I didn't recognize.

'Most of what we have here is demotic, which was the language of the people. Even though the Greeks were the rulers of the world at that time, you and I would have been speaking demotic to each other. That is ancient Egyptian.'

The chant relied on repetition, on the reworking of sounds, going over and over them, again and again, making small shifts up or down a note. It was these sounds that Dr Moftah had spent the best part of his life identifying, clarifying, transcribing and recording. He had started on this mission as a reaction to a modernizing movement that appeared in the Coptic Church back in the 1920s and that sought to introduce organs and other elements that he thought foreign to the time-honoured tradition. Newly returned from university in Germany, where he had been trained in agriculture to work on his family's extensive farm, Dr Moftah decided something had to be done to preserve his church's musical tradition. 'I thought the best way to subvert their movement would be to transcribe all the hymns and thus preserve them for all eternity.'

After more than half a century of listening and recording, he has finally succeeded. The liturgy has been purged of any outside influences, recorded, transcribed and lodged with the American Library of Congress.

'What you are hearing now,' he explained as another recording crackled over the speakers, 'is the liturgy of St Basil, as it was performed one thousand years ago, and as it was performed almost one thousand years before that. And what I am certain of – and I have spent my whole life testing this – is that the Christians used the tradition which already existed for their own purposes, that this is also the sound of the ancient priests.' Assuming he was right – and no one was better qualified than Moftah to make that statement – then this was as vivid a survival as any I had found. Sitting in his plain, dusty office, I was listening to a sound and a language that would have made as much sense to people eighteen hundred years ago as it did to Moftah, while the modulations, the overall sense of movement and timing, would have conjured sacred thoughts in the minds of the ancients.

E. M. Forster once recommended to novelists that they 'only connect'. I could do no more than that. I sat in silence, those long musical vowels reverberating around me, until I noticed Dr Moftah begin to tire, his eyes close, his head dip on to his chest. I left him in his office, his assistant moving forward to take his arm, door open, volume turned up, and the insistent, timeless praise of God followed me down the corridor and out into the street.

CHAPTER 8

The Tree at the End of the Book

A tree that affords thee shade, do not order it to be cut down.
J. L. Burckhardt, *Arabic Proverbs*, 1830

They cut down the palm in front of our building. It was there when I left for the monastery at Wadi Natroun, but had gone by the time I returned, a hole in the ground where it had stood. The bats had also gone and the morning chorus seemed a note or two quieter, the rumble of traffic that much more noticeable. It was another victory for the advancing army of contractors, developers, builders, Cairo-in-the-year-3000 planners and cement-factory owners. Another step away from paradise.

There is another book to be written on this subject of survivals, one which might be called *Losses: Travels in Search of Vanished Egypt*. I have been misleading if I have suggested anything other than that most of Egypt's ancient culture has vanished as decisively as the palm outside my window. Misleading, too, if you think many modern Egyptians spare its passing a moment's thought.

The physical remains are the most obvious losses. When a building comes down in Cairo or Alexandria, people look forward to the opening of a faster-food joint, another slick bar-restaurant, more shops. Very few wonder what lies beneath the foundations or lend their voices in support of the Egyptologists who have to fight to get reconstruction put on hold for a week or a month so they can excavate and save something of the past.

Where are the houses and palaces of the ancient Egyptians? Where are buildings like the Middle Kingdom temple at al-Ashmunayn? Two hundred years ago it was recorded by Napoleon's *savants* in their

Description de l'Egypte and drew the following comment from Baron Dominique Vivant-Denon: 'Is it the Egyptians who have invented and brought to perfection such beautiful art? . . . Even on a first glimpse of this edifice we may pronounce, that the Greeks have never devised nor executed anything in a grander style.' The *Blue Guide* now describes it as 'large mounds of rubble, mud-brick and potsherds'. Sir John Gardner Wilkinson provided an explanation as to what had happened when he wrote, back in 1843, that 'unfortunately built of calcareous stone, it was destroyed by the Turks, and burnt for lime like the monuments of Antinoë.' And what of the tomb of Seti I in the Valley of the Kings, which Wilkinson described as standing 'pre-eminently conspicuous, as well for the beauty of its sculpture as the state of its preservation'? In the current edition of my own guide to Egypt it is listed as having been closed for many years. 'Restoration is underway but it is not certain when, if ever, it will be opened again.'

There are more fundamental entries to be made in the register of the departed. Where is the Nile flood, that annual lottery which brought feast or famine, which at times overwhelmed villages, at others left their fields parched? What of Herodotus's observation that during the flood 'the whole country is converted into a sea, and the towns, which alone remain above water, look like the islands in the Aegean'? What of mudbrick, used to build houses since the beginning of dynastic Egypt but now gradually replaced by concrete as the material of choice? The lotus plant, an essential part of most temple offerings, does not now grow along the Nile. Modern wheat bears very little resemblance to *emmer*, the grain ancient Egyptians used to make bread, which was so gritty that it wore down their teeth by the time they were in their mid-twenties (though some modern Egyptian bread does have the same qualities). The whole of Nubia, Egypt's southern frontier, has disappeared under the waters of Lake Nasser, created by the Aswan Dam, and with it have gone many of the works of the ancients. Inscriptions carved on the walls of caves along the Nile valley in Nubia, now to be found among the archaeological salvage along the new shoreline, show prehistoric carvings of elephants and giraffes. The only living specimens are to be found cowering in cages in Cairo's zoo. It is evolution as Darwin saw it, certainly, but it is hard to be pleased about it, just as it is hard to be pleased as the city's magnificent medieval buildings are left to crumble. So I decided that I would not stay in Egypt to watch it go, nor to see many of the survivals I had found disappear.

There are also many more survivals to add to the list of current customs, but you will not find them here. My intention when travelling in Egypt was to discover if connections could be made, to be suggestive, not encyclopaedic. I was more interested in what lay at the heart of the matter than in discovering its extent. Perhaps one day Umm Seti's manuscript will find a publisher, or more of Winifred Blackman's notes will emerge. Or someone might take up Warren Dawson's suggestion in *The Times*, in 1926, and 'collect, systematically, and publish, the survivals of ancient customs and beliefs among the modern inhabitants of the Nile Valley'.

There is another reason for not being exhaustive on the subject: any list I could make at the moment would soon be out of date as the twin forces of Islamic fundamentalism and creeping Americanization erode the soft borders of Egypt's traditional life.

One more topic, however, I do want to write about. Both Umm Seti and Winifred Blackman touched on it, and I wasn't sure I would include it when I started my research, but it has now a central place in my story and in my feelings about Egypt. It is the heart of the matter, and it follows on from the cutting down of the palm tree outside my window, the tree I looked on as I sat at my desk during the day, watching birds peck at the fruit, and at night when bats swung out of its fronds.

Against the advice of friends and officials, I decided to visit Abydos, out of respect for Umm Seti, who has been part of the animating force behind my search, to see the place where she claimed to have lived two lives and died two deaths. Abydos was ancient Egypt's most sacred place of pilgrimage. It stood at the edge of the agricultural land on the west bank of the Nile, beneath limestone hills which hedge in much of the Nile valley and hold back the desert. A sudden gap in the hills led to Abydos's fame. To ancient Egyptians, this was the entrance to Amenti, the beautiful West, the Kingdom of the Dead, and pharaohs from the dawn of dynastic Egypt, around 3000 BC when the country was ruled from a town called This, were buried at nearby Abydos. Later, kings and nobles buried elsewhere had a 'symbolic' grave built for themselves at Abydos. By the time the cult of Osiris was in full swing 1500 years later, people sought access to Abydos to be near what they believed was the dead god's final resting place; mummified corpses were sent on a pilgrimage to Abydos before interment elsewhere in the country.

A state of crisis had overwhelmed Egypt. Since the attack on the temple of Hatshepsut in Luxor and the death of sixty-seven Egyptians and foreigners, state security forces had clamped down heavily on known fundamentalist Islamist supporters, using extraordinary powers handed them by a state of emergency that had been in place since 1981 when President Anwar Sadat was assassinated. They had also restricted the movements of foreigners: tour buses travelled with armed escorts while private cars carrying foreigners were formed into convoys sandwiched between army vehicles. Foreigners who tried going it alone were turned back at the roadblocks and checkpoints that had become a feature of almost every town along the Nile. Neither tour buses nor convoys were going to Abydos.

I flew to Luxor to avoid the worst-affected areas of middle Egypt and in the hope that I could make a day trip to Abydos from there. In Luxor, the army had pitched tents on the ridges above the Valleys of the Kings and Queens to deter anyone else from taking shots at the few foreigners brave enough to come to town. At night, their lights glowed like fallen stars. Mostly the soldiers were protecting vacant spaces, as beds in the refurbished Winter Palace Hotel remained empty, the swimming pools of Nileside hotels lay undisturbed, calèche drivers dropped their prices to something close to the official tariffs and cruise boats sat six-deep at the moorings. Five months after the attack, there was a still sadness about the place, a sense that it had been defiled.

The night before I left Luxor, I went to pay a visit to Dr Boutros. He had been busy with a late-night patient in the surgery adjoining his mudbrick house and came out wiping his hands. 'They come at all times of the day and night. There's no peace for a doctor.'

I settled on to one of the *mastabas*, a new CD of Bernstein's *Requiem* playing, while he went to find some glasses. When he came back he asked, 'So how did you get on with your research?'

I remembered how sceptical he had been of my project and was careful not to be too specific. 'I have found plenty of material.' When I mentioned some of the places I had been and the people I had met, he nodded in approval. 'But I suspect that a lot of what survives here in

Egypt can also be found in India, in Britain and in other places, though perhaps in different ways.'

'This word "survival" makes me uneasy. That was part of the reason for my reluctance to talk to you before. It makes it sound as if we Egyptians are living fossils. I hate this. It's not true.'

'What would you prefer me to use?'

'It's not a matter of survival. Survival sounds passive, but it's more a question of reusing old material. Reusing and reusing and reusing and sometimes restructuring.'

'For example?' I held my breath, wondering whether he would reply. When he did, it was without any of the reserve he had shown earlier.

'For example . . . take Virgin Mary. Egyptians quickly took to Virgin Mary all over the country. Why? Because she had a role model. She supplanted the goddess Isis directly. You don't need to search else-where. You can see that the icon was already there.' I mentioned a statue I had seen of Isis with baby Horus at her breast. 'Exactly,' the good doctor replied. 'Just the names were changed and there was a new situation. But to the people she was essentially still the same. And when Muslims came, Sayyida Zaynab took her place. Like Isis and Virgin Mary, Sayyida Zaynab is the mother of the weak, of the poor and of the sick.

'And what happened to Mr Horus?' he asked rhetorically. 'Dear Mr Horus who sat on Isis's lap? He became not Jesus Christ but our St George.'

'A case of restructuring rather than reusing?'

'You got it. Our Egyptian St George has two sites, one in the delta and one in the south, just like Horus. And at the same time, the Coptic name for St George is Abu Girg. Do you know what the word *girg* means? Harpooner. And that was one of the titles of Horus. He's a harpooner.'

'Do you think much else has come down from the past?'

'A lot. Like Sham en-Nessim, the ancient Egyptian feast to celebrate the day after the resurrection of Osiris. We celebrate it as a harvest feast after the equinox of spring, when plants are coming out of the body of Osiris. People go out to smell the breeze, be alive, get back to life, just like Osiris. And it takes place on the Monday after our Easter, just like the resurrection of Jesus Christ. Christ is Osiris in a certain way, or rather Osiris is a prototype of Christ. He's a son of God, who came to earth and was killed. He came back to life, went to heaven and was given the power to judge the good and bad. There was a different language, a different conception, but in a certain way the whole structure already existed before Christ came along.'

'What else?

'There is more. Yes sir. The calendar. The measurements of the land. The division between the northern people and the *Saiidis*, the two lands as they used to call it. And on a more philosophical level, you could say monotheism was ancient Egyptian – they didn't refer to "the gods" but simply to God, to *neter*. In Coptic it became *notair*.' He took a slug of whisky. 'I could go on, but you know what I think is more interesting? To consider how all this is changing.'

'Why change now, after all this time?'

'A big part of the population still believes in these things, but there is a new consciousness about what is right and what is wrong, what is unIslamic. Youngsters are getting more sceptical about going to the tombs of sheikhs, the magic crafts, spells, that sort of thing, because they don't think it is orthodox.'

'They are probably right about that, but these are some of the essentials of what makes an Egyptian Egyptian. So they are becoming sceptical, as you put it, about what it means to be Egyptian.'

'I think you're right,' the doctor replied darkly. 'Even the most fundamental things are changing. Think about the relationship with the river. After 1972, 1973, Egypt's relationship with the river suddenly changed. Radically. People in their fifties and sixties still call a certain season the season of the flooding. In their minds, things are as they were. But the young ones see it differently. They never knew the river flooding. So when the older ones die, that will be the end of old Egypt. *Khalaas*, finished. You cannot believe how fast the end is coming. Things are changing. A lot. A lot.'

I was at the taxi station early the next morning looking for a *beejo*, a communal Peugeot 504 taxi, heading north around the great loop in the Nile, past Qena and the aluminium works at Nag Hammadi to Baliyana. If I had to, I was prepared to pay for a seat to Cairo and get out as we passed Baliyana. I'd even pay for two seats, as they sometimes made foreigners do on the assumption that they don't like to be squashed like Egyptians. Or perhaps because if the drivers had as much money as they assume Europeans have, they would pay for the extra seat. As the stretched Peugeots only left when they had their minimum quota of nine, it was also a way of cutting down the waiting time.

I was used to being hounded when I walked into a taxi station, but this time I wasn't. I found a car going to Qena, about halfway to Baliyana, but the driver refused to take me. Others approached, asked what I wanted, then turned me down. I ended by offering to pay for a whole car, plus a bonus if I got to Abydos and back, but not even bribes were going to help.

At the bus station around the corner, the clerk told me there were no direct buses to Baliyana.

'Change at Qena. The next bus is at eleven.'

'Can I buy a ticket to Qena?'

'No.'

'Because?'

'Because I don't know if they will let you on.'

The bus came at 11.45, an old crate that had lost most of its furnishing over the past twenty years. It was packed to the top of its racks with people and bags, but a child was shuffled on to its father's lap, several other people moved and I was squeezed in beside a grandfather in patched blue *galabiyya* and grey jacket. The young, toothless bus conductor spoke a language which only partly resembled Arabic. Yes, I could have a ticket. 'Just one?' he asked.

When I opened the book I had brought for the journey – Umm Seti's biography – the neighbourly grandfather looked at it as though it was a vital clue in understanding a lifetime's vendetta against him. Unable to stand the pressure of his inquisitiveness, I put the book in my bag on the rack and stared at the hypnotic passage of countryside.

We pulled into Qena bus station at a minute to one. Qena was not a place I wanted to stay for any length of time – too many people had died there in the past few years. 'If you run,' the toothless conductor mouthed, 'you might just catch the one o'clock to Baliyana.' It was just moving off as I hit its footplate.

There was a roadblock outside Nag Hammadi, aluminium town. Eight years ago I had spent a night in the Russian-built smelting compound, at a hotel where the greatest dangers were from the lift – you had to insert a finger into the electrical socket before it would move – and from a waiter who attempted a clumsy seduction as he served an inedible dinner and warm beer. Since then, hospitality had given way to security. At the checkpoint on the outskirts of town, by the Nile, the driver killed the engine. We sat beneath the guns of an armoured vehicle, while tin-helmeted soldiers leaning against a sandbag emplacement stared down the barrels of their machine guns at us.

Three policemen stormed the bus. Two of them stood up with the driver, their World War II-issue .202s at the ready, while an officer with a low-slung gunbelt swaggered cowboy-style up the aisle, head down, demanding ID cards with menace. When he reached me he looked up at my face, flicked through my passport and handed it back without comment. I was through.

At three-fifteen I jumped off the moving bus at the checkpoint outside Baliyana. Abydos, and the village of Arabat al-Madfouna which had grown around it, was a couple of kilometres inland from the river and I was hoping to find a passing bus or *beejo* to take me there, but the officer at the checkpoint had other ideas. His jaw dropped and he blanched a little. He demanded my passport. 'What are you doing? Where have you come from? *How did you get here?!*'

'On the bus,' I said, smug as anything. 'From Qena, and Luxor.'

'Don't you know it is forbidden? Forbidden! You cannot be here.'

'Well I am and they didn't say anything at the Nag Hammadi checkpoint. I have come to see the temple. I am a tourist.'

'You must return. Immediately.' He began rapping the table with my passport. 'I cannot take responsibility for you.'

'I have just spent four hours on a bus getting here and I want to see the temple before I go.'

'All foreigners must have protection. Do you know what would happen to me if anything happens to you?'

I drew a suggestive finger across my throat.

'Worse,' he laughed. 'Much worse.'

'So protect me, but let me go to the temple.'

He made a call on the sort of 1950s Bakelite phone that has become a collector's item in London, and then detailed two plain-clothed agents in sweeping blue *galabiyyas* to escort me. To help me on my way, he flagged down a car and directed it along the palm-lined, refuse-strewn track towards Abydos. 'Half an hour. That's all you've got.'

'Make it three-quarters.'

'Why do you British always want to argue?'

The afternoon light fell on Seti's grand temple and made the squat, fortress-like facade gleam like toast and honey.

My own shadows, who had something other than poetry and reincarnation on their mind, left me alone to walk up the slope, through the outer courts and into the temple. To Umm Seti, this was a magical place. 'One leaves the modern world outside in the glare of the sunshine, and, in the soft, subdued light of the interior, enters the world of the past . . . a world of magic such as the modern mind, and particularly the western mind, has difficulty in understanding.'

She had also written that 'to be alone in the Temple of Sety is to feel watched over by benevolent, all-seeing eyes, and to know an overwhelming sense of peace and security.' I had hoped to get a sense of that mystery, but the two temple guards had other ideas. They hadn't seen many foreigners recently, hadn't received much in the way of *baksheesh*, and I was too good an opportunity for them to pass by. They kept calling me to look at carvings and chambers, spouting inaccurate facts and implausible explanations. Soon after they left me alone, a group of boys appeared, asked me to take their photograph and then thanked me by throwing stones as soon as I turned my back.

The temple guards hurried back to stop them and wouldn't leave me after that. I asked if they had known Umm Seti.

'Sure,' said the elder, 'everyone knew her. Very good woman. She died ten years ago.' It was almost exactly seventeen years.

Umm Seti had built herself a tomb in the garden of her house in the village. 'On the west wall I carved a nice little false door,' she once explained, 'just as they did in ancient tombs . . . Then I also carved an offering prayer asking for "1,000 jars of beer, 1,000 loaves of bread, 1,000 oxen, 1,000 geese, 1,000 jars of wine, perfume and every good and pure thing." At the head of the tomb I finally carved a figure of Isis.' She might have prepared herself for the obstacles that Osiris and the other gods would put in her way, but she hadn't reckoned on the local bureaucracy. When she died, the department of health refused to allow her to be buried in her tomb. One account stated that she had been buried far out in the desert. Her biographer, Jonathan Cott, thought she was buried in the desert near the Coptic cemetery.

'She's sleeping in the desert,' the guard assured me, 'a few kilometres from here.'

'Have you been?'

'Sure. You want to go? I can take you.'

'The police will not allow it.'

The old man looked over his shoulder towards my shadows. '*Maalesh*,' he said and wandered off.

The sun was low, my time almost up. There was one more thing to see before I went. The massive columns of the inner hypostyle hall formed an arcade, a stone thicket in front of the seven vaulted sanctuaries to the protector gods of Abydos. Everywhere, decorations, but I soon found what I was looking for. To my left, on an upper register, the Pharaoh Seti was on his knees beside a tree. This was the Tree of Life of Heliopolis, and beside it stood Ra-Harakhty, the falcon-headed god, writing Seti's name on its leaves. Ptah, the creator god of Memphis, held out a figure of a man kneeling with two stripped palm branches, the symbol of eternity in his hands. I was still studying it when the old man started shuffling nervously behind me.

The plain-clothed agents were waiting at the entrance. 'It is time,' they said solemnly, as though leading me to an execution.

At the checkpoint outside Baliyana, the officer was still on duty. 'Luxor,' he ordered. 'Yes,' I replied, 'and no argument.'

The ancient Egyptian vision of paradise is one of the oldest in the world. The first thing they prayed to see when they reached the world of the dead was a large tree whose long, leafy branches would provide them with shade – appropriate for people who lived in a country that was mostly desert. The second part of this fantasy involved Hathor, one of the most ancient gods, known as 'the Lady of the Sycamore', who was to appear from inside the tree to offer cool water and delicious fruit. Most later interpretations of paradise drew on or were curiously similar to this ancient Egyptian vision. And an echo of this vision is still found in a popular Egyptian song which refers to 'you who are going up the tree', to a cow and the quenching of thirst.

A decoration on one of the two pillars in the tomb of Tuthmosis III, in the Valley of the Kings, shows the pharaoh drinking from a breast attached to a tree. A hand emerges from the other side of the tree to guide the breast to the pharaoh's mouth. Images like this, of gods and goddesses inhabiting trees, recur throughout Egypt's ancient history and mythology.

One of the most famous legends involves the god Osiris, who floats in his coffin as far as the shores of Lebanon, where a tree grows around it. Years later, the tree is cut down and used as a pillar in the King of Byblos's palace. It is there that Isis, Osiris's grieving sister/wife, finds it. Osiris is cut out of the wood and returned to Egypt, perhaps to Abydos, for burial.

Sir James Frazer in *The Golden Bough*, his nineteenth-century study of magic and religion, mentions an ancient Egyptian ceremony described by one Firmicus Maternus. 'A pine tree having been cut down, the centre was hollowed out, and with the wood thus excavated an image of Osiris was made, which was then buried like a corpse in the hollow of the tree.' A year later the image was burned and presumably another one carved to take its place. To this description, Frazer added: 'It is hard to imagine how the conception of a tree as tenanted by a personal being could be more plainly expressed.'

It wasn't just the sycamore and pine that were believed to be inhabited. In the conclusion to her masterful study of the date palm, Dr Warda H. Bircher described the dom palm as 'symbolic of the male principle in nature and believed to be the tree of Thot, the god of Science. The . . . date palm . . . is the tree of Hathor, representing the female quality of fecundity and ever-renewing life.' These trees have their counterparts in the trees of the garden of Eden, as described in the Book of Genesis: 'the tree of life in the midst of the garden, and the tree of knowledge of good and evil'. Ancient Egyptians also revered the fig, the tamarisk and the *persea* – whose kernel is shaped like a heart – because of their divine associations, although all trees were considered to be touched with the sacred as their branches reached up to heaven.

Amongst Winifred Blackman's papers in the University of Liverpool, I found the following note on a Sheikha Khadra:

A tree only marks the burial place of this sheikheh. At Senaru, in Fayoum province. The sheikheh is said to be 'in the tree'. Candles are placed on the tree as offerings, as well as bunches of hair, charms enclosed in cotton cases, etc. The tree is a *nebkh* (*zizyphus*, or *rhamnus spina Christi*) and people eat the fruit as a cure for various illnesses, and for possession by *afarit*.

A small light is seen darting about in and around the tree every 'night of Friday'. This is believed to be the *roh* (soul) of the sheikheh. Candles are burned every 'night of Friday'.

The tree is very old, and the sheikheh is said to have been in it *min zaman*, for some time – one man said for eighty years. The tree stands in the midst of fields outside the village of Senaru.

Where are we going this time?' Alan asked, a little apprehensive after the beating at the moulid in Dahshur, the brush with cobras, the story I told about meeting the magician.

'To look for a tree.'

'Naturally. Where?'

'In Fayoum.'

'Good place. Plenty of trees in an oasis.'

We found the sheikha's tree with surprising ease. It was large and gnarled, and it stood on the edge of a village a couple of hours' drive from Cairo. Beside it there was a ramshackle tomb of mud and burned bricks, with a wood-slat roof. A young woman was sitting on a mat inside the tomb and half a dozen others were hanging around, squatting in the corner or leaning in through the paneless window. The girl, the 'servant of the sheikha', had a pretty face and a flirtatious manner and was unable to hide her surprise and delight at the appearance of foreigners. She liked to joke, too, so everyone was in a good mood.

The sheikha's grave was swaddled with fabrics. You could tell this was a woman's grave because on top of the traditional green grave covering, people had placed other flowery fabrics and necklaces and dried garlands were hung around the head of the tomb.

We paid our respects to the sheikha, following Umm Seti's rules for observing the courtesies on visiting a saint's tomb. First we addressed ourselves to the face of the saint. 'The face of the deceased is turned to the east. This means that the visitor is facing west, the traditional stance of the Ancient Egyptian when addressing or making offerings to the dead in front of the false-door.' We then made a circuit around the tomb, a custom that is unknown in other Islamic countries. I was reminded of the edict of the Roman Emperor Theodosius, the one who outlawed pagan rites, who specifically forbade people from going 'around the temples'. Umm Seti noted that it was customary to go around an odd number of times. Three, five or the magical seven, but it occurred to me that one was also an odd number.

We joined the pretty girl on her mat. The sheikha only received visitors on Friday, she explained; many people from the village had already visited that day and brought offerings. 'This again reminds one of Ancient Egypt,' Umm Seti wrote, 'where scenes and inscriptions tell us that food and drink stands stood in the cemeteries, in front of the tombs.'

'Please,' said the girl, holding out some food and glasses of tea which a grandmother had cooked up on a primus stove. While we drank, I asked the girl about the sheikha.

'The sheikha is from a time before we were born, but she lived around here and she is very well known. When there is a sick child, we dig a hole in the sand here, near where the sheikha lives, and put him in it. Later the child will be cured.'

I was wondering whether she believed the sheikha was still alive, when Alan asked, 'Do many people come to be cured?'

'Many, from all around, because she is known to be very, very beneficial. It usually takes a week for these things to happen. If a child comes on Friday, the following Friday it will be well. Old people come, and others with troubles, and they put their heads on the tomb,' she stood up and showed us how, 'and the sheikha strokes their heads and calms their problems.'

'Tell me about the tree,' I asked, as innocently as I could.

'There is lots of *baraka* in the tree. So much. It is the sheikha's tree.'

'How do you know?'

'Twenty years ago, someone wanted to cut it down, but the sheikha appeared to them and said, "Don't do it. This is my tree. And my name is Sheikha Khadra." Another time magicians came and cut the tree. It started to bleed.'

'Red blood?'

'Red blood,' she said with untainted sincerity. 'But the sheikha dealt with them. She cut off their hands.'

I waited to see if she would smile, but she didn't.

'What does the sheikha do to people who light candles?'

'Sometimes people pray and say that if the sheikha helps them then they will bring her a dozen candles, and she does help them, so she must like candles.'

'Do you light them in the tree?' I asked leadingly.

'We used to. Plenty of them, along the branches. On Thursday night.'

'Last night?'

'No. We stopped doing it some time ago.'

'Why?'

'Because now we have electricity. Much better. We don't need candles.'

The word *khadira* translates as 'to be green', *khadir* as 'green, verdant', *khudra* as 'green, greenness'. It is from this word that the sheikha derived her name. There was another entry in the dictionary: *al-khadir*, *al-khidr*, 'a well-known legendary figure'. And to add to the connections, there was another word of interest from the same root, *al-khudaira*. Paradise.

Sheikh Muhammad Mustafa Gemeiah, the Muslim cleric at Al-Azhar, protested that instead of worshipping God people were worshipping trees.

The sheikh had given me a copy of Ibn Kathir's *Stories of the Prophets*, which he had translated, which includes 'The Story of Moses and al-Khidr'. The story is a strange one about God sending Moses to find another man who had been given the gift of knowledge. That man was al-Khidr (also transliterated as al-Khedr), from whom Moses hoped to learn. But Moses found him strange indeed: he scuttled a ship on which he had been given free passage, killed a seemingly innocent boy and refused to be paid for his labour. The point, which Moses learned, was that not everything is the way it looks and that al-Khidr was working according to God's wishes.

Gamal al-Hajjaji, outside his shop near Luxor station, had also told me a story about al-Khidr. In his version, the saint was a Robin Hood (or, as he is called in French, Robin *du Bois*, Robin of the Wood) who stole from the rich and helped the poor. In Alexandria I had heard yet another version, in which the Sheikh al-Khidr was none other than the Green Man. In whatever guise, it was becoming obvious that all these stories had a strong connection with ancient Egypt and touched on some fundamental longing.

You need a large-scale map to find the village of Kinayyiset ad-

Dahariyya, buried in the heart of the Nile delta, yet it compensates for lack of size by being blessed with the tombs of no less than thirty-nine saints. What seemed most remarkable at the village was that one of those saints was not a man but a tree and 'he' was called Sidi Khadr.

I slipped through from Cairo to Tanta, from Tanta to Kafr az-Zayyat, from Kafr az-Zayyat across the western, Rosetta branch of the Nile to Kinayyiset ad-Dahariyya. As I went deeper into the countryside the means of transport became smaller and more decrepit, from the Cairo–Alex train to a large bus to a mini-van to an open-backed pick-up. In the pick-up, I asked my neighbour if I was on the right track for the village.

'What are you looking for?' he asked.

'A tree.'

'Ah,' he said, looking as though he suspected he was having his leg pulled.

'Do you know Sidi Khadr?'

'Sure,' he said and immediately averted his eyes, which made me think that perhaps he didn't.

The pick-up stopped at the end of a dirt track which cut through green fields to the village. The tree was easy to find, the man had said, just outside the village, not far from some of the other tombs.

It was early afternoon by the time I got there and the village was quiet, but I found a man called Gabr near a twenty-metre-high tree.

'This is the tree of Sidi Khadr,' he assured me. 'And in the tomb over there, with the yellow dome and white wall, is Sidi Merai. Sheikh Ahmad az-Zakeri is across the field under the palms.' He went on naming the local sheikhs, sounding like a well-rehearsed guide.

'Do many people come to visit?'

'Some, from around here, because we have so many saints.'

'Thirty-nine, so I have been told.' Gabr looked at me with suspicion. 'But tell me about Sidi Khadr,' I said. Getting close to the massive trunk of the tree, I could see marks on its lower branches, which might have been candle burns. Incisions had been made in the trunk where the bark or sap had been taken.

Before long, others from the village joined us and conflicting accounts of which tree represented Sidi Khadr began to emerge. Gabr slipped away. 'He doesn't know what he's talking about,' one of the newcomers whispered. 'Come, I can show you Sidi Khadr.'

We walked into the village. Ten or at most twenty years ago, this would have been a place of mudbrick and if there was electricity, there would have been little to connect to it beyond street and house lights. But out of the shells of mudbrick houses, new three- and four-storey concrete blocks had emerged, new apartments for a growing population, and each one had sprouted a TV antenna or satellite dish.

By this time a crowd had grown around me and we jostled each other as we pushed through the streets.

'Here is the Sidi,' said one man, pointing to a stump at the base of the wall. 'We cut him down. He was in the way.'

I was incredulous, imagining the reverse-*baraka*, the utter damnation they were bringing down on themselves. 'You killed Sidi Khadr?'

'Yes,' said one.

'No,' said another.

'Look, he is over here,' said a third, and led me to a locked gate of what looked like a mosque.

Gamal Salman appeared with the key. His grandfather, Fathallah Salman had built this place, he said. He pointed to the date stone. 1281 AH. AD 1895. It was not a mosque but the tomb of Sidi Daou er-Rassoul. Two trees stood in the large courtyard, a palm and a *lebbakh*, like the Trees of Life and of Knowledge in Eden.

'So which one is Sidi Khadr?'

'Neither,' Gamal replied, and began to tell me the story of Sidi Daou er-Rassoul and his rival, one Abu Neshabi, both of whom wanted to be buried in this place. 'They staked their claims by planting these trees,' Gamal explained, patting each one in turn, 'Abu Neshabi the *lebbakh* and Sidi Daou the palm. Sidi Daou was so enraged by the actions of Abu Neshabi that he went to Cairo to seek justice. He *walked* to Cairo. It was a long, long way,' he added, in case I didn't know.

I can't tell you what happened to Sidi Daou in Cairo because at this point several large men pushed their way into the crowd and took me by the arm.

'You cannot be here,' one of them said. 'We must take you to the police.'

'Why?'

'Where is your permit to be here?'

'I don't need a permit to visit the sheikhs of Kinayyiset ad-Dahariyya.'

'We will take you to the house of the sheikh al-balad, the village head, and he will decide whether you do or not.' They marched me out of the tomb compound, through the streets, across a field to the edge of the village. The people we passed looked at me as though I were some criminal caught red-handed.

The sheikh al-balad was still resting after his midday meal and the men's determination of purpose was softened by deference. They left their shoes outside and me in an armchair in a blue room whose only decoration was a pair of fake-ormolu wall sconces. One of them went softly, apologetically in to the main part of the large house to call for their leader.

The sheikh was a fine-looking man, with a sleek, almost hairless, well-oiled head, trim moustache, big chest and even bigger belly. By the time he was installed in his chair, an entire council of elders had gathered, including Gabr, the first man I had met in the village. They debated my case freely in front of me.

'We should turn him over to the police,' said a thick-necked old man in an immaculately pressed *galabiyya* and white knitted cap. 'Foreigners are not allowed to leave the road. It is the law.'

'That was for during the troubles with the Jews [Israeli's],' another man sitting opposite him, one Abdel-Nasr, protested.

'He could be spying,' said the first.

'It's the prison for him,' said another.

'He was asking about Sidi Daou,' Abdel-Nasr replied.

They slugged it out like tennis players caught in a marathon point and both I and, opposite me, the sheikh turned from end to end as the exchanges became more heated.

The sheikh had my passport in his hand. Now my accusers suggested they go through my bag. I pulled out a small bottle of water, a pen and finally an illustrated guidebook I had written about Egypt.

At the sight of the book, the sheikh broke his silence. 'Show me that,' he ordered.

He began flicking through the pictures. 'Ah ha,' he said knowingly. 'Alexandria.' A couple of the men shuffled over so they too could see the pictures. 'The mosque of Husayn. Look at Cairo. And Luxor. *Ya salaam*, look at the beautiful Nile at Aswan. Oh my eyes.' He looked sternly at me.

'I wrote that book,' I explained, meek as a schoolboy.

They looked at me in silence.

'What?'

'The book. It's one I wrote.'

The sheikh couldn't read English, that much was already clear, but I pointed to my name on the title page and made him compare it with the one in my passport. He looked from me to the book to the passport several times.

'Why? Why did you write the book?'

'Because Egypt is beautiful,' I began and then delivered the other clichés. 'Because Cairo is the mother of the world. Because Egyptians are good people. Because I wanted to tell others about it.'

'How do you know about the sheikhs of our village?'

'Who does not know of the fame of your village? How many others can claim so many saints?'

The prosecution seemed almost convinced by this outburst, but one thing still niggled. 'Why were you asking for Sidi Khadr?' Gabr asked.

I took a risk and told the truth. 'I had heard about your famous tree and wanted to place a candle on it.'

There was a sudden contraction in the room, a wincing that confirmed I had touched an exposed nerve.

'The tree is no longer there,' said Abdel-Nasr, 'and that . . . that . . . doesn't happen any more.'

'It is finished,' said the sheikh, having passed judgement on both the tree worship and my prosecution, 'and now you must eat.' His son, as immaculately turned out as his father, placed a large tray of food on a low table in front of me. Defence, prosecution and judge sat and watched as I fulfilled my part of the hospitality obligation by tucking into *kofta*, meat in tomato sauce, rice and bread.

After I had eaten, Abdel-Nasr said to the sheikh, 'It is better that we tell him than he hears it from someone else.' There was no reply, but no one stopped him. 'For Sidi Khadr, people used to put lights on the tree each Monday and Thursday.'

One of the other men added, 'It still goes on, but not much now. Maybe only one in a thousand of us still does it.'

'Sidi Ahmad az-Zeheri also had a tree,' Abdel-Nasr continued. 'Two, in fact. *Gemmezas*. Sycamores. And they lit up each Monday and Thursday, but they did so by themselves.'

'What do you mean?'

'There was a flame in the tree, but none of us lit it. Sidi Ahmad made the light. To show us he was there.'

'Can I see the tree?'

The sheikh al-balad stood up to indicate that the crisis had been avoided and the was session over. 'Before you go,' he said, leading me towards a green box hanging outside his house, 'it is tradition that everyone who passes this way makes a donation to my new mosque.'

Abdel-Nasr was a councillor and the local historian. He led me to the cemetery, pointing out tombs of some of the saints as we passed them. The cemetery was on a raised mound, just off the track out of the village. Sidi Ahmad az-Zeheri's sycamores were old, wizened, strange-looking growths, their trunks split open and hollowed out as though they had been zapped by a celestial thunderbolt. One of them had just one side still standing. On closer inspection, there were no signs of cutting, but there was still some black oily substance on the trunk. 'This is what burned,' Abdel-Nasr explained. 'It gave off a very small amount of smoke and light and it burned all evening. I wouldn't have believed it, except that I saw it many times with my own eyes.'

'How do you explain it?' I said, and immediately wished I had been able to suppress my rational thoughts in the face of his convictions.

'No one knows because no one would go into the cemetery at night.'

'Could someone have been lighting them?'

'Could have, but why?'

'A traveller sleeping in the cemetery? A child with a cigarette?'

'Why go to the cemetery when there is all the countryside to go to?'

'So what, then?'

'Perhaps it was the sheikh who made the tree burn.'

'But not now?'

He said not. But the haste with which he hurried me down the track to the road, the fact that he waited for me to get on to a pick-up and that he told the driver I was going back to Cairo made me think otherwise. The sun was setting and the night, Thursday night, the night of illuminations, was coming on.

I allowed Ibrahim to drive me to Heliopolis, not because of his claim to be the best driver in town, nor because he insisted his fifteen-year-old Peugeot was both slick and sleek, but because I was leaving this place to which I had become unexpectedly attached, which I could not imagine I would never see again and I was feeling sentimental, touched with a terrible sadness. As we kangarooed through the solid traffic, I looked out at Cairo with the tenderness of a departing lover. *Umm ed-Dunya*, Mother of the World, long in the tooth, saggy breasted, grown fat, smelling bad. But did I see any of that? Did I care? Did I hell.

While I was mourning my impending loss, Ibrahim had been thinking about my lack of luggage. 'Ya basha, you are going on a journey without a bag?'

'What makes you think I'm going on a journey?'

'We are going to the airport, no? To Heliopolis?'

'We are indeed going to Heliopolis, Ibrahim, but to the old one, not the new.'

According to one of several ancient Egyptian legends about the creation, the first piece of land to emerge from the primeval slime was at On, the ancient Egyptian city of the sun, which the Greeks called *Helios polis*, sun city, Heliopolis. The place is now part of a mixed city within the city, part luxury shops and apartments, part neglected, over-crowded, low-rent housing. In the middle of the latter lie the remains of perhaps the most important of all ancient Egypt's religious centres, where the sun-god Ra, the primal god who fathered later deities such as Osiris and Isis, was worshipped. The cult at Heliopolis appears to have centred around the Spring of the Sun and the holy *persea* tree, the Tree of Life, which it nourished. This was the tree I had seen represented in the temple at Abydos, the tree before which the Pharaoh Seti kneeled and on which his name was written, ensuring long life, the tree that stretched back to the beginning of time.

We drove to the place where the great gates of the temple of Heliopolis might have stood. Of the avenue of obelisks that lined the way, a single one remains, the oldest still standing in Egypt. Its twenty-two metres of pink granite, erected in glory in 1941 BC, now towers over a small park and a large expanse of flat, barren, unexcavated land.

Not far from the obelisk, there is an old well in a walled compound. Some rubbish had floated into the well but beneath the fetid water where the sun-god was said to have performed his ablutions on the first morning of the world, I could make out a vault or arch from an earlier building, submerged as the ground- and water-level rose.

The guardian, a Copt, took us to the ticket office. Ibrahim insisted on paying for his own ticket. 'For the *baraka*,' he explained.

In the centre of the compound, an ancient tree had spread itself. This has come to be known as the Virgin's Tree because, according to a Coptic legend, the Holy Family rested here during their flight from Herod. One account has the Holy Family actually hiding in the tree. Another suggests that Jesus called forth the Spring of the Sun. A very ancient tree survived here until 1656. When it fell, the Franciscan Fathers took a cutting which they were able to replant in 1672. That tree fell in 1906, but another sapling was grafted and had grown into the mass of gnarled trunk and branches that Ibrahim, the guardian and I were admiring, a direct descendant, perhaps, of a tree that had lived in antiquity.

The guardian recited tales of miracles performed and disasters averted. The tree, I noticed, had suffered from souvenir hunters and not a leaf or a sprout was within reach. The guardian, master of the situation, lopped off some higher buds with a stick. '*Baraka*,' he chanted as he handed one to Ibrahim, another to me.

'No more,' I insisted, as he went to have another go at the tree, 'or you will kill the tree and have nothing to show the next visitors.'

Undeterred, he produced a piece of metal and scored the tree, which started to weep. While the guardian anointed us with sap, Ibrahim invoked Allah and his Prophet.

'Now you will live a long long time, *inshaallah*,' the guardian said in the same tone he used a few minutes later when he said, 'Now you will light candles.' Seeing my surprise, he added, 'All the people light candles when they come here.'

The sun filled the enclosure with dazzling light and above us the sky was eternally blue. A bored housewife looked down at us from her top-floor window. If Ibrahim was to be believed then God was also looking down at us just then, to which the guardian added the Virgin Mary, to which I added the ghosts, the shades, the memory of all the people who had stood in that spot before us.

The guardian struck his match, Ibrahim and I lit our candles. After the magic, the sheikhs, the ancient chants, this was something I understood instinctively. This was a hotline back to the origins of our civilization and it made me think of Lucia, of Hannukah and other festivals of light with their promises of renewal. With the candles and the tree and the prayers it also reminded me of Christmas. Wax dripped to the ground as it did in ancient libations, while the three of us stood around the holy sycamore, the Tree of Life, the tree of paradise, murmuring prayers for survival and salvation.

By the time Sylvie and I left Egypt, I had found what I was looking for. In the fertility rites and funerary customs, the devotion to sheikhs and to magic, in the relationship of Egyptians with the Nile and the agriculture that it makes possible, in the rites of the Coptic Church and the form of its places of worship – in these and a thousand other ways I saw the shadows cast by pharaohs and their people. When I left I did so with enough new pointers and leads to have filled several more volumes with survivals.

But there are other questions, beyond the 'what' of survivals, that I now find more interesting. Will they survive? When I left I was certain they would not. I remembered what Professor Shenouda from the Coptic Institute for Higher Studies had said, that the Copts were finished in Egypt. I imagined them chased out of the valley, as they had been under the Romans, living in exile outside the country or in remote communities in Wadi Natroun and the monasteries of the Eastern Desert. I also remembered what Dr Boutros had said about the pace of change and the growing number of people who no longer remembered the Nile flooding. But the changes cut deeper than that: in the past generation, the great move away from the country into cities has coincided with the arrival of global culture in the shape of American soap operas on TV, trainers in the markets, burger bars, mobile phones, mass tourism – the list is long. The pro-western government is sufficiently concerned about the way Egypt is perceived in the world to discourage the filming of images of traditional life that might look 'primitive'. And this process of rejecting the past can only fast-forward, with Egypt's population set to grow by some fifty per cent, up to around ninety million, in the next twenty years.

I did go back though, and not just to prove the prophesy of Amr, the boy who started this adventure many years ago, that he who drinks from the Nile will always return. Ahmad, the herbalist–decorator, had told me that I would find eternity only in myself, but I disagree. I found it in Egyptians, even though many of them had understood neither my quest nor my curiosity. They had maintained their survivals without questioning, as though by instinct. That lack of awareness encourages me to believe that even if the domes of the tombs of Egypt's countless sheikhs fall in, even if the Copts emigrate, the magicians are outlawed and high walls and barbed wire are placed around every ancient shrine in the country to keep the women out, somehow Egypt's ancient culture will survive.

I remember a second-century pagan prophesy, quoted by fifth-century St Augustine in *The City of God*. It is a text full of doom and gloom. 'The gods, on leaving the earth, will return to heaven; they will abandon Egypt,' it warned. 'That holy earth, land of sanctuaries and temples, will be completely covered with coffins and corpses. Oh Egypt, Egypt, nothing will remain of your cults, but fables, and later, your children will not even believe them!' The prophet ended with the conviction that 'there will be more dead than living; as for those who survive, it is only by their language that they will be recognized as Egyptian; in their manners they will seem to be men of another race.'

It hasn't turned out that way yet, for it is precisely by their manners, by their customs and traditions and their relationship with the Nile that these people are seen to be Egyptians. Dr Boutros pointed out that Egyptians are constantly changing. They have survived the change of religion and language that the Arabs brought and so perhaps they will survive the onslaught of our global culture by shifting, by adjusting, accommodating, mutating. And in the same way, I will carry the memory of them – their imprint on me, the taste of that tin-rusted water – wherever I go and however I change.

London/Cairo June 1999

Glossary

abuna, Coptic monk, also form of address, 'O my Father'
afrit, afarit (pl.), spirit or ghost
afwan, you're welcome, not at all, by your leave
alhamdulillah, God be praised, thank God
Allah karim, God is generous
arusa, bride
aywa, yes
bab, gate or door
baladi, of the country, popular, vulgar (can have one of these meanings
   or all at once)
baraka, blessing
be izn illah, if God wills
berseem, mediterranean clover (*trifolium Alexandrium*)
calèche, horse-drawn carriage
caliph, lit. successor (to Muhammad), Muslim leader
deir, monastery
djinn, ghost(s)
eid, feast, religious holiday
emir, prince
fatheh, the first sura of the Koran
fellah, fellahin (pl.), peasant farmer
ful, bean stew
galabiyya, traditional Egyptian robe, similar to a kaftan
gebel, mountain

gemmeza, sycamore tree

Hadith, sayings of the Prophet that make up a body of tradition

haikal, altar sanctuary in church

haram, forbidden, wrong, a sin

hawi, snake-charmer, magician, conjurer

helwa, sweet

inshaallah, God willing

itfaddal, please, go ahead

izzayyak (m), *izzayyik* (f), how are you?

khawaga, western-looking foreigner

kofta, minced meat

kufiyya, traditional headscarf worn by Arab men

kushari, a mix of macaroni, rice, lentils and onions

maalesh, never mind, too bad

madrassa, (Koranic) school

mamnou, forbidden

mastaba, built-in bench of stone or mudbrick

min zamaan, long ago

moulid, saint's festival

qarin, *qarina* (f.), *aqran* (pl.), colleague or companion

rayyis, leader, ruler

Saiidi, Upper Egyptian

salaam, peace

sharia, street

Sharia, Islamic law

shaytan, devil

sheikh, sheikha (f), a respected person; also a saint

shisha, waterpipe

shukran, thank you

sihr, magic

sitt, lady, also used as form of address

souq, market

Sufi, a Muslim mystic

sura, a verse (of the Koran)

taamiyya, Egyptian version of falafel

umm, mother

waqf, a religious endowment

yallah, let's go

zagharit, ululations
zikr, repetition of religious formulas in praise of God
zir, large clay water jar

Bibliography

Published sources

Abu Salih, *Churches and Monsateries of Egypt*, Oxford, Oxford University Press, 1895

Aldridge, James, *Cairo*, London, Macmillan, 1969

Andreu, Guillemette, *Egypt in the Age of the Pyramids*, London, John Murray, 1997

Armour, Robert, *Gods and Myths of Ancient Egypt*, Cairo, American University in Cairo Press, 1989

Ayrout, Henri, *The Egyptian Peasant*, tr. John Williams, Boston, Beacon Press, 1963

Badawi, Alexandre, *Guide de l'Egypte Chrétienne*, Cairo, Société d'Archéologie Copte, 1953

al-Baghdadi, Abd al-Latif, *The Eastern Key*, tr. K. A. Zand and John and Ivy Videan, London, Allen & Unwin, 1965

Bagnall, Roger S., *Egypt in Late Antiquity*, Princeton, Princeton University Press, 1993

Biegman, Nicolaas, *Egypt: Moulids, Saints and Sufis*, London, Kegan Paul International, 1991

Bircher, Warda, *The Date Palm*, Cairo, Elias Modern Publishing, 1995

Blackman, Winifred, *The Fellahin of Upper Egypt*, London, Harrap, 1927

Brier, Bob, *Ancient Egyptian Magic*, New York, Morrow, 1980

Brunton, Paul, *A Search in Secret Egypt*, London, Rider, 1936

Budge, E. A. W., *Egyptian Magic*, London, Routledge & Kegan Paul, 1975

Burckhardt, John Lewis, *Arabic Proverbs*, London, Darf, 1990

Butcher, E. L., *The Story of the Church of Egypt*, London, Smith, Elder, 1897

Butler, Alfred, *The Ancient Coptic Churches of Egypt*, Oxford, Oxford University Press, 1884

Charles-Roux, F. *Bonaparte: Governor of Egypt*, London, Methuen, 1937

Chuvin, Pierre, *A Chronicle of the Last Pagans*, Boston, Harvard University Press, 1990

Clayton, Peter, *Chronicle of the Pharaohs*, London, Thames & Hudson, 1994

Cott, Jonathan, *The Search for Umm Seti*, New York, Doubleday, 1987

Critchfield, Richard, *Shahhat, an Egyptian*, Cairo, American University in Cairo Press, 1988

Dalby, Andrew, *Dictionary of Languages*, London, Bloomsbury, 1998

Dawson, Warren, *Magician and Leech*, London, Methuen, 1929

—, *The Bridle of Pegasus, Studies in Magic, Mythology and Folklore*, London, Methuen, 1930

Devonshire, Mrs R. L., *Rambles in Cairo*, Cairo, Les Editions Universitaires d'Egypte, 1947

Duff Gordon, Lady Lucie, *Letters from Egypt, 1862–1869*, London, Routledge & Kegan Paul, 1969

Early, Evelyn A., *Baladi Women of Cairo*, London, Rienner, 1993

Erman, Adolf, *Life in Ancient Egypt*, New York, Dover, 1971

Evelyn-White, H. G., *The Monasteries of the Wadi 'n-Natrun*, New York, 1933

Forster, E. M. *Alexandria, a History and Guide*, London, Michael Haag, 1986

Fowden, Garth, *The Egyptian Hermes*, Princeton, PUP, 1993

Frazer, Sir James, *The Golden Bough*, London, Wordsworth, 1993

Gardiner, Alan, and Kurt Sethe, *Egyptian Letters to the Dead*, London, Egyptian Exploration Society, 1928

Ghallab, Muhammad, *Les Survivances de l'Égypte antique dans le folklore égyptien moderne*, Paris, Librarie Orientaliste, 1929

Gilsenan, Michael, *Saints and Sufis in Modern Egypt*, Oxford, Clarendon Press, 1973

Haas, Christopher, *Alexandria in Late Antiquity*, Baltimore, John Hopkins University Press, 1997

Harris, J. R. (ed.), *The Legacy of Egypt*, Oxford, Oxford Univeristy Press, 1988

Hassoun, Jacques, 'The Jews' in *Alexandria 1860–1960*, ed. Robert Ilbert and Ilios Yannakakis, Alexandria, Harpocrates, 1997

Henein, Nessim H., *Mari Girgis, Village de Haute-Egypte*, Cairo, IFAO, 1988

Herodotus, *The Histories*, tr. Aubrey de Selincourt, London, Penguin, 1972

Hewison, R. Neil, *The Fayoum*, Cairo, American Univeristy in Cairo Press, 1986

Hourani, Albert, *A History of the Arab Peoples*, London, Faber, 1991

Ibn Kathir, Imam, *Stories of the Prophets*, tr. Sheikh Muhammad Mustafa Gemeiah, Mansoura, El-Nour Publishing, 1997

Ilbert, Robert, and Ilios Yannakakis (eds), *Alexandria 1860–1960*, Alexandria, Harpocrates, 1997

Kamal, Hassan, *Dictionary of Pharaonic Medicine*, Cairo, National Publication House, 1967

Kamal, Moharam, *Athar Hadaret al-Fara'ena fi Hayatena al-Haleya*, Cairo, 1998

Kanatawi, Naguib, *The Tomb and its Significance in Ancient Egypt*, Cairo, Egyptian Ministry of Culture, 1987

Kees, Herman, *Ancient Egypt: a Cultural Topography*, tr. Ian Morrow, Chicago, Univeristy of Chicago Press, 1978

Lane, Edward, *An Account of the Manners and Customs of the Modern Egyptians*, London, Ward, Lock, 1890

Leeder, S. H., *Modern Sons of the Pharaohs: Manners and Customs of Copts*, London, Hodder and Stoughton, 1918

—, *Veiled Mysteries of Egypt*, London, Eveleigh Nash, 1912

Legrain, Georges, *Une Famille Copte de Haute-Égypte*, Brussels, Édition de la Fondation Égyptologique Reine Élisabeth, 1945

Lewis, B. (ed.), *Land of the Enchanters*, London, Harvill Press, 1948

Ludwig, Emil, *The Nile*, New York, Viking, 1937

M'Leod, Walter, *Atlas of Scripture Geography*, London, 1860

McPherson, J. W., *The Moulids of Egypt*, Cairo, NM Press, 1941

el-Mahdy, Christine, *Mummies, Myth and Magic*, London, Thames & Hudson, 1989

Malek, Jaromir, and John Baines, *Atlas of Ancient Egypt*, Oxford, Andromeda, 1980

Manley, Deborah, *The Nile: a Traveller's Anthology*, London, Cassell, 1991

Maspero, Gasto, *Popular Stories of Ancient Egypt*, London, H. Grevel, 1915

Meinardus, Otto, *Monks and Monasteries of the Egyptian Deserts*, Cairo, American University in Cairo Press, 1992

—, *Christian Egypt, Ancient and Modern*, Cairo, American University in Cairo Press, 1977

Morris, Jan, *Among the Cities*, London, Viking, 1985

Murnane, William, *The Penguin Guide to Ancient Egypt*, London, Penguin, 1983

Murray, Margaret A., *The Splendour That Was Egypt*, London, Sidgwick & Jackson, 1987

Nightingale, Florence, *Letters from Egypt, a Journey on the Nile 1849–50*, ed. A. Sattin, London, Barrie & Jenkins, 1987

Parker, R., R. Sabin and C. Williams, *Islamic Monuments in Cairo*, Cairo, American University in Cairo Press, 1985

Pettigrew, T. J., *History of Egyptian Mummies*, London, Longman, 1834

Pinch, Geraldine, *Magic in Ancient Egypt*, London, BMP, 1994

Plutarch, *De Iside et Osiride*, ed. J. G. Griffiths, Cardiff, University of Wales Press, 1970

Ray, John, 'The Tale of al-Zir', in C. Eyre (ed.), *The Unbroken Reed*, London, EES, 1995

Reeves, N., and R. Wilkinson, *The Complete Valley of the Kings*, London, Thames & Hudson, 1996

Roberts, Alison, *Hathor Rising, Serpent Power of Egypt*, London, Northgate, 1995

Rodenbeck, Max, *Cairo, the City Victorious*, London, Picador, 1998

Romano, James F., *Death, Burial and Afterlife in Ancient Egypt*, Pittsburgh, The Carnegie Museum of Natural History, 1990

Rufinus, Tyrannius, *Church History*, tr. Philip R. Amidon, S. J., New York, Oxford University Press, 1997

St John, Bayle, *Village Life in Egypt*, London, Chapman & Hall, 1852

Salih, Ahmad Rushdi, *Al-Adab ash-Sha'bi*, Cairo, Dar al-Ma'rifah, 1954

Sattin, Anthony, *Lifting the Veil*, London, Dent, 1988

Sauneron, Serge, *Villes et Légendes d'Egypte*, Cairo, IFAO, 1983

Savary, C. E., *Letters on Egypt*, London, Robinson, 1786

Scott-Moncrieff, Philip, *Paganism and Christianity in Egypt*, Cambridge, Cambridge University Press, 1913

Sety, Omm and Hanny el Zeini, *Abydos: Holy City of Ancient Egypt*, Los Angeles, LL Co., 1981

Seton-Williams, V., and P. Stocks, *Egypt Blue Guide*, London, A & C Black, 1984

Shah, Sayyed Idries, *Oriental Magic*, London, Octagon Press, 1956

Siculus, Diodorus, *The Antiquities of Egypt: Bibliotheca Historica, Book 1*, tr. Edwin Murphy, New Brunswick, Transaction, 1990

Stewart, Desmond, *Great Cairo, Mother of the World*, Cairo, American University in Cairo Press, 1981

Theodoret of Cyrrus in English Recusant Literature, 1558–1640 ed. D. M. Rogers, Aldershot, Scholar Press, 1976

Thomas, E. S., *Catalogue of the Ethnographical Museum of the Royal Geographical Society of Egypt*, Cairo, Société Royal de Géographie d'Egypte, 1924

Thompson, Jason, *Sir Gardner Wilkinson and his Circle*, Austin, University of Texas Press, 1992

Walker, John, *Folk Medicine in Modern Egypt*, London, Luzac, 1934

Watson, Helen, *Women in the City of the Dead*, London, Hurst, 1992

Wente, Edward, *Letters from Ancient Egypt*, Atlanta, Georgia, Scholars Press, 1990

Wickett, Eleanor Elizabeth, *For Our Destinies: the Funerary Laments of Upper Egypt*, Ph.D. thesis at the University of Pennsylvania, 1993

Wikan, Uni, *Life Among the Poor in Cairo*, London, Tavistock, 1980

Wilkinson, Sir J. Gardner, *Modern Egypt and Thebes*, London, John Murray, 1843

—, *The Ancient Egyptians, their Life and Customs*, London, Senate, 1996

Wind, Edgar, *Pagan Mysteries in the Renaissance*, London, Faber, 1958

Yannakakis, Ilios, 'The Death of Cosmopolitanism', in *Alexandria, 1860–1960*, ed. Robert Ilbert and Ilios Yannakakis, Alexandria, Harpocrates, 1997

Zaki, Pearl, *Our Lord's Mother Visits Egypt*, Cairo, Dar al-ʿAlam al-ʿArabi, 1977

Journals and Periodicals

Abaza, Mona, 'The changing image of women in rural Egypt', *Cairo Papers in Social Science*, 10 (1987)

Bachatly, Charles, 'Le bosquet sacré du Guizeh: étude relative à un article de M. Hornblower', *Bulletin de la Société Géographique d'Egypte*, 18 (1932), 97–101

Bell, Harold, 'Popular religion in Graeco-Roman Egypt, 1: the pagan period', *Journal of Egyptian Archaeology*, 34 (1948), 82–97

Blackman, Winifred, 'Sacred trees in modern Egypt', *JEA*, 11 (1925), 56–7

—, 'Some occurrences of the corn-aruseh in ancient Egyptian tomb paintings', *JEA*, 8 (1922), 235

—, 'An Englishwoman in Upper Egypt', *Wide World*, 52

—, 'The karin and karineh', *MAN*, 26:56 (1926), 163–9

—, 'Ancient Egyptian symbol as modern Egyptian amulet', *L'Annuaire de l'Institut de Philologie et d'Histoire Orientales*, 3 (1935), 176

—, 'An ancient Egyptian custom illustrated by a modern survival', *MAN*, (1925), 65–7

—, Obituary, *The Times*, 14 December 1950

Blanchard, R. H., 'Notes on Egyptian saints', *Harvard African Studies*, (eds. Oric Bates and F. H. Sterns), 1 (1917), 182–92

Dawson, Warren, 'Pettigrew's demonstrations', *JEA*, 20 (1934), 170–82

—, 'Notes on Egyptian magic', *Aegyptus*, 11 (1931), 23–8

Eady, Dorothy, 'A question of names', *ARCE Newsletter*, 71 (1969), 10–15

—, 'Warding off an eclipse', *ARCE Newsletter*, 80 (1972), 25–7

Galal, Mohamed, *Essai d'Observations sur les rites funeraires en Egypte actuelle*, Revue des Etudes Islamiques, 11, 1938

Griffiths, J. G., 'A modern Egyptian fertility rite', *MAN*, 39:131 (1939), 183

Hassan, Salim, 'Al-adat al-misriyyah al-qadimah al-baqiyah ila al-an fi misr al-hadithah', *Bulletin de l'Association des Amis de l'Art Copte*, 2 (1936)

Hornblower, G. D. 'The laying of a ghost in Egypt', *MAN*, 31:167 (1931), 164

—, 'A sacred grove in Egypt', *MAN*, 30:16 (1930), 17–19

—, 'Survivals in modern Egypt', *MAN*, 38:136 (1938), 119

—, 'Osiris and fertility rites', *MAN*, 41:9–10 (1941), 71

—, 'Further notes on phallism in ancient Egypt', *MAN* 27: (1927)

Hornell, James, 'Boat processions in Egypt', *MAN*, 38:177–188 (1938), 144–46

Keimer, Louis, 'Histoires des serpents dans l'Egypte ancienne et moderne', *Mémoires présentés à l'Institut d'Egypte*, 50 (1947)

Legrain, Georges, 'Légends, coutumes et chansons populaires du Said',

Revue Egyptienne, 1: (1912), 171–81, 205–11, 243–5, 269–76, 300–07, 345–58

—, 'Abou Seifeine et les fous', *Revue Egyptienne*, 1:9 (5 September 1912), 257–63

Maspero, Gaston, 'Chansons populaires recueillies dans la Haute-Egypte de 1900 à 1914', *Annales de Services des Antiquités*, 14 (1914), 97–210

Mogheis, Dr Kamal, 'Legend of the tombs', *A Quarterly Women's Human Rights Journal*, 3 (December 1996)

Padwick, Constance, 'Notes on the jinn and the ghoul in the peasant mind of lower Egypt', *Bulletin of School of Oriental Studies*, 3 (1923–25), 421–46

Piccione, Peter, 'Mehen, mysteries and resurrection from the coiled serpent', *Journal of the American Research Center in Egypt*, 27 (1990)

Ritner, Robert K., 'The Mechanics of Ancient Egyptian Magical Practice', *SAOC*, (Oriental Institute, Chicago), 54 (1993)

Sadek, Ashraf, 'Du désert des pharaons au désert des anchorètes', *Le Monde Copte*, 21–2

el-Shamy, Hassan, 'Folk practices in Egypt', *Catalyst*, 6 (1972), 13–28

Sobhy, George, 'The persistence of ancient Coptic methods in medical treatment', *Bulletin of Byzantine Institute* 2 (1950), 185

Taylor, Christopher, 'The cult of saints in late medieval Egypt', *ARCE Newsletter*, 129 (1987), 13–16

Toureille, C., 'Quelque superstitions populaires Egyptiens', *Bulletin de la Société Khédiviale de Géographie*, 6:4 (1904)

Tribier, Paul, 'Les fêtes coptes et le Nil', *Revue Egyptienne*, 1:10–11 (5 October 1912), 318–22

Wickett, Eleanor Elizabeth, 'Women's songs of celebration and lament from Luxor', *ARCE Newsletter*, 149 (1990), 7–11

Wissa Wassef, Ceres, 'Les survivances pharaoniques dans la tradition égyptienne', *Quaderni dell Instituto Italiano di Cultura Pas de la RAE*

Unpublished material

Winifred Blackman archive:
Many of Miss Blackman's papers, including her notebooks from her years in Egypt, were given to the University of Liverpool, where her brother, A. M. Blackman, was Professor of Egyptology.

Umm Seti Manuscript:

I first read about the manuscript in Umm Seti's obituary, carried by the newsletter of the American Research Center in Egypt, in Cairo. The ARCE authorities, who were credited with owning the manuscript in the obituary, knew nothing about the pages. Professor Kent Weeks, who had seen it when Umm Seti was alive and knew that it contained 'wonderful things', gave me the lead when he remembered that the late Walter Fairservis had taken the pages to the United States. Why would pages belonging to the ARCE be taken to the States? Mrs Jano Fairservis, Professor Fairservis's widow, generously agreed to let me have a copy and also clarified the question of ownership: 'My husband commissioned the articles from Umm Seti and sent the money for them. He recognized her unique position and her story-telling ability – and she was struggling to support herself. The American Research Centre in Egypt handled the money and she sent the manuscripts there – where they sat. We expected the ARCE to publish them but they did not.' They are still looking for a publisher.

Index

Abbas II Hilmi, Khedive 190
Abdallah (Egyptian ruler) 83
Abdel-Nasr (villager) 209–11
Abdel Shafy, Hideyb 114, 116
Abdel-Wanis, Muhammad (magician)
  163–7
Abduh (Cairo tomb-dweller) 88–93,
  96–8
Abu Atla, Sheikh Muhammad 111–13
Abu Bakr 100
Abu Neshabi 208
Abu Rawash (village) 148–53
Abu Sayfein (St Macarius) 127
Abu'l-Hajjaj, Sheikh
  festival of 122–33, 174
  tomb of 124,130
Abu'l-Latif, Sheikh, tomb of 115–17
Abydos 18–19, 195–8, 200–4, 212
African Association 76–7
Ahmad (herbalist) 154–8, 214
Alaa ad-Din, Sheikh 73–4, 108
Alan (Scottish friend) 55, 111–17, 154,
  158–62, 204
alchemy 138
Alexander of Abonotica 141
Alexander the Great 24, 25, 26, 35,
  38–9, 82

Alexandria 22–45
  ancient 23–9
  Cecil Hotel 25
  and Coptic Christians 170, 174, 175
  cult of Serapis 38–40, 41, 42–5
  Great Synagogue 34–8
  Hebrew School 34
  Jews 34–8, 170, 180
  library 24
  Nebi Danial mosque 26–8
  Pompey's Pillar 25–6, 28, 40–4
  Serapeum 39, 41–2, 44, 48
  tombs of Alexander 25, 26, 28
  writers on the myth of 25–6
Ali, Sheikh 144
Amenhotep III, Pharaoh 129, 130
Americanization of Egypt 195, 214
Amr (guide) 1–5, 14, 57, 214
Amun (god) 64, 119–21, 129, 130, 132
Anba Younus (Coptic saint) 136
Andreu, Guillemette 50
Annianus 174
Antar (Arab hero) 1, 2, 4–5
Arab-Israeli wars 35, 87
Arabat al-Madfouna (village) 200
Arabic language 189
arusa (bride)

sacrifices to the Nile 49–50, 74
sugar dolls 125–8
al-Ashmunayn, Middle Kingdom
    Temple at 193–4
Aswan Dam 69, 194
Attiyat (wife of Abdua) 88–9, 90
Attiyat (wife of Munir) 154, 157
Augustine, St, *The City of God* 215
Augustus, Emperor 26, 31
Avicenna (Ibn Sina) 155–6
Ayyubid sultans 83
Al-Azhar university and mosque
    104–8, 121, 129

Balasseano, Victor 34–8
Barquq, Sultan 85–6
Bastet (cat-goddess) 119
Bedawi, Dr Zaki 56
Belzoni, Giovanni 78
Beni Hassan, tombs of 2
Bentresch (daughter of the prince of
    Bakhtan) 127
Biegman, Nicolaas, *Egypt: Moulids,
    Saints, Sufis* 109
Bircher, Dr Warda H. 203
Blackman, Aylward 15, 16, 17
Blackman, Winifred 15–17, 21, 134,
    139–41, 151, 195
    archive at Liverpool University
        16–17
    The Fellahin of Upper Egypt 16, 17,
        46, 93, 114, 143, 156
    on fertility rites 58–9, 74
    in Lahun 114–17
    on magic 143, 162
    obituaries of 17
    on snake-charmers 147
    on the tombs of sheikhs 109–15,
        117, 140, 141
    on women mourners 93
Boutros, Dr 68–9, 73, 142, 143, 196–8,
    214, 215
Brunton, Paul 60, 139, 146–7

A Search in Secret Egypt 139
Bryaxis 42
Budge, Sir E.A. Wallace 18
Burckhardt, Jean Louis (Sheikh
    Ibrahim) 76–81, 193
burials *see* funerary customs; tombs
Burton, Harry 132
Burton, Richard 80

Cairo 5–10
    Al-Azhar University 104–8, 121,
        129
    City of the Dead 84, 86–98, 135
    compound of the Coptic Patriarch
        170–3
    Coptic Museum 177–8
    feast of Husayn 99–104, 159
    old city (Gamaliyya) 101
    Pyramids Road 169
    saints in 118
    Sultan Qalawun's complex 84–5
    tomb and mosque of Sultan Barquq
        85–6
    tomb of Sheikh Ibrahim 76, 78–81
Calvino, Italo 1
Cambyses, Persian king 31
Caracalla, Emperor 26
Carter, Howard 15, 110, 132
Cavafy, Constantin 26
children, Egyptians' attitude to 50–1
Christianity
    and the cult of the dead 82
    and the cult of Serapis 39–44
    and the end of ancient Egyptian
        culture 31
    and *moulids* 117, 118–19, 127
    see also Coptic Church
Clement of Alexandria 137
Cleopatra 31, 138
Constantine, Emperor 31, 40
Coptic Church 170–92, 213, 214, 215
    and ancient Egypt 170–5, 186,
        187–9, 190–1

and change 186-7
and the cult of the dead 82
iconography 175-7
and Islam 109
liturgies 190, 192
magicians 143, 164
and miracles 178-9, 183
monasteries 172, 179-87, 214
and *moulids* 126-8
music 190-2
and the Nile 48
and saints 136, 197, 213
Coptic language 188-90
Cott, Jonathan, *The Search for Umm Seti* 18, 20, 202
Critchfield, Richard 61-2, 64, 69, 70, 71, 143
Curzon, Lord George 181-2

Dahshur, moulid at 158-61
Dalby, Andrew, *Dictionary of Languages* 189
Danial, Prophet, tomb of 26-8
Darwin, Charles 194
David (friend of Zeitoun) 63, 142
Dawson, Warren 195
Deir al-Bahari temple 59
Deir al-Medina (ruins of village) 10-13, 176-7
Deir Anba Bishoi monastery 181-7
deities
  ancient Egyptian 119-21, 138
  and Coptic Christianity 172, 177, 188
  and fertility rites 60-1
  inhabiting trees 202-4
  survival of 197-8
Devonshire, Mrs R.L. 87, 97-8
  Rambles in Cairo 98
Deya, Sheikha 143-6
Digby, Jane (formerly Lady Ellenborough) 110
Dimocrates (ancient architect) 25

Diocletian, Emperor 30, 40, 174
Dionysus, feast of 117-18
Djedefre Pyramid 148
Duff Gordon, Lady Lucie 124, 125, 129, 167, 173
Durrell, Lawrence 33

Eady, Dorothy see Umm Seti (formerly Dorothy Eady)
Eberhardt, Isabelle 110-11
Efendi Ismail, Abd ar-Rahman 55
Egypt Exploration Society 16
Egyptian Antiquities Organisation 19

Fairservis, Jano 20-1
Fanous, Dr Isaac 175, 176, 182-3
Farouk, king of Egypt 63, 169
Fathy, Hassan 63
Fatimid sultans 83, 104
Fayoum 15, 111, 204
Fayoum Portraits 176
fertility rites 4, 13, 50-75, 133, 214
  and the Habu temple 71-5
  and sheikhas 52-4, 55-6
  Umm Seti on 59-61, 74
  women passing over the dead 54-5, 59
festivals see moulids (saints' festivals)
Forster, E.M. 23, 28, 30, 33, 35, 39, 192
Fortunes of War 96
Franquet, Sylvie 78, 79
Frazer, Sir James, *The Golden Bough* 203
Frith, Frances 70
funerary customs
  ancient Egypt 171-2
  Coptic 171-2
  Islamic 82-3, 93, 94-5
  and women mourners 92-3, 172
  see also tombs

Gabr (villager) 207-8, 209

Gemeiah, Shiekh Muhammad
    Mustafa 104–8, 129, 187, 206
Gibbon, Edward 42, 43, 180
Girgis 126–8, 174
Giza Pyramids 60, 82, 85, 148, 178
Gomaa (Cairo cemetery guardian) 80,
    81, 88
Gomaa (driver) 111, 112, 114
Griffiths, J. Gwyn 59
Gulf War 14

Hadrian, Emperor 22, 40
al-Hajjaji, Gamal 134–7, 142, 146,
    154, 158, 164, 206
Hamdi (electronics engineer) 6–7, 9
Hamida 69–75, 108
Hapi (deity) 47
Hardjedef (Old Kingdom sage) 81, 82
Haridi, Sheikh 140–1
'Harpists' Songs' 82
Hathor (goddess) 119, 202, 203
Heliodorus (ancient chronicler) 48
Heliopolis 121, 202, 211–14
hermits, Coptic Christians 180,
    184–5, 185–6, 187
Herodotus (ancient Greek historian)
    99, 129, 164, 167, 177, 179
    on ancient festivals 119, 127
    on the feast of Dionysus 117–18
    on the Nile 194
    on women mourners 94
Horus (falcon-headed god) 119
house-building 63–4
Husayn (saint) 7, 58, 108
    feast of 99–104, 121, 159
A Hymn to the Nile 47

Ibn Abdallah, Sheikh Ibrahim see
    Burckhardt, Jean Louis (Sheikh
    Ibrahim)
Ibn al-As, Amr (Arab general) 23, 31,
    49, 82–3, 171
Ibn Kathir, Stories of the Prophets 206

Ibn Sina (Avicenna) 155–6
Ibrahim (taxi-driver) 62–3, 99, 104,
    121–2, 179, 181, 211–12, 213–14
iconography, Coptic 175–7
Ihy (god) 60
Iphy (ancient sculptor) 10–11, 13
Isis (goddess) 47–8, 59, 197, 203, 212
    and Coptic Christians 172, 177
Islam
    and Burckhardt 80–1
    and burials 82–3, 93, 94–5
    and childless women 58
    and the Coptic Church 178
    fundamentalism 9–10, 14, 96,
        122–3, 195, 196
    language of 189
    and magicians 143
    and moulids 103–9, 117, 127,
        128–9
    and saints 197
    and Sheikh Abu'l-Hajjaj 123
    and snake worship 139
    Sunni and shia factions 100
Ismail Pasha (Egyptian ruler) 102

Jackson, James G. 76
Jews, in Alexandria 33–8, 170, 180

Karima 50, 52, 56
Karnak temple 120, 131
Kha-em-West 165
Khadr, Sidi, tree of 207–8, 210
Khadra, Sheikha 203–6
Khalid (Islam fundamentalist) 6–10,
    13–14, 101, 123
al-Khidr, Sheikh 206
Khonsu (god) 127, 129, 130
Kinayyiset ad-Dahariyya (village)
    206–11
Kom Lolah 68–75

Lahun (village) 114–17
Lane, Edward

on the Coptic Christians 173–4
on fertility rites 54–5
on the Rifai 139
on sacrifices to the Nile 49
on snake charmers 139–40
visit to tomb of Sheikh Ibrahim 76
on women mourners 93, 94
The Manners and Customs of the Modern Egyptians 173
Lear, Edward 169
Legh, Thomas 77
Legrain, Georges 127
Libianus (fourth-century historian) 48
Lutfallah, Dr (professor at Alexandria University) 24–5, 27, 31
Luxor
Deir al-Medina 10–13, 176–7
fertility rites in 62–75
funerals in 95–6, 97
massacre of tourists at 179
moulids (saints' festivals) in 121–33
and Sheikh Abu'l-Hajjaj 123–4
Temple 128–33
Valley of the Kings 11, 15, 66, 83, 194, 196, 202

McPherson, Bimbashi, *Moulids of Egypt* 117–18, 139
magic 134–66, 198, 205
in ancient Egypt 137–8, 165
books of spells 164–6
and healing 154–8
at *moulids* 158–61
origins of 138
and Satanism and sorcery 153–4
and snakes 138–41, 142, 146–7, 148–53
Mahfouz, Naguib 33
Mahmoud 122–3, 129–33
Maimonaides, Moses 35–6
Mamelukes 83–4, 86, 127

Manning, Olivia, *Balkan Triology* 96
al-Maqrizi (historian) 30, 189
Marina 50–6, 74, 167
Mark, St 39, 170, 174, 190
Medinet Habu Temple 66–8, 108, 142, 143
Meinardus, Dr Otto 179
Merai, Sidi, tomb of 207
Min (fertility god) 117
miracles, and Coptic Christians 178–9, 183
Mitchell, Timothy 61–2, 69
Moftah, Dr Ragheb 189–92
Mona 56–8
Montifiore, Sir Moses 35
Montu (god of war) 120
Morris, Jan 25
Moses (prophet) 38, 134–5, 138, 206
moulids (saints' festivals) 99–109, 117–33
Abu'l-Hajjaj 122, 123–33, 174
in ancient Egypt 119–21
and Christianity 117, 118–19, 127
and the feast of Opet 129–30, 131–2
Husayn 99–104, 121, 159
and Islam 103–9, 117, 128–9
and magic 158–61
and ritual fighting 126, 127
Sayyida Zaynab 6–8, 14
Mousa el-Hawi, Sheikh 146–7
Muhammad Ali (Egyptian ruler) 32, 35, 77, 102
Muhammad, Prophet 7, 96, 100, 109, 155, 157
burial of 83
Muhammad (Zeitoun's neighbour) 142, 143, 144, 146
Muhanni, Sheikh 147
Munir Fayed 154, 157, 167
Murnane, William 118, 130
Murray, Margaret 45
music, Coptic 190–2
Mut (goddess) 129, 130

Nag Hammadi (aluminium town) 199–200
Napoleon Bonaparte 35, 48, 78, 193
Nasser, Gamal Abdel 35, 172
Nasser, Lake 194
Newlandsmith, Ernest 190
Nile, River 2, 46–75
    annual rising 44–5, 47–50, 194, 198, 214
    deities 47–8
    drinking the waters 5
    ferry 122
    sacrifice tradition 49–50, 76
Nilometers 44, 48–9, 68, 74
Nubia 194
    temple of Abu Simbel 77, 78

Olympius (pagan philosopher) 43
Opet, feast of 121, 129–33
Oqbah, Sidi 83
Osiris (god) 44, 47–8, 66, 74, 126, 127, 197–8, 212
    and Abydos 195–6
    and Coptic Christians 172
    and tree legends 203

paradise, ancient Egyptian vision of 203
Park, Mungo 77
Pasht (lion goddess) 3
Peter (monk) 184–5
Petra 77
Pharos, lighthouse of 24
Philo 191
Pliny 48–9
Pompey (Roman general) 23
Ptah (god) 202
Ptolemy I 38, 42
Ptolemy III Euergetes 39
Ptolemy Philadelphus 35
pyramids 167–8
    Abu Rawash 148
    Giza 60, 82, 85, 148, 178

Lahun 114

Qalawun, Sultan 84–5
qarin (soul or spirit) 156–7, 158
Qayt Bey, Sultan 87

Ra (sun god) 2, 138, 212
Ra-Harakhty (god) 202
Ramses III, Pharaoh 10, 61, 77, 120
    mortuary temple of 61, 64–8, 71–5
er-Rassoul, Sidi Daou 208, 209
René, Dr Stephane 175–7
Rifai (snake catchers) 137, 138, 142, 146–7, 149–53
al-Rifai, Sheikh Ahmad 139, 147
Rodenbeck, Max 84
Roman Empire 23, 24, 30
Rosetta Stone 39
Rufinus of Aquileia 41–4

Sadat, Anwar 14, 172, 198
Said Pasha 27
St John, Bayle 141
saints see moulids (saints' festivals);
    sheikhas; sheikhs
Saladin 83, 86
Salem, Professor As-Said Abdel-Aziz 22–4
Salman, Fathallah 208
Salt, Henry 30, 78
Samy (Karima's husband) 54–6
Satanism 153–4
Savary, C.E. 140–1
Sayyed (driver) 168–70
Schliemann, Heinrich 28, 29
Selim 102–4
Senusret II, Pharaoh 114
Serapis, cult of 38–45
Serapis (god) 180
Seth 47–8
Seti I, Pharaoh 18–19, 194, 202, 212
    grand temple 201
Shah, Sayyed Idries 134, 138

Shahhat (*fellah*) 61–2, 64, 68, 143
Shakespeare, William 24
Sham en-Nessim (feast) 197–8
sheikhas
    and fertility rites 52–4, 55–6, 167
    and magical powers 143–6, 205
    tombs of 203–6
sheikhs
    and magical powers 134, 136–7, 139
    snake catchers 149–51
    tombs of 109–10, 111–17, 130,
        140–1, 198, 207–9, 215
    see also moulids (saints' festivals)
Shenouda, Dr Zaki 171–3, 179, 186,
    189
    History of the Copts 172
Shenouda III, Pope, Patriarch of
    Alexandria 170, 180, 182, 183,
    184, 214
Sidrak, Abuna (monk) 181, 182–3
Sladen, Percy 15
snakes, and magic 138–41, 142,
    146–7, 148–53
Speos Artemidos 2–5, 13, 14, 57
Stanhope, Lady Hester 110
Strabo (Greek geographer) 25, 48,
    180
Suez Canal 27, 32, 190
Suez Crisis 19, 87

Tatius, Achilles (fifth-century bishop)
    26
Ta-urt (goddess) 60
Thebes (capital of ancient Egypt) 31,
    25, 30
    deities and festivals 119, 120–1
Theodoret, Bishop of Cyrrus 42, 43–4
Theodosius the Great, Emperor 40,
    42–4, 204
Theophilus, patriarch of Alexandria
    40–4, 74
Tibb ar-Rukka 55
Tolba, Masr 153

Tolba, Sheikh 149–51
tombs 103
    in Cairo 76, 78–81, 84–98, 118
    and ka-servants 81–2
    of sheikhs 109–10, 111–17, 130,
        140–1, 198, 215
    tala (visits to) 93
    trees at 112, 203–6
    of Umm Seti 201
Toth, Margit 190
Towzah, Sitt 123
trees 193
    in the ancient Egyptian vision of
        paradise 202
    at Heliopolis 212–14
    images of deities inhabiting
        202–4
    at tombs of saints 112, 203–11
Tutankhamun 110, 130, 132
Tuthmosis III 120
    tomb of 202

Umm Seti (formerly Dorothy Eady)
    17–21, 134, 139, 154, 195, 199
    Abydos, Holy City of Ancient
        Egypt 20
    and *arusa* sugar dolls 126
    burial of 201–2
    on Copts and ancient beliefs
        187–9
    on fertility rites 59–61, 74
    on magic 147–8, 165
    manuscript 20–1
    on natroun 181
    obituary of 20
    and ritual fighting 127
    on tombs of saints 130, 204–5
    on women mourners 94
    The Search for Umm Seti 17

Valley of the Kings 11, 15, 66, 194,
    196, 202
Valley of the Nobles 94

Vivant-Denon, Baron Dominique
194

waaf (system of religious endowment) 83, 84
Wadi Natroun monasteries 179–87,
214
Weeks, Professor Kent 19–20
western influence in Egypt 14, 96,
195, 214
Wickett, Elizabeth 94–5, 132
Wilkinson, Sir John Gardiner 30, 99,
124, 141, 180, 194

Modern Egypt and Thebes 30
women
and fertility rites 4, 13, 50–75
mourners 93–6, 172

Zaki, Pearl, *Our Lord's Mother Visits
Egypt* 178–9
Zaynab, Sayyida (saint) 6–8, 14, 58,
101, 123, 197
az-Zeheri, Sidi Ahmad 210–11
Zeitoun (friend in Luxor) 62–70, 72,
73, 75
visit to sheikha with 142–6